# EDINBURGH GUILDS AND CRAFTS

# EDINBURGH GUILDS
## AND CRAFTS

A SKETCH OF THE HISTORY OF BURGESS-SHIP,
GUILD BROTHERHOOD, AND MEMBERSHIP OF
CRAFTS IN THE CITY

BY THE LATE

SIR JAMES D. MARWICK, LL.D.

EDINBURGH

PRINTED FOR THE SCOTTISH BURGH RECORDS SOCIETY

MDCCCCIX

J. M. Alston, Esq., Writer, Coatbridge.
Robert Anderson, Esq., 142 West Nile Street, Glasgow.
E. Beveridge, Esq., St. Leonard's Hill, Dunfermline.
Sir William Bilsland, Bart., Lord Provost of Glasgow, 28 Park Circus, Glasgow.
Most Hon. The Marquis of Breadalbane, Taymouth Castle, Kenmore, Aberfeldy.
J. A. Brown, Esq., 208 St. Vincent Street, Glasgow.
Alex. Bruce, Esq., Clyne House, Sutherland Avenue, Glasgow.
A. W. Gray Buchanan, Esq., Parkhill, Polmont, Stirlingshire.
P. MacGregor Chalmers, Esq., I.A., Architect, 95 Bath Street, Glasgow.
W. R. Copland, Esq., 146 West Regent Street, Glasgow.
John M. Cowan, Esq., M.D., D.Sc., 14 Woodside Crescent, Glasgow.
Rt. Hon. The Earl of Crawford and Balcarres, Haigh Hall, Wigan.
John Cumming, Esq., 12 Melrose Gardens, Kelvinside, N., Glasgow.
Ralph Dundas, Esq., C.S., c/o Richard Cameron, Bookseller, 1 St. David Street, Edinburgh.
John Edwards, Esq., 4 Great Western Terrace, Glasgow.
Andrew Gilmour, Esq., J.P., 212 High Street, Linlithgow.
Robert Gourlay, Esq., 5 Marlborough Terrace, Kelvinside, Glasgow.
Daniel Graham, Esq., 8 Royal Crescent, Glasgow.
Sir John Macpherson Grant of Ballindalloch and Invereshie, Bart., Ballindalloch Castle, Ballindalloch.
George Gray, jun., Esq., Town Clerk, Blairtum Park, Rutherglen.
Rt. Hon. The Earl of Haddington, Tyninghame House, Prestonkirk.
William H. Hill, Esq., LL.D., Barlanark, Shettleston, Glasgow.
Thomas Hunter, Esq., Town Clerk, Edinburgh.
George Harvey Johnston, Esq., Edinburgh.
Sir James King, Bart., LL.D., Carstairs, Lanarkshire.
Messrs J. MacLehose & Sons, Publishers, 60 St. Vincent Street, Glasgow (3 copies).
Rev. Wm. H. MacLeod, Manse of Buchanan, Drymen.
Messrs Martin & Co., 27 Abingdon Street, Westminster, London, S.W.
William Melven, Esq., 7 Jedburgh Gardens, Kelvinside, Glasgow.
Duncan Menzies, Esq., Architect, 31 Regent Terrace, Edinburgh.
Sir Arthur Mitchell, K.C.B., 34 Drummond Place, Edinburgh.
Geo. Mitchell, Esq., 9 Lowther Terrace, Kelvinside, Glasgow.
Alex. Moncrieff Mitchell, Esq., 8 Kew Terrace, Kelvinside, Glasgow.
David Murray, Esq., LL.D., Moore Park, Cardross.
George Neilson, Esq., LL.D., Wellfield, Partickhill Road, Glasgow.
James Ness, Esq., LL.B., 216 West George Street, Glasgow.
John F. Orr, Esq., 184 West Regent Street, Glasgow.
Messrs Philip, Son & Nephew, Booksellers, South Castle Street, Liverpool.
Rees Price, Esq., 163 Bath Street, Glasgow.
James A. Reid, Esq., 172 St. Vincent Street, Glasgow.
Robert Renwick, Esq., 8 Balmoral Crescent, Glasgow.
Rt. Hon. The Lord Ruthven, Newland, Gorebridge.
Rt. Hon. The Lord Sempill, Craigievar Castle, Leochel-Cushnie, Aberdeen.
J. Guthrie Smith, Esq., 205 St. Vincent Street, Glasgow.
Messrs J. Smith & Sons, Booksellers, 19 Renfield Street, Glasgow.
J. J. Spencer, Esq., 121 West George Street, Glasgow.
Messrs B. F. Stevens & Brown, Booksellers, 4 Trafalgar Square, London (2 copies).

# LIST OF PUBLICATIONS.

I.—THE ANCIENT LAWS AND CUSTOMS OF THE BURGHS OF SCOTLAND. Edited by Professor COSMO INNES.

II.-V.—FOUR VOLUMES OF EXTRACTS FROM THE BURGH RECORDS OF EDINBURGH—(1) 1403-1528; (2) 1529-57; (3) 1557-71; and (4) 1573-89. Edited by Sir J. D MARWICK, LL.D.

VI.—INDEX TO THE FOUR EDINBURGH VOLUMES.

VII.—CHARTERS AND DOCUMENTS RELATING TO THE CITY OF EDINBURGH, 1143-1540. Edited by Sir J. D. MARWICK, LL.D.

VIII., IX.—TWO VOLUMES OF EXTRACTS FROM THE BURGH RECORDS OF ABERDEEN—(1) 1625-42; and (2) 1643-1747. Edited by JOHN STUART, Esq., LL.D.

X.—CHARTERS AND EXTRACTS FROM THE BURGH RECORDS OF PEEBLES, 1165-1710. Edited by WILLIAM CHAMBERS, Esq., of Glenormiston, LL.D.

XI., XII.—EXTRACTS FROM THE RECORDS OF THE BURGH OF GLASGOW—(1) 1573-1642; and (2) 1630-62. Edited by Sir J. D. MARWICK, LL.D.

XIII.—MISCELLANY OF THE SCOTTISH BURGH RECORDS SOCIETY. Edited by Sir J. D. MARWICK, LL.D. The Volume contains: (1) Report by Thomas Tucker to the Commissioners for Appeals as to the Trade and Shipping of Scotland in 1656; (2) Reports made to the Convention of Royal Burghs in regard to the State and Condition of the Royal Burghs in Scotland in 1692; and (3) A Collection of the Setts of the Royal Burghs made by the Convention in 1708.

XIV., XV.—CHARTERS AND DOCUMENTS RELATING TO THE CITY OF GLASGOW, Vol. I., Parts 1 and 2, 1175-1649. Edited by Sir J. D. MARWICK, LL.D.

XVI.—EXTRACTS FROM THE RECORDS OF THE BURGH OF GLASGOW, 1663-90. Edited by Sir J. D. MARWICK, LL.D., and ROBERT RENWICK.

XVII.—CHARTERS AND DOCUMENTS RELATING TO THE CITY OF GLASGOW, Vol. II., 1649-1707, with Appendix, 1434-1648. Edited by Sir J. D. MARWICK, LL.D., and ROBERT RENWICK.

XVIII.—CHARTERS AND DOCUMENTS RELATING TO THE COLLEGIATE CHURCH AND HOSPITAL OF THE HOLY TRINITY AND THE TRINITY HOSPITAL, EDINBURGH, 1460-1661. Edited by Sir J. D. MARWICK, LL.D.

XIX.—EXTRACTS FROM THE RECORDS OF THE BURGH OF GLASGOW, 1691-1717. Edited by Sir J. D. MARWICK, LL.D., and ROBERT RENWICK.

XX.—THE RIVER CLYDE AND THE CLYDE BURGHS: THE CITY OF GLASGOW AND ITS OLD RELATIONS WITH RUTHERGLEN, RENFREW, PAISLEY, DUMBARTON, PORT-GLASGOW, GREENOCK, ROTHESAY, AND IRVINE. By Sir J. D. MARWICK, LL.D.

XXI.—EDINBURGH GUILDS AND CRAFTS: A SKETCH OF THE HISTORY OF BURGESS-SHIP, GUILD BROTHERHOOD, AND MEMBERSHIP OF CRAFTS IN THE CITY. By Sir J. D. MARWICK, LL.D.

# PREFACE.

To tell in his own words the circumstances under which Sir James Marwick entered upon the preparation of this work, it is only necessary to quote two passages from his "Retrospect," printed a few years ago for the use of his family and intimate friends. Referring to the proposal of the Town Council, in the year 1868, to confer on the Baroness Burdett-Coutts the freedom of the city of Edinburgh, "if this were found to be consistent with constitutional usage," Sir James says: "The proposal was a novel one, in support of which no modern precedent could be cited, so I was requested to apply such antiquarian and constitutional knowledge as I possessed to the solution of the question. It was quite understood that my report would be accepted, and that if it was in favour of the appointment of a woman as a burgess, and if the Baroness were so elected, the precedent would no doubt be followed by other burghs. Going back to the oldest extant burghal records, I satisfied myself that women had been burgesses, though not guild sisters, and I so reported, stating the grounds of my opinion. It was accepted, and the Baroness received the freedom." At a subsequent part of the "Retrospect" the following paragraph occurs: "The investigation which I found it necessary to make in 1868 as to the early practice of the Royal Burghs of Scotland in regard to the admission of women as burgesses led me to continue my investigations as to the main condition of membership in these early communities; the power which burghs assumed to regulate the conditions of burgess-ship and to admit burgesses; the privileges which such admission conferred; the right which the burgess possessed of disposing of his heritable property; the rights of his widow and children in regard to succession in heritage and in moveables; the rights of burgesses in the election of their own magistrates; the constitution of merchant guilds; the claim of these guilds to represent the entire community; the position and right of craftsmen, and their struggles with the merchant guilds. On these and other branches of the burghal law, as illustrated specially in Edinburgh, I had written and printed off for the Burgh Records Society the sheets of a work on 'Burgess-ship, Guild Brotherhood and Membership of Crafts in Edinburgh,' carrying the subject down to 1584-5, and had made progress in the completion of the work when the negotiations with Glasgow and my settlement in that city prevented further progress."

When the foregoing was written, Sir James seems to have been under the impression that the printing of the book was stopped at the time of his removal to Glasgow, but in this respect his recollection was not quite exact. Continued at intervals and under obvious disadvantages, it was still going on in 1878, as is shown by a reference on p. 114 to the second volume of the Privy Council Register, which was published that year. It must have been after this that Chapter II. was completed, and, with the exception of a couple of sheets, printed off. A first proof of the remainder of the book, chiefly made up of extracts from the Town Council Registers down to the year 1872, had been obtained and was waiting revisal for the press and the writing of a connecting narrative; but at this stage the printers, seeing no early prospect of the release of their type in the ordinary way, took it down, thus removing at least one incentive to speedy publication.

Subsequent to his retirement from the Town-Clerkship of

Glasgow, the completion of the book was one of the objects which Sir James had in view; but other undertakings had precedence, and at the time of his death the print remained in the condition in which it had been left about thirty years before. Though the work was not so complete as the author intended to make it, and though nearly one-half of the pages required to be re-set, the information brought together was considered too valuable to be longer withheld from publication, and arrangements were accordingly made for the book being issued. Access to the MS. Council Registers was readily granted by Mr. Hunter, Town Clerk, and, with the assistance obligingly rendered by Mr. Jarvis, of the Town-Clerk's Office, the Revd. Walter MacLeod, Edinburgh, was enabled to collate the unrevised proofs with the original record, thereby ensuring accuracy in the extracts. The late Mr. Adam, City Chamberlain, had furnished the statistics derived from the Guildry Accounts, and his successor, Mr. Paton, has been kind enough to supply a few supplementary particulars.

The portrait forming the frontispiece is from a photograph of the Author taken about the time the book was written.

R. RENWICK.

Glasgow, *April* 1909.

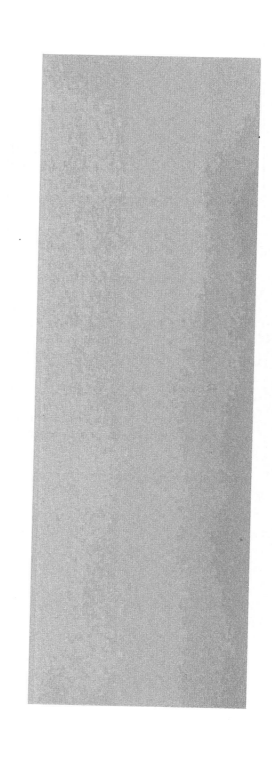

# CONTENTS.

———◆———

# CORRECTIONS.

Page 10, line 16, *for* " 1389" *read* " 1369." Footnote 7, *for* " 92 " *read* " 192."

Page 24, line 25, *for* " south " *read* " north."

Page 39, line 6, *for* " blacksmiths), goldsmiths " *read* " blacksmiths, goldsmiths." Line 7, *for* " armourers, fleshers " *read* " armourers), fleshers."

Page 127, footnote 4, line 2, *for* " Lord " *read* " of."

Page 158, line 6, *for* " burgh " *read* " burghs."

Page 183, line 23, *for* " the following " *read* " an." Lines 26–30 should be transposed to follow " stent " in line 33.

# BURGESS-SHIP, GUILD-BROTHERHOOD,

AND

# MEMBERSHIP OF CRAFTS
# IN EDINBURGH.

A

# CHAPTER I.

THE earliest glimpses of Scottish burghs are obtained in the Laws of the Four Burghs of Edinburgh, Roxburgh, Berwick, and Stirling, compiled in the reign of David I. (1124–1153);[1] in the legislation of William the Lion (1165–1214); in the Statutes of the Guild, enacted for the regulation of the guild of merchants of Berwick, before the end of the thirteenth century, but soon generally adopted and quoted as authoritative among the burghs of Scotland; in the Articuli Inquirendi in Itinere Camerarii,[2] which seem to belong to the latter half of the reign of Robert I. (ending in 1329); and in the Iter Camerarii,[2] which is apparently of the end of the fourteenth century.

In these collections,[3] and in the charters granted by successive monarchs to the burghs of Scotland, these burghs are presented as compact, well organized bodies, possessing recognised public rights

---

[1] Of the Laws of the Four Burghs, Mr. Burton observes: 'Altogether the Laws of the Four Burghs are more complete and compact, and have in them more of the qualities of a body of statute law, than any other fragments of ancient legislation in Scotland.'—*History of Scotland* (2d edition), vol. ii. p. 91.

[2] Both the Articuli Inquirendi and the Iter Camerarii relate to the procedure of the Great Chamberlain in his eyres or circuit courts. This high officer was charged with the supervision of all matters connected with burghs, and held his eyres periodically for the determination of questions of burghal administration.

[3] The references to these, and to the other old burghal laws and customs quoted in the footnotes, will be made to the collection issued by the Scottish Burgh Records Society, under the title, 'Ancient Laws and Customs of the Burghs of Scotland, 1124–1424.'

and valuable monopolies, and enjoying the advantages of local government.

The main condition of membership of these early communities appears to have been the possession of real property within the burgh. Thus, it is declared by the Laws of the Four Burghs that—

'na man may be the kyngis burges bot gif he may do service to the kyng of als mekyl as fallys till ane rude of land at the leste.'[1]

Again, ' Ilke burges sall geyff to the kyng for his borowage at he deffendis for ilke rud of land v d. be yhere.' [2]

Further, ' Gif ony mannis thryll, barounis or knychtis, cummys to burgh and byis a borowage, and duellis in his borowage a tuelfmoneth and a day foroutyn challange of his lorde or of his bailye, he sall be evirmare fre as a burges wythin that kyngis burgh and joyse the fredome of that burgh.'[3]

The law under which a serf obtained freedom by acquiring a burrowage, and occupying it for a year and a day unclaimed for his lord, is also stated in the Regiam Majestatem.[4] It existed in England in the reign of Henry I.[5] It obtained in the cities of France, and a similar custom was established in Germany; but the

---

[1] Leges Burgorum Scocie, § 49. It is declared by § 54 of the Fragmenta Collecta that 'the rude off the land in the burghe mesurit off a midlyng mane sal be xx. fute.'

[2] Ibid., § 1.                                    [3] Ibid., § 15.

[4] Lib. ii. c. ix. 'Gif ane natiue bondman, whais bond that ever he be, remaine quietlie the space of ane year and ane day in anie privileged toun, sic as the king's burgh in thair communitie or gild, and is not challenged be his maister, nor be nane in his name, sic as his bailie or steward, in that case he sal be frie and delivered fra bondage.'

[5] The customs of Newcastle-upon-Tyne, in the reign of Henry I., as set forth in a report drawn up in the time of Henry II., declare, 'Si rusticus in burgo veniat manere, et ibi per annum unum et diem sicut burgensis maneat in burgo, ex toto remaneat, nisi prius ab ipso vel domino suo prælocutum sit ad terminum remanere' [Acts of the Parliament of Scotland, vol. i. pp. 33, 34]. Glanvil's treatise, ' De legibus et consuetudinibus Angliæ,' written in the reign of Henry II., and from which treatise a large portion of the Regiam Majestatem has been copied, contains the following passage: ' Si quis nativus quietè per unum annum et unum diem in aliqua villa privilegiata mauserit, ita quod in eorum communem gyldam tanquam civis receptus fuerit, eo ipso a villenagio liberabitur.' L. v. c. 5.

time of prescription was, in some places at least, much longer than a year and a day.[1]

What was necessary to the acquisition of freedom and burgess-ship in Scotland in early times was the purchase of a burrowage, and residence in it for a year and a day without challenge. A bondman might, no doubt, escape into a town and elude observation for that time; but unless he brought with him the means of purchasing a burgage tenement, and actually acquired one, his residence was ineffectual. Property in those days, however, consisted mainly of stock, which could not be sold except in the presence of witnesses, with all the formalities prescribed by the law; and it is almost inconceivable that any bondman or person attached to the soil could realize the means wherewith to purchase a burrowage without the knowledge and challenge of his lord. The attainment of freedom and burgess-ship under this law, therefore, cannot have been a thing of easy accomplishment.

The object of the provision was, doubtless, to prevent bondmen or native men from settling in burghs and prosecuting their callings for the benefit of their lords. But for this salutary law, it would have been the interest of the lords to encourage the settlement of their bondmen in towns. The servile element would thus have existed to a large extent among the burgesses, with what deteriorating effect it is not difficult to imagine. But the declaration that the possession and occupancy of a burrowage for a year and a day secured the freedom of the owner, and entitled him to all the privileges of burgess-ship, effectually prevented such a result, and made every burgh a centre of freedom.

After a time burghal communities assumed the power of regulating the conditions of burgess-ship, and exercised exclusively the discretionary and arbitrary power of making burgesses. Formal admission by the magistrates, with the consent of the community,

[1] Hallam's Middle Ages, vol. i. p. 260.

and subsequent enrolment, were prescribed;[1] and with a view, probably, at once to enhance the value of the right and to provide funds for the public works and other requirements of the burgh, admission both as a burgess and guild brother came to be sold at prices fixed by tariffs approved of from time to time by the governing body. On admission, every burgess had to

'swer fewte to our lorde the kyng and to the bailyeis, and to the communyte of that burgh in the whilk he is made new burges.'[2]

His name was thereupon inserted in the roll of burgesses, and that roll had to be produced at the eyres of the Great Chamberlain.[3]

Various charters to royal burghs refer to residence as a condition of burgess-ship. Thus, in his charter to Ayr, William the Lion granted peculiar privileges to the burgesses 'who shall come and inhabit his said burgh, and shall there settle and remain.'[4] And when Alexander II. made a burgh at his new castle of Dumbarton, in 1221, he gave to the burgh and to his burgesses remaining therein all the liberties and free customs which his burgesses in Edinburgh and remaining therein had. He also granted a variety of privileges[5] to the burgesses who should come there to inhabit his said burgh, and there settle and remain.[6] But such residence does not appear to have been essential in the earliest burghs, except with a view to a bondman acquiring freedom. The Laws of the Four Burghs, for example, provided that a rustic living out of the burgh, but having a burrowage within it,

---

[1] Iter Camerarii, § 28.

[2] Leges Burgorum, § 2. The form of oath to be taken by a burgess is given in the Juramenta Officiariorum in the Ayr MS., which is of the time of Robert I. (1306–1329).

[3] Iter Camerarii, § 3.

[4] 'Burgensibus qui illuc venient ad burgum meum inhabitandum, et ibi sedentes et manentes erint.'

[5] See copy of charter, as given in Irving's History of Dumbartonshire, 2d edition, p. 45.

[6] The same words precisely as those employed in the charter to Ayr.

should be held to be a burgess only in that burgh in which his burrowage was.[1] Again, failure on the part of a non-resident burgess to attend the three head courts of the burgh subjected him to a fine of 8s., while the resident burgess had to forfeit only 4d., the difference being accounted for by the fact that the non-resident burgess was required to attend only these head courts.[2] The existence of non-resident burgesses, with limited rights and privileges, is also recognised in the legislation of William the Lion, and in the Statutes of the Guild,—the former enacting that no burgess who dwelt out of burgh should buy or sell or be free in any burgh except that in which he was burgess;[3] and the latter providing that no burgess or guild brother dwelling beyond the burgh should buy or sell merchandise belonging to the guild in the burgh except on the market day, and that no non-resident burgess should buy victual imported in ships to sell or retail, but only for the sustentation of his house, under the penalty of a cask of wine to the guild.[4] The Iter Camerarii also directed that all burgesses, non-resident as well as resident, should appear before the chamberlain or his depute when he held his eyre in burgh; and that the roll of burgesses, which had to be produced on such occasions, should contain the names of all the burgesses resident within the burgh as well as beyond it.[5] Non-resident burgesses, like those persons who sold their goods at stalls, and were known as 'stallengers,'[6] were pro-

[1] Leges Burgorum, § 11.
[2] Ibid., § 40.
[3] Fragmenta Collecta, § 9.
[4] Statuta Gilde, § 51.
[5] Iter Camerarii, § 3.
[6] Stallengers were required by the Leges Burgorum to pay the provost (*prepositus*) such sum as might be agreed upon betwixt them, or, failing that, a half-penny each market day for the privilege of being permitted to sell at a stall in the street. Each merchant ('*mersar*,' '*mercenarius*') who used a covered booth in the market on the market day had to pay the *prepositus* a half-penny for custom, and if his booth was not covered he had to pay a farthing. —Leges Burgorum, § 37. Stallengers were, however, prohibited from buying or selling within burgh as burgesses, or from brewing, making malt, or holding mills.—Articuli-Inquirendi, § 66.

hibited from having *cut* or *cavil*[1] with a burgess of any kind of merchandise, except during the time of fairs.[2] But burgesses resident beyond burgh were declared to have the same delay on law days as one resident burgess was entitled to have against another.[3]

✝Residence, however, came to be regarded as essential to burgess-

---

[1] The words *lot* or *cut* and *cavil* occur three or four times in the old burgh laws. The Statutes of the Guild ordain that no one but a brother of guild shall have *lot* or *cavil* 'with brother of our guild' (§ 23), and that no brother of guild ought to have *lot* or *cavil* with another in less than a half-quarter of skins, and half a dakir (probably one dozen) of hides or two stones of wool (§ 48). The Court of the Four Burghs enacted in 1405 that no outland burgess should have *lot or cavil* with burgesses dwelling within burgh (§ 3). In these cases the words seem to mean a share of something, or a place or position determined by lot. Jamieson says that in their strict and appropriate signification, as used in the passage referred to in the text, they refer to what seems to have been a very ancient custom at fairs in Scotland, 'a custom which still prevails in the north at least. As multitudes of *chapmen* have been accustomed to repair to these fairs from various parts of the country, and to erect *stalls*, or temporary booths, in the street, or wherever the fair was held, for exposing their goods to sale; in order to prevent the broils, and even bloodshed, which often resulted from their struggles to obtain the best situations, it was reckoned necessary that all who meant to erect stalls should give in their names, and cast *cavils*, or draw cuts, as to the place that each was to occupy.' 'The words, as they occur in the Statutes of the Guild,' he adds, 'must be understood in the same sense, and the meaning obviously is, that strangers who came to a fair should not be allowed to cast lots in common with the *gild brether*. The latter were to have the preference; and after they had cast lots for their places, strangers might do it among themselves for those that were unoccupied.'—(Scottish Dictionary, *voce* CAVIL.) The limitation in the 48th section of the Statutes of the Guild was probably intended to prevent guild brethren who had a small quantity of merchandise to sell, from competing for places in the market with those whose stocks were greatly in excess of the specified minimum. The enactment by the Court of the Four Burghs excluded non-resident burgesses from competing for places with burgesses who resided in the burgh.

[2] Leges Burgorum, § 54. The fair in burghs was a time of license, and none but the outlaw, the traitor, or malefactor who had offended so as to be beyond sanctuary, could be arrested during its continuance; all others were free from attachment, unless they broke the peace of the fair (Leges Burgorum, §§ 3, 86, 87, 92), in which case they were tried, not by the magistrates of the burgh, but by the court of the fair, known as the court of *pies poudress*, or *dusty feet, i.e.* the travelling pedlars or merchants.

[3] Fragmenta Collecta, § 7.

ship. This appears from the frequent legislation of Parliament, of the Convention of Burghs, and of the Town Council, to which reference will afterwards be made.

From the earliest times women appear to have exercised the privileges of burgess-ship and membership of the guild. This is shown by the 116th section of the Laws of the Four Burghs, which commences thus:—'Gif a man or a woman that is burgess dee in the burgh,' etc.;[1] and by an enactment of the same code, to the effect that, if a widow living in burgh wished to buy and sell with her neighbours, she had to bear her share in all aids with them. But widows were exempted from the duty of watching the burgh.[2] The 11th section of the Statutes of the Guild also declares that no persons shall be received into the guild for less than forty shillings, except 'they be gild sonnes and gild daughters.' Entries also occur in the early records of various burghs of the admission of women as burgesses and guild brethren,[3] but nowhere do women appear to have taken any part in the administration of the affairs of burghs or guilds.

Burgess-ship implied submission to various duties and obligations. The burgess had, as has been seen, to defend his burrow-

[1] 'Si homo vel femina burgensis in burgo moriatur,' etc.
[2] Leges Burgorum, §§ 104, 81.
[3] Extracts from the Records of the Burgh of Edinburgh (Scottish Burgh Records Society), vol. i. p. 2. Extracts from the Records of the Burgh of Peebles (Scottish Burgh Records Society), pp. 113, 133, 151, 162. Records of the Burgh of Prestwick (Maitland Club), pp. 12, 16, 20, 60, 61, 89.

In later times the practice in this respect became much less liberal, and the admission of women to the privileges of burgess-ship, or of the guildry, was unknown. The question came up, however, for consideration by the Town Council of Edinburgh in 1869, and, on a report by the town-clerk, the right of women to become burgesses, if otherwise qualified, was recognised. Burgess-ship is now therefore attainable in the capital of Scotland without distinction of sex. The principle was carried still further recently, when the Baroness Burdett Coutts was created an honorary burgess of the city.

Merewether and Stephens state that females were by the common law exempted from service at the court leet, and were never admitted as burgesses,

B

age.[1] He was also bound to maintain a house upon it; and if he was made a burgess of a waste land, and had no inhabited house within the burgh, he behoved to have a house built and occupied after a year.[2] He had to attend the three head courts of the burgh, held after the feast of St. Michael, Yule, and Easter.[3] He had to be provided with measures and weights, sealed with the seal of the burgh,[4] and he behoved, whether resident or non-resident, to attend the chamberlain's eyre, and to answer to his name when the roll of burgesses was called.[5] He was bound to watch the burgh,[6] and, in addition to these duties imposed upon him by statute, he was subject to all the obligations incident to the possession of real property, viz. liability to pay a share of common civic burdens, and to sustain in turn such offices as the law imposed on the free inhabitants of burghs. These obligations were known in Scotland, as they were in England, by the term _Scot_ and _Lot_. An Act of David II., in 1389, prohibited burgesses from leaving Scotland without the permission of the king or the chamberlain.[7]

On the other hand, burgess-ship conferred important privileges.

No foreign merchant could buy wool, hides, or other merchandise, except within burgh and from a burgess;[8] and no one

though they were admitted as members of guilds (History of Boroughs, vol. i. p. 565). But in Scotland there seems to be no reason to doubt that every member of the merchant guild of a burgh had first to be a burgess, and so to become free of the burgh.

The widows of freemen in London appear to have been authorized for the first time to carry on their husbands' arts and occupations in the city by the charter of Charles I., dated 18th October 1638.

[1] Leges Burgorum, § 1.

[2] Ibid., § 27; Articuli Inquirendi, § 36; Curia Quatuor Burgorum (1405), § 2. The only exception to this rule was, when the house of a burgess was laid waste by fire or war; in which case, if he had other land built upon, he might delay till he was able to build, paying the king's rent in the meantime.

[3] Leges Burgorum, § 40.      [4] Ibid., §§ 48, 68.      [5] Iter Camerarii, § 3.

[6] Leges Burgorum, § 81; Articuli Inquirendi, § 52. At the stroke of a staff on the door of each burgher's house, a watchman was bound to come forth with two weapons, and to watch the town from _coûre feû_ till day dawn.

[7] Acta Parliamentorum Regis David II., p. 92.      [8] Leges Burgorum, § 16.

but a burgess could buy wool to dye, or make or cut cloth.[1] Churchmen, barons, and other secular persons were prohibited from buying wool, skins, hides, and such like merchandise, and were bound to sell the same to merchants of burghs within the sheriffdom and liberty in which they resided.[2]  Salt and herrings arriving by sea had to be sold on shipboard; but all other sea-borne merchandise had to be landed before being sold.[3]  Subject apparently to the above exception, all merchandise was appointed to be presented at the market cross, and there offered to the merchants of the burgh in good faith.[2]  Merchants from abroad were prohibited from selling their merchandise elsewhere than in burgh, or to others than the merchants of the burgh.  They were also prohibited from cutting cloth or selling in retail, but only in great,[4] and within burgh, to merchants of the burgh.[5]  No one but a burgess could have an oven on his land,[6] or keep hand mills,[7] or make lard for sale.[8]  Commerce was thus rigidly forbidden to any class except the burgesses, who were free to buy and sell throughout Scotland, by water and by land.[9]  The freedom of trade thus enjoyed by the burgess extended to his son so long as he lived in family with him; but when the son left the family, the privilege ceased until he purchased the freedom of the burgh, and, in the language of the vernacular, was ' maid free man.'[10]  William the Lion also granted to the burgesses of Scotland and their heirs—

'That thai salbe quyt of tol and lastage, of pontage, of passage alswele within as without of all the hevynnis of the sey, within the kinrik of Scotland, alswele on this side of the Scottes sey [11] as beyond.'[12]

---

[1] Leges Burgorum, § 20.          [2] Assise Willelmi Regis, §§ 38–40.
[3] Leges Burgorum, § 9.  [4] i.e. wholesale.  [5] Assise Willelmi Regis, § 41.
[6] Leges Burgorum, § 18.  For the manner in which ovens had to be kept, see §§ 61, 62.
[7] Articuli Inquirendi, § 58.     [8] Ibid., § 61.    [9] Fragmenta Collecta, § 29.
[10] Leges Burgorum, § 14.          [11] i.e. the Frith of Forth.
[12] Fragmenta Collecta, § 8.  The charters by the same king to Aberdeen and Ayr confer similar privileges upon the burgesses of these burghs respectively. See charters in Appendix to General Report on Municipal Corporations, pp. 6, 7.

All suits and actions arising within burgh, except such as appertained to the Crown, behoved to be determined in the burgh court. The burgess might decline the jurisdiction of any court outside of the burgh; and in all matters he had the right, in common with every Scottish freeholder, to be tried by his peers.[1] When challenged of any suit, and required to answer in the king's court, he might appear and claim to be tried in the court of his burgh, before his alderman or bailie (*prepositus*). But he was bound to show due respect to the royal authority by appearing in obedience to a lawful citation, and pleading his privilege, otherwise he was amenable to the jurisdiction of the king's court.[2] No burgess, however, could be summoned by a king's sergeant unless accompanied by a sergeant of the burgh;[3] and no person residing in burgh who was attached for any cause by a king's bailie could be removed beyond the liberty of the burgh, either to the castle or to any other prison, unless he failed to find surety.[4]

From the earliest times the laws and customs of the burghs were designed to foster the spirit of peace, so essential to commercial and manufacturing enterprise. Outside of the burgh the wager of battle was a recognised institution, to which even the Church lent its most solemn sanction; and for the burghal code to have prohibited it altogether would have been, as Mr. Burton observes, a radical measure, which might, indeed, have compromised the rank taken by the burgesses in the body politic. If, therefore, two burgesses resident in the same town desired to settle their quarrel by an appeal to arms, there does not appear to have been anything to prevent them. If, however, a rustic, or non-resident burgess, challenged a resident burgess, the latter was not bound to fight— he might defend himself by law; but if, on the other hand, the resident burgess challenged the rustic, or non-resident burgess, the

---

[1] Leges Burgorum, §§ 6, 7; Fragmenta Collecta, § 8.
[2] Leges Burgorum, § 57; Fragmenta Collecta, § 34.
[3] Leges Burgorum, § 110.            [4] Ibid., § 117.

rustic had to defend himself by battle.[1]  If, again, an 'upland man,' not connected with the burgh, challenged the burgess, the latter was required to defend himself by law of burgh, and not to fight, unless the challenge were of treason or of 'theme,'[2] in which case he was bound to defend himself by combat.  And under any circumstances, when a burgess was to fight an upland man, he behoved to go out of the burgh to do so.[3]  The other provisions of the burghal code on this subject were all such as to favour the king's burgess.  Thus it was declared that a king's burgess might have battle of the burgesses of an abbot or friar, and of an earl or baron, but they could not require him to fight.[4]  And again, when a burgess was challenged to battle and was too old to fight, he might plead his age, and purge himself, by the oaths of twelve men such as himself, of that whereof he was accused.[5]  The privileges thus conferred on burgesses were renewed by William the Lion, except in respect to such pleas as fell to the Crown.[6]

The burgess also enjoyed the right, when in sound health, but not on deathbed, of disposing as he pleased of all lands within burgh purchased or acquired by him of conquest,[7] and of selling or mortgaging, under certain conditions, such lands as he had succeeded to by inheritance.  The provisions of the Laws of the Four Burghs on this subject are precise.

Every burgess was at liberty, except when on deathbed, to give or sell to whomsoever he pleased all the lands within burgh which he had purchased or acquired of conquest.[8]  He was not at liberty, however, to alienate or sell, to the prejudice of his heir,[9] such property

---

[1] Leges Burgorum, § 11.

[2] i.e. question of freedom.

[3] Leges Burgorum, § 12.

[4] Ibid., § 13.

[5] Ibid., § 22.

[6] Fragmenta Collecta, § 8.

[7] Conquest in Scotland is such heritage as a person acquires by purchase, donation, or exchange, and not as an heir.

[8] Leges Burgorum, §§ 21, 42.  Fragmenta Collecta, § 23.

[9] The Regiam Majestatem declared the heir of a burgess to be of perfect age when he could number and tell silver, or measure cloth with an ell-wand, and attend to his father's other business and affairs (lib. ii. c. 35).

as he had acquired by inheritance, unless when compelled by poverty
to do so, and after offering it in the first instance to the next heir at
three head courts of the burgh.   Then, if the heir wished to have
the land, he had to provide the seller with such meat and clothes
as he needed—the clothes being grey or white in colour; but if
the heir either did not wish the land, or was unable to acquire it,
it might be sold to any other person.[1]   In like manner, except when
under the pressure of poverty, a burgess was not entitled to alienate
his principal messuage from his heir, nor could he endow his wife
therewith if he had any other land with which he might dote her.[2]
In consistency with these provisions, which were all intended for
the benefit of the heir, a burgess might, when in sound health, give
all his lands—those to which he had succeeded equally with those
which he had acquired—to his heir; but if the father afterwards
became impoverished, and the son failed to provide for him, the
father might, notwithstanding his previous gift, lawfully sell or
mortgage the lands for the relief of his necessity; but before such
sale or mortgage was effectual, the necessity of the father had to
be established by the oaths of twelve leal and worthy men of the
burgh.[3]   If, however, a father who had several children and sundry
lands conveyed a portion to each, retaining the fruits during his
lifetime, the heir was not entitled to impugn the bequests, on the
ground that the children were in minority.[4]   When lands were
sold by a burgess under the pressure of necessity, after having
been offered to his nearest friends, it was not competent for these
friends, when the lands were built upon and furnished by the purchaser, to come forward to redeem them with money borrowed
for the purpose.   The title of the purchaser was absolute and

---

[1] Leges Burgorum, § 42.   An interesting illustration of this law is found in
a charter granted by Robert de Methyngby to the Archdeacon of Glasgow
in 1280-90.—Charters and Documents relating to the City of Glasgow
(Scottish Burghs Records Society), No. xiii. p. 17.   See also Leges Burgorum,
§ 114.

[2] Leges Burgorum, § 106.         [3] Ibid., § 107.            [4] Ibid., § 108.

irredeemable.[1]  The superior, and the heir of the superior, of lands
within burgh which had been let in feu-farm, were entitled to a
right of pre-emption of these lands, in the event of the feuar or
his heirs being necessitated to sell them.[2]

According to the custom of burghs, as ascertained on a consultation between the burghs of England and Scotland at Newcastle,[3]
no burgess while on deathbed could give or sell, or in any way
alienate from his heir, any lands in burgh acquired by succession
or conquest, unless under the pressure of absolute necessity, and
when the heir either could not or would not supply his father's
needs or pay his debts.[4]

If a burgess died possessed of lands in burgh, either by succession or conquest, leaving a widow and a child, the child inherited
all the lands, with the exception of the inner half of the principal
house, which was called 'the flett.'  The outer half was retained by
the heir if he chose to occupy it.  If, however, the widow had been
otherwise provided for by the husband, the heir took the whole of
the principal house.[5]  If the heir was in minority, he remained
with his 'chattels' in the custody of his mother's relatives, his
father's kindred taking care of the heritage till he came of age.[6]
If a burgess who had been married oftener than once, and had a
family with each wife, died, leaving many lands, all the lands of
which he died possessed, acquired by him either by succession or
conquest during the first marriage, belonged to the children of the
first marriage.  All the lands, on the other hand, which had been
similarly acquired during the second marriage belonged to the
children of the second marriage; and so on.  The widow, whether
of a second or subsequent marriage, was not entitled to remain

---

[1] Leges Burgorum, § 91.          [2] Ibid., § 95.
[3] Scotland in the Middle Ages, p. 154.
[4] Leges Burgorum, § 101.  See also Fragmenta Collecta, §§ 17, 18.
[5] Leges Burgorum, § 23.  See also Fragmenta Collecta, § 19.
[6] Leges Burgorum, § 98.

longer than forty days after the death of her husband in the house which belonged to the heir.[1]

As regarded lands acquired in burgh through a marriage of which there was issue, the husband was entitled, after the death of his wife, to enjoy the property during his lifetime, and on his demise it passed to the issue. The husband was equally entitled to the liferent if there was a living child of the marriage, though it may have died immediately after birth, provided it could be proved, by the evidence of two leal men or women, to have been heard 'crying, or greeting, or braying.' On the dissolution of the marriage by the death of the wife, without a living child having been born, the land passed to the heir of the wife.[2]

These and other provisions of the Laws of the Four Burghs prove indisputably that the burgesses of the twelfth century were vested in the absolute property of their burrowages; that the succession of their heirs was anxiously secured; and that, while alienation to strangers was discouraged, it was competent in cases of necessity.

Twelve witnesses were required to the sale of lands within burgh, and afterwards formal possession or sasine was given or taken, in presence of the alderman or bailie (*prepositus*), in this wise: The seller, being within the land sold, passed out, and the purchaser, being without, entered, and both paid a penny to the magistrate, the one for his outgoing, and the other for his entry and sasine. When lands were excambed (exchanged), each of the parties paid twopence to the magistrate.[3] After lands thus sold had been possessed in peace and without challenge for a year and a day, the purchaser could not be deprived of them unless the person challenging his right was under age or out of the kingdom, in either of which cases the challenger's right existed till he attained majority or returned to the country.[4] On the other hand,

---

[1] Leges Burgorum, § 24.          [2] Ibid., § 41.          [3] Ibid., § 52.
[4] Ibid., § 10. The same law existed in England, and is thus expressed in the charters by Henry II. to Lincoln and Nottingham: 'Concedo etiam eis,

if the purchaser had passed on pilgrimage, or had gone beyond sea on business, before the challenger had shown the king's letters in court, it behoved the challenger to delay proceedings till his return, unless he remained away fraudulently, in which case the challenger was not bound to delay longer than forty days.[1]

The same anxiety to prevent the land of a burgess from passing out of his family for debt is evinced in the Laws of the Four Burghs. Before a creditor could sell lands held by him in security of a debt which was past due, he behoved to offer them to the debtor at three head courts, and failing the debtor then redeeming the lands, the creditor might sell them, paying over to the debtor any surplus of the price.[2] If one burgess became surety for another, who died leaving no means for the relief of the surety except his lands, the surety was bound to hold the lands for forty days, and during that time to offer the lands to the nearest friends of the debtor at three head courts. If they did not pay the debt or purchase the land, then the surety was at liberty to sell them to any person, paying over to the heirs of the debtor whatever surplus of the price remained after settling the debt.[3] In like manner, if a burgess had no other means than his lands wherewith to pay his debt, the creditor was bound to hold the lands for a year and a day, offering them during the currency of that time to the nearest heirs; and if they did not pay the debt or purchase the lands, the creditor might sell them to any person, paying over the surplus of the price to the debtor.[4]

The Laws of the Four Burghs also contain a statement of the

quod si aliquis emerit aliquam terram infra civitatem de burgagio Lincoln et eam tenuerit per annum et unum diem sine calumpnia, et ille qui eam emerit, possit monstrare quod calumpniator exteterit in regione Angliæ infra annum et non calumpniatus est, eam ex tunc est in antea bene et in pace teneat eam et sine placito' [Fœdera (Record Edition), vol. i. p. 40]. 'Et quicunque burgensium terram vicini sui emerit, et possident per annum integrum et diem unum absque calumpnia parentum vendentis si in Anglia fuerint postea eam quietè possidebit' [Ib. vol. i. p. 41].

[1] Leges Burgorum, § 45.    [2] Ibid., § 79.    [3] Ibid., § 89.    [4] Ibid., § 90.

custom in the burghs of Scotland as to succession in moveables, embodying the result of a consultation at Newcastle between the burghs of England and Scotland. On the death of a burgess leaving lawful children, a third portion went to the children, sons or daughters, the eldest son and heir taking an equal share with the other children unless he had been forisfamiliated.[1] The enumeration in these laws of the articles, pertaining to the house, which the heir was entitled to take, in the case of intestate succession, is interesting, as affording information in regard to the furnishing of the dwelling of a burgess in early times.[2] To the best of all these and other household articles the heir had right. The burgess was not even entitled to sell them unless compelled by necessity, and then only in the presence of witnesses.

Scarcely, if at all, inferior in importance to the right enjoyed by burgesses of transmitting and selling their property, was the right which they possessed of electing their own magistrates, to whom were entrusted the administration of their laws in the courts of the burgh.

On this subject the Laws of the Four Burghs enact that—

'at the fyrst mute nexte eftir the feste of Sancte Mychael, the alderman and the bailies [*prepositi*] sal be chosyn thruch the consaile of the gud men of the toune, the whilk aw to be lele and of gud fame.'[3]

---

[1] Leges Burgorum, § 115.  Fragmenta Collecta, § 21.

[2] Leges Burgorum, § 116.  The following is the enumeration referred to :— The best board, with the trests or supports, a table cloth, a towel, a basin, a laver, the best bed, with the sheets and all the clothes that belonged to it, the best feather bed, and if there were no feather bed, the best wool or flock bed, a leyd with a maskfat or vat for brewing, a vat for fermenting wort, a barrel, a caldron, a kettle, a gridiron, a small porringer, a chimney, a pitcher, and a crook or instrument for suspending a pot over the fire.  All buildings on the ground, and everything sown or planted, also fell to the heir, who was also entitled to have a chest, a shearing hook, a plough, a waggon, a cart, a car, a brazen pot, a pan, a roasting iron, a girdle, a mortar, a pestle, a drinking cup, a large wooden platter, a cup, twelve spoons, a bench or seat, a form, a stool, a balance and weights, a spade, an axe.  See also Fragmenta Collecta, § 20.

[3] Leges Burgorum, § 70.

And the Statutes of the Guild ordain—

' that the mayor and bailies [*maior et prepositi*] shall be chosen at the sight and by the consideration of the whole community.' [1]

No record of the elections of magistrates in Edinburgh previous to the fifteenth century is in existence. But the valuable records of Aberdeen set forth the appointment of the magistrates of that burgh, on the Monday after Michaelmas 1398, in the following terms :—

' On which day, William of Chamber, the father, with the consent and assent of the whole community of the said burgh, is elected to the office of alderman, and Robert the son of David Simon of Benyer, John Scherar, and Master William Dicson are elected to the office of bailies.' [2]

The election of the alderman, bailies, and sergeants for the following year is also made in the same terms : ' *cum consensu et assensu totius communitatis dicti burgi.*' [3]  It thus appears that by the Laws of the Four Burghs, and by the practice of Aberdeen, which recognised and held itself bound at a very early period by these laws,[4] the alderman or provost and the bailies were elected at the first court after Michaelmas, through the consent of the good men of the town, as it is expressed in the Laws of the Burghs, or at the sight and consideration of the whole community, as it is expressed in the Statutes of the Guild.[5]

---

[1] Statuta Gilde, § 38.

[2] General Report of Commissioners on Municipal Corporations, p. 18.

[3] Extracts from the Burgh Records of Aberdeen (Spalding Club), vol. i. p. 374.

[4] Ibid., vol. v. p. 1.

[5] The old usages of the city of Winchester, which are written in a hand of the fourteenth century, and refer to a still earlier period in which they were observed, contain many provisions which.throw light on the old burgh laws and customs of Scotland.  In that document it is set forth, ' that the mayor should be chosen every year by twenty-four sworn men and by the commonalty, that there should be twenty-four sworn men " in stede of the moste. gode men, and of the wysest of the toun, for to treuleche helpe and counseyle the forsaid meyer for to saue and susteyne the franchyse," and that they should

Who were ' the gudemen of the toune, lele and of gud fame,' the
' *probi homines fideles et bone fame*,' referred to in the Laws of the
Four Burghs, or the whole community, ' *tota communitas*,' referred
to in the Statutes of the Guild and in the record of the Aberdeen
elections, has been made the subject of controversy. It cannot be
supposed, however, that a right so important as that of the election of the magistracy rested on anything other than a distinct
and intelligible basis; and there seems to be little room for doubt
that the ' *probi homines* ' and the ' *tota communitas* ' were one and
the same, viz. the permanent free inhabitants of the burgh,—the
holders of the burrowages, duly admitted, sworn, and enrolled as
burgesses, who performed the duties and enjoyed the privileges
incident to that relation.

Singularly enough, the Laws of the Four Burghs contain no
distinct reference to the body known as the town council. That
code, no doubt, contains an enactment that—

' in evir ilk burgh of the kinrik of Scotland, the mare or alderman of that ilk
burgh (*superior illius burgi*) sal ger xii. of the lelest burges and of the wysast of
the burgh suer be thair gret athe that all the lawys and the usyt custumys
lauchfully thai sal yeme an mantene eftir their power.'[1]

But this information is very indefinite. Whether the alderman
was to select the twelve, or whether his duty was the purely
ministerial one of seeing that they were elected by the burgesses,
and of administering the oath prescribed, does not appear. Nor
is it stated for what period the persons so sworn were to hold
office—for a year, like the alderman and bailies, or for life, like
justices of the peace in the present day; nor in what manner they
were to exercise their functions. The body thus appointed was,
however, in all probability what originally received and afterwards

attend the mayor on his summons; that two bailiffs should be chosen by the
commonalty out of four named by the twenty-four, at the Michaelmas burgh
moot, with four sergeants to do the bidding of the mayor and bailiffs.'—English
Guilds (Early English Text Society), pp. 349, 350.

[1] Leges Burgorum, § 112.

retained the name of the *duodene* or *dusane,* long after the number of its members exceeded the limit of twelve.[1]

A more distinct reference to a body which may correspond with the town council is contained in the later Statutes of the Guild, enacted, as has been already observed, for Berwick, but subsequently accepted by the other burghs of Scotland. In that capitulary the following provisions occur :—

'We ordain, moreover, by common consent, that the community of Berwick shall be governed by twenty-four good men, of the better, more discreet, and more trustworthy of that burgh thereto chosen,[2] together with the mayor and four bailies. And whensoever the said twenty-four men are summoned to treat concerning the common business, he who comes not at the summons before night shall give two shillings to the Guild.'[3]

It is further enacted, by the following section, that—

'if any controversy be in the election of the mayor or bailies, then their election shall be made by the oaths of twenty-four good men (*proborum hominum*) of the said burgh, elected to choose one person to rule the said community.'[4]

The twenty-four upon whom was thus conferred the power of declaring who should be the magistrates, in the event of any controversy as to their election, were probably the same as those who by the previous section were appointed to govern the com-

[1] There are other well-known illustrations of the practice of bodies or institutions retaining names derived from the number of members of which they were originally composed long after such names had ceased to be applicable. Thus the Danish burghs were called indifferently the 'Five' and the 'Seven' Burghs. Palgrave supposes that the confederation originally consisted of the five towns of Lincoln, Nottingham, Derby, Leicester, and Stamford, and that when York and Chester were added, it continued to be called by the original as well as by the actual number. [Commonwealth, p. 49. See also Kemble's Saxons in England, vol. ii. p. 320.] The Cinque Ports afford another illustration of the same thing ; and in Scotland, the confederation of burghs known as the Court or Parliament of the Four Burghs retained that name long after it consisted of representatives of all the free burghs of the realm.

[2] Probos homines de melioribus et discretioribus ac fidedignioribus eiusdem burgi ad hoc electos.

[3] Statuta Gilde, § 37.

[4] Ibid., § 38. See, as to the usages of Winchester, footnote 5, p. 19.

munity. These, it has been seen, were. elected by the good men of the town. And in conformity with the principle of popular election thus recognised, the election of twenty persons as common councillors in Aberdeen, in 1399, was made on the same day with that of the aldermen and bailies, and apparently also with the consent and assent of the entire community.[1]

There is thus every reason to believe that at a very early period, if not, indeed, at the earliest period, of the municipal history of Edinburgh, it was governed by magistrates, consisting of the *prepositus*—known first as the alderman, and afterwards as the provost —and the bailies, and by a body of burgesses called the *duodene, dusane,* or council. The magistrates, and probably also the *dusane* or council, were elected annually at or about Michaelmas, so that the municipal year must be regarded as extending from the beginning of October in one year to the beginning of October in the year following.

The burgess also possessed a variety of other privileges.

He was exempted from bludwit,[2] stingisdynt,[3] merchit,[4] herezeld,[5] and such like things.[6] What the precise meaning or effect of this provision was it is not very easy to say. It, however, may be accepted as indicating that the burgess was free from many of the exactions to which the vassal was liable under the feudal tenure. He could not be poinded without leave of the *prepositus*.[7]

If a burgess claimed a debt from any one resident out of the burgh, by which was probably meant a non-resident burgess, the

---

[1] Eodem die electi sunt in communes consiliarios dicti burgi Willelmus de Camera pater, and nineteen other persons.—Extracts from the Burgh Records of Aberdeen (Spalding Club), vol. i. p. 374.

[2] The fine for the effusion of blood.

[3] A stroke with a baton or stick.

[4] The tax payable by a vassal to his superior on the marriage of his daughter.

[5] The best horse, ox, or cow belonging to the vassal or tenant, which on his death was given to the superior or landlord.

[6] Leges Burgorum, § 17.         [7] Ibid., § 4.

non-resident burgess, if he admitted the claim, behoved to pay it ;
if he denied the claim, he had to answer to it in the court of the
burgh.[1] If a burgess claimed a debt from any one except a knight,
and the debt was denied, he might require the oath of the person
so denying the debt. If, however, he could not establish his claim
against the knight by witnesses at common law, the knight might
put forward his steward or grieve (*prepositum suum*), and other
free men, to make the oath required.[2] If a burgess was accused of
theft by an upland man, he might free himself by his own oath and
the oaths of twelve of his neighbours.[3] When a king's burgess was
absent with the leave of the Church and of his neighbours on a
pilgrimage to the Holy Land, or to any other sacred place, his house
and means were declared to be in the king's peace and in the
bailies' peace till his return.[4]

In order, probably, to foster the spirit of good neighbourhood
by the interchange of friendly services, the Laws of the Four
Burghs imposed on burgesses reciprocal duties. If a burgess
was attached beyond the burgh for a debt or for any misdeed,
his co-burgesses were bound to go and bail him at their own
expense if he was within the sheriffdom, or at his cost if
beyond the sheriffship.[5] If challenged of any misdeed, and unable
to find bail, his co-burgesses were bound to keep him 'in fasten-
ing' in his own house for fifteen days. If after the expiry of that
time he still had failed to find surety, his neighbours were bound
to deliver him to the king's bailie, by whom he behoved to be
placed in the custody of the king's sergeant if the burgesses had
no prison ; and the sergeant had to provide good and strong fasten-
ing for the burgess placed in his charge, and to keep him from
his challengers.[6] One of the provisions of the Fragmenta Collecta
sets forth the duty of burgesses to be security or pledge for each

[1] Leges Burgorum, § 5.      [2] Ibid., § 28.
[3] Ibid., § 26.      [4] Ibid., § 77.
[5] Ibid., § 51.      [6] Ibid., § 57.

other once, twice, thrice, until loss resulted, after which the loser
was relieved from the obligation to be security further for the
person through whom he had suffered, unless of his own free will,
and on being compensated for the loss he had sustained. This
principle was specially applied to bakers, brewers, and fleshers,—
all of them probably as dealing in what were regarded as the
necessaries of life,—who were required to accommodate their
neighbours with bread, ale, and flesh as long as they had these
articles for sale ; but it was provided that if the person so favoured
failed to pay for the articles so supplied, he should be dis-
trained, and would not be entitled to similar accommodation in
future.[1]

Possessing these privileges, it seems to have been intended that
the respectability of the burgess class should be maintained, as far
as this could be done, by prohibiting burgesses from engaging in
certain avocations which in early times were regarded as incom-
patible with the status of a burgess. Thus, in the Articuli Inquirendi, inquisition was appointed to be made in the chamberlain's
eyre whether fleshers who were burgesses put to their hands to
kill 'mairts,'[2] and whether dyers who were burgesses put their
hands in the wadd.[3]

Such, then, were the rights and privileges of the burgesses of Edinburgh, as disclosed in the oldest burgh laws and forms of procedure;
and there can be little doubt that the rights and privileges of the
burgesses of the other royal burghs south of the Tweed were essen-
tially similar. But within the burghal community there were other
organizations, which, though subordinate, were of great influence.
The most ancient as well as the most important of these was the
guild of merchants,—an association for purely trading purposes,
apart from mechanical pursuits, — which frequently attained a
position that enabled it to overshadow, and sometimes apparently
even to absorb, the municipal organization.

[1] Fragmenta Collecta, § 1.      [2] Leges Burgorum, § 75.      [3] Ibid., § 76.

How early merchant-guilds[1] were established in the Four Burghs it is impossible to say; but their existence in Edinburgh, and in Berwick, Roxburgh, and Stirling, is recognised in an enactment of the Laws of the Four Burghs, to the effect that dyers, fleshers, shoemakers, and fishers should not be in the merchant guild unless they abjured the practice of their trade with their

[1] As associations for mutual help, guilds have existed in England from Anglo-Saxon times, and are referred to in the laws of Ina (A.D. 688, 725) [Thorpe's Anglo-Saxon Laws, Ina, 16, vol. i. p. 113] and of Alfred (A.D. 871, 901) [Ibid., Alfred, 27, 28, vol. i. pp. 79, 80]; in the Judicia Civitatis Lundoniæ of the time of Athelstane (A.D. 924, 940) [Ibid., Athelstane, v. 2, 3; 8, clauses v. vi., vol. i. pp. 229, 230, 237]; in the canons enacted under King Edgar (A.D. 959-975) [Ibid., vol. ii. p. 247]; and in the Laws of Henry I. (A.D. 1100-1135) [Ibid., Henry I., lxxv. § 10; lxxxi. § 1; vol. i. pp. 580-588]. Several guilds, partaking very much of the nature of hundreds, existed in London in the time of Athelstane (A.D. 925-941); and one in particular, known as the Knighten Gild, or Young Men's Gild, continued distinct from the rest of the civic body all through Saxon times [Madox, Firma Burgi, pp. 23, 24; Herbert's Livery Companies, vol. i. pp. 5-7; Merewether's Municipal Corporations, vol. i. p. 307]. Another guild of the same name existed, Kemble says, in Canterbury at a still earlier period, in the reign of Ethelbert (A.D. 860) [Saxons in England, vol. ii. p. 335]. There were also guilds at Cambridge, at Abbotsbury, and at Exeter, and their ordinances, the originals of which are in Anglo-Saxon, are still preserved [Turner's History of the Anglo-Saxons, vol. iii. pp. 98, 99; Kemble's Saxons in England, vol. i. pp. 511-513]. Reference is made in Domesday Book to a guild of burgesses and another of clergy in Canterbury [Domesday Book, fols. 2a, 3a. See also Somner's Canterbury, part i. p. 178], and to a guild hall in Dover [Ibid., fol. 1a]. The word guild or gild, with its varieties gield, geld, gyld, is of Saxon origin, and meant a contribution or rateable payment; and it seems that by a natural association the term came to be attached to the fraternities who levied from each of their number a certain payment of money, or contribution of service, towards the common stock or object. But, as Mr. Kemble points out, 'these gylds, whether in their original nature religious, political, or merely social unions, rested upon another and solemn principle: they were sworn brotherhoods between man and man, established and fortified upon oath and pledge; and in them we consequently recognise the germ of those sworn communes, which in the times of the densest seignorial darkness offered a noble resistance to episcopal and baronial tyranny, and formed the nursing-cradles of popular liberty.'—Saxons in England, vol. ii. p. 310.

D

own hands, and conducted it exclusively by servants.[1] The establishment of merchant-guilds, embracing the whole merchants of the realm, was also sanctioned by the assise of King William, which provided that the merchants of the realm should have their merchant guild, and should enjoy and possess the same, with liberty to buy and sell in all places within the bounds of the liberties of burghs, so that each was content with his own liberty, and that none occupied or usurped the liberty of another.[2] The servants of the guild were also empowered by the same assise to apprehend all persons who invaded the rights and privileges which it conferred on the merchants of the realm.[3] His successor, Alexander II., also conferred on the burgesses of Aberdeen, by special charter in 1222, the right to *have*, which probably meant to *continue* and *uphold*, their merchant-guild.[4] Twenty-seven years later, the mayor of Berwick and other good men of that burgh framed what is known as the Laws of the Guild of Scotland, which referred to the existence of more than one guild in the burgh, and enacted that 'all particular guilds' previously existing should be abolished, and the property reasonably and of right belonging to them should be given to the general guild; and that thereafter no one should presume to establish another guild in that burgh, but that all the members should be united in one society, under a common head, in 'suthfast friendship.'[5] These statutes soon came to be adopted and quoted as authoritative in Edinburgh, and amongst the burghs of Scotland generally.

How the mayor of Berwick and the other good men of that town should have abrogated the several guilds which previously existed in the burgh, should have created a new guild, and should have trans-

---

[1] Leges Burgorum, § 94.   [2] Assise Willelmi Regis, § 39.   [3] Ibid., § 41.

[4] 'Ut habeant gildam suam merchatricem.' Kennedy's Annals of Aberdeen, vol. i. p. 13. General Report of Commissioners on Municipal Corporations in Scotland, p. 14.

[5] Statuta Gilde, § 1.

ferred to it all the property of the others, is not explained. It is probable, however, that their action rested upon and gave effect to the resolution of the whole body of the citizens. It seems strange, also, that a code enacted for the regulation of the merchant-guild should have dealt, as this code does, with the election of the magistrates and governing body of the entire community. Merewether and Stephens refer to the sections relative to the election of the mayor and bailies, and of the twenty-four men of the burgh, as if these persons were officers of the guild,[1] distinct from those of the burgh; but it seems difficult to read the 37th and 38th sections as referring to the officers of anything else than the burgh, as distinct from, though including, the guild. Some of the sections deal with matters affecting the whole community,—the administration of the affairs of the town, the police of the markets, and other points of general municipal interest; while others legislate as to matters specially concerning the guild as a separate and subordinate association of persons engaged in mercantile pursuits;[2] and the remainder may be held to deal with subjects that equally affect both the general community of the burgh and the special interests of the brotherhood of the guild.[3] How a code of ordinances for the regulation of a mercantile guild should be made so comprehensive, may be explained on the hypothesis that in Berwick, as in Wallingford in 1266, and in other burghs at a subsequent date, the merchant-guild was under the jurisdiction of the aldermen, bailies, and burgesses, who regulated it as well as the burgh; or it may still more probably be, that the merchant-guild in its re-organized form, including the members and goods of all the other

[1] English guilds often had their own head officer, called alderman,—a term which strictly belongs to the guild, and not to the municipality as such,—and subordinate officers, called stewards, dean, and clerk.

[2] Among the former are articles 18, 19, 20, 21, 22, 24, 26, 27, 28, 29, 30, 31, 32, 33, 34, 35, 36, 37, 38, 40, 41, 42, 43, 44, 45, 46, 48, 49, 50, 51; while among the latter may be classed sections 3, 4, 10, 11, 12, 13, 14, 15, 16, 50.

[3] Among these may be included 2, 5, 6, 7, 8, 9, 17, 23, 25, 39, 47.

guilds of the burgh, comprehended so large a proportion of the burgesses as to be practically co-extensive with and equivalent to the burghal community. This seems to be substantially the opinion of Dr. Brentano, who says that the way in which this statute was drawn up shows clearly that 'citizen' and 'gild brother' were considered identical.[1]

In England, it would appear, a commercial constitution was sometimes engrafted upon burghs, which then took the name of guilds. In many cases the great bulk of the burgesses, certainly the most influential of them, were traders, and members of the guild. · From the guild brethren, therefore, the magistrates and holders of burghal offices would naturally be selected; and as the same individuals would be appointed officers of the guild also, the distinction between the functions appropriate to the respective offices would be very apt to disappear, and the bye-laws of the guild would come to trench upon matters of proper burghal administration. In some towns, moreover, the merchant-guild, as including a large proportion of the wealthy burgesses, appears to have succeeded in negotiating with the Sovereign for a lease or purchase of the *firma burgi*, or for special privileges, and in obtaining charters in favour of themselves, not as members of the *communa*, but as citizens of the guild. Such transactions, it can easily be conceived, must have done much to forward the pretensions or usurpations of the guild. Of such transactions the charters to Winchester by Henry II. (1154–89)[2] and by Richard I. (1190)[3] may be regarded as illustrations. Maddox also refers to

[1] On the History and Development of Gilds, English Gilds (Early English Text Society), p. xcix.

[2] 'Præcipio quod cives mei Wintonienses de gilda mercatorum cum omnibus rebus suis sint quieti de omni thelouio, passagio, et consuetudine,' etc.—Milner's Winchester, ii. 300.

[3] 'Sciatis nos concessisse civibus nostris Wintoniæ de gilda mercatorum, quod nullus eorum placitet extra muros civitatis Wintoniæ de ullo placito præter placita extra muros civitatis Wintoniæ de ullo placito præter placita de tenuris

charters granted to Gloucester and Worcester in the reign of Henry
III. (1216–1272), by which the qualification of citizenship was
made dependent upon possession of the freedom of the merchant-
guild as well as residence.[1]

In some such way the merchant-guilds of Berwick and Edinburgh may have come to represent the entire community, and the
acts of the *probi homines* or *tota communitas* may have been
regarded and designated as the acts of the guild. This conjecture receives confirmation from the fact that the first election
of the provost, dean of guild, bailie of Leith, treasurer, sergeants,
appraisers of flesh and wine, and *duodene* of the burgh, of which
the particulars are recorded, sets forth that the officers above
enumerated—whom it designates 'officers of the guild'—were
elected 'at the first Head Guild held after the feast of St.
Michael, in the tolbooth of the burgh, the brethren being called
and compearing on 3d October 1403.'[2] There can scarcely
be a doubt, however, that the date 1403 has been erroneously
transcribed for 1453. Moreover, the loose leaves from which the
above extract, and the others to be immediately noticed, bear to
have been transcribed, are called 'louse leiffes of guild courts.'
An entry, dated 17th March 1406–7, records that Alison Duscoull
is made sister of the guild;[3] and another, on the 15th November
1407, sets forth that 'dyuers persons " were " made gild brether for
the dewty of x s.'[4] On 12th January 1450 the craft of skinners
established statutes for the maintenance of the altar of St. Christopher, in St. Giles' Church, which statutes are referred to in an
instrument, which it is said 'the skinners forthwith required the

---

exterioribus exceptis monetariis et ministris nostris. Concessimus etiam eis
quod nullus eorum faciat duellum, et quod de placitis ad coronam nostram
pertinentibus se possint directiocinare secundum antiquam consuetudinem
civitatis,' etc. etc.—Foedera, vol. i. p. 52.

[1] Maddox, Firma Burgi, pp. 270–272.

[2] Extracts from the Records of the Burgh of Edinburgh, vol. i. pp. 1, 2.

[3] Ibid., vol. i. p. 2.                                      [4] Ibid.

common clerk, notary, and scribe of the burgh to register and
engross in the common book of the guild of the said burgh;' and
it is added, ' it is ordained to be so done by the provost, Thomas
of Cranston, and by the bailies, John of Halkerstoun, Matthew of
Chambers, and Richard of Farneley, Adam Cant, dean of guild,
John Lamb, treasurer, the council and dusane of the said burgh.'[1]
The recording of the admission of guild brethren on ' leaves of the
guild court' along with the election of officers of the burgh, and
the application by the craft of skinners to the town clerk to record
an instrument connected with the craft in the common book of
the guild, sustained as that application was by the magistrates
and council, seem to imply that the guild was then regarded as
one and the same with the community of the burgh.

Be that as it may, the code of the guild of Berwick—accepted
as it was as a model for the guilds of the other burghs of Scotland—
seems to have partaken largely of the spirit of brotherhood which
characterized the old guilds of England, whether these were terri-
torial, or religious, or social, or for purposes of trade.  It proclaimed the duty of all the members of a community to live in
peace and concord; it recognised the right of its own members to
mutual consideration at all times, to sympathy and assistance in
trouble, to relief in sickness and poverty, to the offices of religion
and the last marks of respect after death, and to kindly help to the
orphan.  It enforced fair and honest trading according to the
notions of the times, and it insisted upon a loyal promotion by
each member of the general interests, with the corresponding obligation to preserve the counsel of the guild.

By the Statutes of the Guild it was enacted that no one should
be received within the fraternity for less than forty shillings,
unless the sons and daughters of burgesses and guild brethren.[2]
If any one, though not a guild brother, bequeathed a part of his

[1] Extracts from the Records of the Burgh of Edinburgh, vol. i. pp. 9–11.
[2] Statuta Gilde, § 11.

property to the guild by testament, he was appointed to be received into the fraternity, and to get its assistance in the recovery
of his debts, and in his other necessities, as if he had been a
brother.[1]   The guild served all the purposes of a charitable society,
and charged itself with the care of sick and decayed brethren,[2]
with the obsequies of such as died in poverty,[3] and with providing
a dowry for their daughters, either on their marriage or on
entering a religious house.[4]   The members stood towards each
other in a fraternal relation, and offensive language used by one
to another was punished, for the first, second, and third offences,
by forfeiture of forty pence ; for the fourth offence, the offender
had to abide the decision of the alderman, the ferthingmen (who
were probably the bailies, each having charge of a quarter of
the town),[5] the dean of guild, and the remainder of the brethren.[6]
Assault by one guild brother on another was punished still more
severely.[7]   The brethren were also bound, if in town, to attend
the funeral of deceased members, under penalty of a boll of
barley malt.[8]   They had also to render good offices to each other
when in trouble.   If a member was challenged, beyond the
burgh, of life or members, it behoved two or three good men of
the guild to pass and remain with him at two diets on the charges
of the guild ; and if it was necessary to do more, they still had to
render service to the person accused, but at his cost.   If, however,
he was found to be justly accused, then he was liable for all the
expenses incurred by the brethren, according to the judgment of
the alderman.[9]   All claim by a brother upon the fraternity ceased

[1] Statuta Gilde, § 4.                [2] Ibid., § 12.  Fragmenta Collecta, § 2.
[3] Statuta Gilde, § 14.  Fragmenta Collecta, § 2.
[4] Statuta Gilde, § 13.
[5] Towns seem to have been divided into quarters from the earliest times.   In
the charter by Henry II. (1154–89) to Lincoln, reference is made to the four
divisions of the city [Foedera (Record edition), vol. i. p. 40].
[6] Statuta Gilde, §§ 5, 6.                [7] Ibid., §§ 7, 8, 9.
[8] Ibid., § 14.                [9] Ibid., § 15.

when he contumaciously neglected the guild. His brethren were then prohibited from ministering counsel or help to him, in word or deed, within or without the burgh, even should he be impleaded and in danger of life or member, or in any other deadly peril.[1]

The privileges of a member of the guild, as set forth in the statutes, so closely resemble those which have been found to appertain to burgesses, as to support the conclusion that guild-brotherhood rested on burgess-ship, and was but a higher grade of burghal organization. No one but a guild brother, or a stranger merchant for sustentation of his office, was at liberty to buy hides, wool, or wool-skins to sell again, or to cut cloth; and no stranger merchant could have lot or cavil with a guild brother.[2]  But even as between guild brethren, a later ordinance, passed in 1284, declared that no brother of guild ought to have lot or cavil with another in less than a half-quarter of skins and half a dakir of hides, or in two stones of wool.[3]  With a view, doubtless, to prevent forestalling, and to secure fair trading, no guild brother was at liberty to buy herrings or other fish, nor any other merchandise, such as corn, beans, pease, or salt, brought by ship to town, until the ship was on dry land and the oars taken out. Contravention of this regulation subjected him to a forfeit of a cask of wine to the guild, or expulsion from the town for a year and a day.[4]  When herrings, salt, corn, beans or pease, or other merchandise, was bought at ships, the purchaser was bound, under forfeiture of a cask of wine to the guild, to sell as much to his neighbour as he might require for the sustenance of his household at the same price as that at which he had bought; but if the neighbour took more than he needed for such sustenance, and afterwards sold the

---

[1] Statuta Gilde, § 16.                    [2] Ibid., § 23.
[3] Ibid., § 48.  Antea, p. 6, note.  A dakir of hides was probably one-sixth of a last, or two dozen.  Half a dakir was thus one dozen.
[4] Statuta Gilde, § 26.

excess, he was liable to a similar penalty on account of his fraud.
No purchaser, however, could be required, under any circumstances, to sell more than three-fourths of his purchase. When
goods were so bought and delivered, payment had to be made on
shipboard.[1] Moreover, when herrings were bought by a guild
brother in presence of his brethren, all those who were present
were entitled to a share at the same price. Such persons as were
not present, and wished to purchase a part, had to give the buyer
twelve pennies for his profit. Contravention of this ordinance
involved forfeiture of a cask of wine to the guild; and the same
penalty was imposed upon the neighbours who, having bought
from the original purchaser, failed to make payment of the price.[2]
An ordinance in 1294 prohibited any one, under forfeiture of a
cask of wine to the guild, from buying corn, beans, pease, salt,
coals, or other merchandise coming to Berwick by sea, unless
at the ship's side by the Rade-brae, or from carrying the goods
from the ship's side before sunrise or after sunset.[3] Non-resident
guild brethren were prohibited, under a similar forfeiture, from
buying or selling within the burgh any merchandise pertaining to
the guild except only on the market day. All non-resident burgesses were also prohibited from buying victual coming to the
burgh in ships for re-sale, or otherwise than for the sustentation
of their houses.[4]

Nothing is said in the Statutes of the Guild as to the election of
the office-bearers of the guild as distinct from the magistrates of
the burgh, who seem to have exercised jurisdiction in regard even
to guild offences,[5] but in conjunction occasionally with the dean
of guild, who is referred to in two sections.[6] The alderman and
the ferthingmen or bailies, however, are alone recognised as the
persons by whom meetings of the guild should be called,[7] and the

[1] Statuta Gilde, § 27.  [2] Ibid., § 41.  [3] Ibid., § 49.
[4] Ibid., § 51.  [5] Ibid., §§ 6, 7, 9, 12, 15, 25, 39.
[6] Ibid., §§ 6, 7.  [7] Ibid., §§ 17, 47.

E

bailies are referred to as presiding in the courts of the guild.[1] Another ordinance provides that all forfeits exceeding eight shillings, except such as were of the king's toll, or such as pertained to the right and freedom of the bailies, should be given to the guild;[2] and an enactment in 1294 declared that all assessments taken from stranger merchants ought to belong to the brethren of the guild and the burgesses of the town, except such as belonged to the king, and were reserved to him by law.[3]

The brethren of the guild were all bound to take part in the deliberations on the common affairs, and were required, under penalty of twelve pence, to assemble at the ringing of the bell, whenever the alderman, ferthingmen, and other good men appointed.[4] An ordinance in 1284 appointed the bell to ring thrice, and subjected such of the brethren as did not assemble before the ringing had ceased to a fine of twelve pennies.[5] What passed at these deliberative assemblies was regarded as secret, and any burgess who, contrary to his oath, revealed the counsel or showed the secrets of the guild, was liable to punishment for the first offence at the discretion of the alderman and other trustworthy men of the guild; for a second offence, he was appointed to lose the liberty of the burgh for a year and a day; and a third offence involved the loss of the liberty of the burgh for life, and the stigma of infamy, which prevented his enjoying the freedom of any other burgh in the realm.[6] Conspiracy against the community, to separate or scatter it, was visited with a fine of a cask of wine.[7]

There are other ordinances in this code which refer to the conduct of business in the courts of the burgh, and to the manner in which commercial transactions were to be conducted, and trades carried on in the town, which all seem to have reference to the general legislation of the burgh, and to establish a community of

---

[1] Statuta Gilde, § 20.      [2] Ibid., § 2.      [3] Ibid., § 50.
[4] Ibid., § 17.             [5] Ibid., § 47.     [6] Ibid., § 39.
[7] Ibid., § 36.

interest and jurisdiction between the guild and the whole body of the inhabitants.

The Statutes of the Guild contain several references to women, who, according to the law and practice, were admissible as sisters of the guild.[1] No one having a husband was allowed to buy wool in the street.[2] No woman was at liberty to buy in the market more than a chalder of oats with which to make malt, under forfeiture of all she purchased, whereof one-third went to the bailies of the burgh, and the remainder to the guild.[3]

It is noticeable that the heavier fines imposed by these statutes in respect of contravention of the regulations in regard to trade, etc., consisted of a cask of wine to the guild.[4]

Whilst the burghs monopolised the export and import and inland trade of the country, they were also necessarily the great centres of manufacturing industry as that was then known, and a large portion of the inhabitants of many of the towns were handicraftsmen,—the masters, or those who carried on business for their own behoof, being free and burgesses, while their servants were unfree, and many of them probably bondsmen. These masters seem in early times to have imported the raw material with which they

---

[1] Statuta Gilde, § 34.      [2] Antea, p. 7.      [3] Statuta Gilde, § 43.

[4] Ibid., §§ 26, 27, 28, 35, 40, 41, 49, 51. The frequency with which this penalty is prescribed for guild offences suggests the suspicion that, in whatever respect the early Scottish guilds differed from the still earlier guilds of England and the Continent, the love and practice of conviviality were common to all. Feasting and drinking were regularly and largely provided for in the oldest Anglo-Saxon guilds of which any record has been preserved. The code of the 'frith-gild' of the city of London, so early as the time of Athelstane, directed a monthly meeting to be held, at which there was to be a 'bytt-filling,' or filling of butts or vats, and a refection. In the statutes of the guild at Exeter, contributions of malt were prescribed, and each member of the four guilds of Battle was required to pay a sum *ad cervisiam faciendam*, and to drink his share of the brewing, either in person or by deputy. Whether all the ale into which the malt was converted, or all the wine levied from offending brethren, was drunk at the meetings of the members does not appear. It may, in so far as not required for personal use, have been sold for the benefit of the guild.

worked. Thus the tailors of London were then great importers of woollen cloth,[1] while the brewers of Hamburg were the principal corn merchants.[2] As traders and merchants, therefore, many craftsmen must necessarily have been members of the merchant-guild; but it is impossible now to ascertain what burgesses were admitted into the early merchant-guilds, and what were excluded. That all guild brethren were burgesses seems evident; but it is also certain that some classes of craftsmen were inadmissible into the fraternity. In Aberdeen, for example, the charter by Alexander II., which in 1222 empowered the burgesses of that town to have their merchant-guild, excepted fullers and weavers. But the crafts thus excluded were two of the most skilled and important. In all the manufacturing towns of England, Flanders, Brabant, and the Rhine, the weavers stood foremost among the craftsmen; and if they were excluded from the Aberdeen guild on the ground of being socially inferior to the mercantile classes, it is difficult to conjecture what craftsmen could be admitted. Long before the date of the Aberdeen charter, the weavers of London, Nottingham, York, Huntingdon, Lincoln, and Winchester had been sufficiently powerful not only to form themselves into craft-guilds, but to have their guilds recognised and confirmed by the Crown. In Cologne, Spire, Mayence, Worms, Frankfort-on-Maine, also, guilds of weavers existed during the eleventh and in the commencement of the twelfth centuries. The conjecture may therefore be hazarded, that in Aberdeen the fullers and dyers had, previous to the reign of Alexander II., succeeded in forming themselves into independent associations, and that the existence of these associations, possibly the jealousy with which they inspired the mercantile classes, may have led to their express exclusion from the merchant-guild. Be that as it may, it is obvious that in process of time the lines of separation between the merchant-guild and the crafts became

[1] Herbert's Livery Companies of London, vol. i. p. 29.
[2] English Guilds, p. cvii.

broader and more marked.  The mercantile classes became wealthier and more important; the handicraftsmen became more and more confined to the poor and the unfree.  Then the merchant-guild made the practice of certain trades a ground of exclusion from the fraternity.  Danish, German, and Belgian guild statutes ordain that no one with 'dirty hands,' or with 'blue nails,' or who 'hawked his wares on the streets,' should be a guild brother, and that no craftsman should be admitted till he had foresworn his trade for a year and a day.  The Laws of the Four Burghs, as has been seen, excluded litsters, fleshers, and souters from the merchant-guild, if they worked with their own hands;[1] and the statutes of the guild of Berwick prohibited any butcher from dealing in wool and hides so long as he carried on his trade.[2]  But the merchant-guild not only excluded craftsmen, it assumed the right to regulate them.  Thus the statutes of the guild of Berwick contain ordinances for shoemakers,[3] glovers and skinners,[4] and butchers.[5]

This condition of matters could not continue long without some effort being made by the craftsmen to improve their condition, and this object obviously could only be effected by organization. The merchant-guild presented itself as a model of the required organization, and so suggested the formation of subordinate fraternities and combinations.  Societies of craftsmen were accordingly formed, which afterwards obtained recognition from the governing body of the burgh, and sometimes from the Crown.[6]

[1] Antea, p. 25.            [2] § 25.                  [3] § 24.
[4] § 40.                    [5] § 44.
[6] From that period the distinctive characters and rights of burgesses, in reference to the two great branches of burghal monopoly, became clear and well defined; and under various denominations of burgesses and guild brethren, or burgesses of guild, or merchant burgesses on the one hand, and burgesses of crafts, or trade burgesses, or craftsmen on the other, these two classes have ever since continued to maintain their respective privileges, not only against unfreemen of the burgh, but against one another.—General Report on Municipal Corporations in Scotland, p. 73.

But even these societies were exclusive in their constitution and aims. They were so many leagues of master craftsmen against the encroachments of the merchant class; but they dominated in turn over the unfree worker, and waged a constant war against the invasion of their own trade monopolies from without. It was, in truth, as has been observed by one of the ablest writers on early Scottish history, 'a hard age for the dependent classes, wherever they were, and the "bondman in burgh" may at times have cast many a wistful glance towards the blue hills in the distance. Monopoly and exclusive dealing were in accordance with the spirit and policy of the age, and must inevitably have arisen in every quarter when it was enacted that every sale and purchase should be made "in port," and in the presence of witnesses chosen "in burgh," which must, of course, have concentrated all the traffic of the district connected with the burgh in the hands of the resident population.' [1]

Of the crafts and occupations prosecuted in the burghs of the twelfth century, the old laws and forms of procedure mention bakers, brewers (male and female), fleshers, millers, fishers, tanners, skinners, shoemakers, dyers of cloth,[2] maltmakers, wine-taverners, tailors, saddlers, and wool-combers. That there were many others cannot be doubted. A capitular of Charlemagne, made in the year 812, required the *judex*, or steward of each of his *villæ* or manors, to have in his employment good artificers, among whom are enumerated blacksmiths, workers in gold or silver, shoemakers, carpenters, shield-makers, fishers, falconers, soap-makers, brewers, bakers, net-makers, and other artisans. The Memorials of London and London Life in the thirteenth, fourteenth, and fifteenth centuries,[3] mentions ropers or ropemakers, ironmongers, nailmakers,

---

[1] Robertson's Scotland under her Early Kings, vol. i. p. 303.

[2] Which in Scotland as well as England seems to have been the staple commodity from the earliest period of record.

[3] Edited for the Corporation of that city by Mr. Riley.

armourers, and a great variety of others, including many the names
of which are now forgotten. In addition to these, however, evidence exists in the records of Edinburgh, and in the charter chests
of the Incorporations of Craftsmen in the city, that seals of cause
were granted to hat-makers, wrights and masons, weavers, hammermen (including blacksmiths), goldsmiths, lorymers, saddlers, cutlers,
buckler-makers, armourers, fleshers, coopers, walkers and scherars,
bonnet-makers, surgeons and barbers, candle-makers, bakers, tailors,
skinners, furriers, and cordiners. No more interesting chapter in
the history of Edinburgh could be written than that which would
describe the gradual development of these crafts, notwithstanding
the hostility they had to encounter from the mercantile classes, as
that took form in the legislation of Parliaments and of the town
council; their incorporation by means of seals of cause granted
by the magistrates; the constitution of these subordinate incorporations; their struggles to participate in the management of the
common affairs of the burgh; and the steps by which they labori-
ously gained their object. But these are matters to which reference can only be made here in so far as they are incidental to the
ascertainment of the conditions of membership of the several trade
associations or incorporations.

# CHAPTER II.

FOR the preceding investigation no materials have been derived from the Council Records of Edinburgh, the regular series of which commences only in 1551. The scanty remains of a previous date consist of transcripts of minutes which have been written on separate sheets or loose leaves, the originals of which have long since disappeared; and the earliest do not go farther back than 1406. Of these, not more than one hundred and twenty-five Acts or Memoranda of burghal legislation are extant of a date previous to 1500. Between that time and 1551 their Acts and Memoranda are much more numerous, though very far from being complete. These, supplemented by the legislation of successive Parliaments during the reigns of the first five Jameses and of Mary, will be used as far as possible in connecting the results of the preceding inquiry with those of an inquiry subsequent to 1551, in which the Council Records afford fuller information.

The first entry in the records of the city relative to admission to the guild of which any trace has been preserved, is dated 17th March 1406-7, and sets forth that Alison Duscou[ll] was made sister of the guild as heir of her brother.[1] On 15th November 1407 divers persons are stated to have been made guild brethren for a duty of ten shillings.[2]

Some years later, viz. on 12th March 1424, a statute of James I. enacted—

‘ that na merchande of the realme pas oure the see in merchandice, bot gif

---

[1] C. R. Ad. Lib. fol. 25. Extracts from C. R. vol. i. p. 2.
[2] Ibid.

he have of his awine propir gudis or ellis committyt till his gouernall thre serplathis[1] of woll, or the valour thairof in other merchandice, the quhilk sall be kend or he pas be ane inquest of his nychtburis vnder the payne of x li. to the king.[2]

That the craftsmen had at this time formed themselves into associations, and possessed sufficient influence to obtain the recognition of the Legislature, is shown by an act of the same Parliament, which required each craft in every town to choose one of its 'wise men,' with the consent of the 'officiaris of the tovne,' to be deacon or masterman, to assay and govern all work done by the men of his craft.[3]  This enactment was, however, modified on 30th September 1426 by an act of Parliament, which declared that the deacons should stand till the next Parliament, but only to see that the workmen were cunning and their work sufficient.  At the same time, the alderman and council of each town were directed to fix the price of the material and the cost of the labour of the workmen of each craft, and to prescribe the manner in which their work should be sold.  And in consequence of complaints to the king and his council against wrights and masons, all workmen were prohibited from taking more work on hand than they might properly execute.[4]  On 1st July in the following year, Parliament declared that the previous ordinances in regard to deacons of crafts had tended to the hurt and common loss of the realm.  These ordinances were accordingly repealed, and it was enacted that the deacons then in office should no longer exercise the functions of deacons, nor hold their usual meetings, which were thought 'to savour of conspiracies.'[5]  On 1st March 1427–8 a Council-general of the realm directed the town council of each burgh for one year to elect a warden of every craft, who, with advice of other discreet men assigned to him by the

---

[1] Serplar, serplathe, eighty stones of wool.
[2] 1424, c. 16, A. P. S. vol. ii. p. 8.
[3] 1424, c. 17, Ibid., p. 8.
[4] 1426, §§ 2, 3, 4, and 5, Ibid., p. 13.
[5] 1427, § 4, Ibid., p. 14.

F

town council, should examine and fix the price of all work. This ordinance was especially applied to masons, wrights, smiths, tailors, websters, and all others whose 'fees and handling' were appraised.[1]

On 1st December 1450 the payment for admission as a burgess was fixed as follows :—By the heir of a burgess, 6s. 8d.; by one admitted in right of his wife, 6s. 8d.; and by those who bought their burgess-ship, 40s. At this time it is added, 'many ar maid burgessis, and callit *postnati et postnate* of thair fatheris.' On the same day David Admuty was made a hereditary burgess in right of his uncle, John Crysteson.[2]

A notarial instrument, dated 12th January 1450–1, sets forth an obligation by the skinners of the town to contribute to the support of a chaplain to officiate at the altar of St. Christopher, then lately founded by them within the church of St. Giles, and to repair the ornaments of the altar. It declares that every one receiving an apprentice to the craft should pay five shillings to the repair of the altar, and that such apprentice should be bound, on the termination of his apprenticeship, to contribute to the same object according to his ability; and it further provides that, should any controversy arise among the skinners, the disputants should abide by the judgment of the brethren of the craft, and the decree of the council and dusane of the burgh.[3]

On 12th May 1451 one Aitkyne, a barber, was admitted a burgess without payment, at the instance of the queen; he was also admitted to the freedom of the guild, and gave spices[4] and wine, but it was declared that no one should succeed him in the freedom of the guild after his death.[5] On 18th May in the same

---

[1] 1427, § 3, A. P. S. vol. ii. p. 15.
[2] C. R. Ad. Lib. fol. 25. Extracts C. R. vol. i. p. 8.
[3] C. R. Ad. Lib. fol. 38. Extracts C. R. vol. i. p. 9.
[4] A general name for dried fruits, as well as the 'spices' of the present day.
[5] C. R. Ad. Lib. fol. 25. Extracts C. R. vol. i. p. 12.

year, one Rede, a dyer, was admitted a burgess as in right of his
father, and gave wine and spices.[1]   On 14th June 1451 Henry
Rafe and Mairtyne Hope were found by an assize to have
wrongously occupied the freedom of the town, and were each fined
twenty pounds.[2]  And on the same day Andrew Mowbray, second
son of his father, was made burgess as in right of his father, and
compounded for 6s. 8d.[3]  On 30th October 1453 John Hiane,
junior, was admitted a burgess as in right of his uncle, Thomas
Spens, and gave 'for the freedom' spices and wine.[4]   On 13th
September 1456—

'it was grantet be the provest, baillies, and counsale of the toun in favoures
of the haill craft of the baxteris that thair sall na man of that craft be maid
burges or freman without the avys and consent of the maist pairt of the
worthiest of the craft, and that it sall be sene that he be worthie and sufficient
to labour, and that he haif cunnying and power to labour, and that thai pay
their dewteis to the alter lyk as the laif of the craft dois.'[5]

A statute of James II., passed on 6th March 1457, ordained, for
the prevention of deceit to the lieges, that in every burgh in which
goldsmiths worked, an understanding and cunning man of good
conscience should be appointed dean of the craft, who should assay
and stamp all gold and silver work.  The same Parliament also
declared it to be—

'sene speedful that lit be cryit up and vsyt as it was wont to be, and that
na litstar be draper, nothir to by claytht, nor yet tholyt to sell, vnder the payne
of eschet thairof.'[6]

Another act of the same date, for the 'restriccione of the
multitude of sailars,' enacted in terms similar to those of 1424—

'that thar saill na personis bot hable and of gud fame and at he haif at the
lest thre serplaris of his awne gudis or ellis committyt till him, or the availl
thairof, and that the saylaris in merchandyce be fre men of burrowis and indwellaris within the burghe.'[7]

---

[1] C. R. Ad. Lib. fol. 25.   Extracts C. R. vol. i. p. 13.      [2] Ibid.      [3] Ibid.
[4] C. R. Ad. Lib. fol. 25.   Extracts C. R. vol. i. p. 14.
[5] C. R. vol. i. fol. 35.   Extracts C. R. vol. i. p. 14.
[6] 1457, c. 9, A. P. S. vol. ii. p. 49.     [7] 1457, c. 10. A. P. S. vol. ii. p. 49.

In subsequent statutes, similar or higher rates in the amount of property were required of dealers in foreign trade, with the view of disabling needy and desperate adventurers from disturbing the regular course of the more opulent class of merchants.[1]

On 3d October 1459 Edward Boncle was made a guild brother *gratis,* for his aid and counsel.[2] On 7th October 1462 John Chappellane was made a guild brother in right of his wife, and compounded by paying 20s.[3] On 7th October 1463 John Greig was admitted guild brother, and paid £3 for the freedom; William Frog, who was the second son of a guild brother, compounded for 20s.; William Vernour, who was the son and heir of a guild brother, was admitted, and gave spices and wine; and another William Vernour, a saddler, was admitted, at the instance of the king, for 20s.[4]

A statute of James III., passed on 31st January 1466, enacted that no one should sail or pass in merchandise out of Scotland—

'bot free men burges duelland within burgh or thar familiaris, factouris, or seruandis being with tham of houshald at mete and drink, saufand that it sal be leful to prelatis, lordis, barouns, clerkis, to send thar propre gudis with thar seruandis, and to by agane thingis nedeful to thar propre vse.'[5]

This reservation would appear to indicate the previous enjoyment by the higher classes of society of privileges of trade in a modified form, and it is repeated in subsequent statutes.[6]

It was also enacted by the same Parliament, (1) that no craftsman should use merchandise by himself, his factors or servants,

[1] General Report by Commissioners on Municipal Corporations in Scotland, p. 74. See the Acts 1466, c. 3. A. P. S. vol. ii. p. 86; 1487, c. 12. A. P. S. vol. ii. p. 178.
[2] C. R. Ad. Lib. fol. 25. Extracts C. R. vol. i. p. 19.
[3] Ibid.          [4] C. R. Ad. Lib. fol. 25. Extracts C. R. vol. i. p. 20.
[5] 1466, c. 1. A. P. S. vol. ii. p. 86.
[6] See the Acts 1567, c. 56. A. P. S. vol. iii. p. 41; and 1633, c. 24. A. P. S. vol. v. p. 42.

unless he renounced his craft without colour or dissimulation;[1] and (2) that only famous and worshipful men, having of their own half a last of goods, or 'samekle in stering and gouernance,' should sail or pass out of the realm in merchandise under pain of £10.[2]

Another statute of the same king, passed on 20th November 1469, to regulate the annual election of the aldermen, bailies, dean of guild, and other officers of burghs, empowered each craft to—

'cheise a persone of the samyn craft, that sall haue voce in the said electioune of the officiaris for that tyme, in likewise yeir be yeir.'.[3]

And on the 27th of the same month, masons, wrights, and other craftsmen 'that ar set for lang tyme or schort for the werk' were appointed to work on Saturdays and other vigils until 4 P.M., and to keep no other holidays than the great church feasts.[4]

As affording some indication of the social position of the burgess class in the fifteenth century, reference may be made to the legislation of the period as to the arms which burgesses were required to have, and the dress they and their wives were permitted to wear, by the sumptuary laws of the time.

An act passed on 11th March 1425 required burgesses and indwellers in burghs to be armed and harnessed according to their means, and to attend weapon-shawing four times a year, at the sight of the aldermen and bailies.[5] A subsequent statute, passed on 6th March 1429, prescribed that each burgess having £50 in goods should be armed as a gentleman ought to be; that a burgess having £20 should be bodin with 'souer hat' and doublet, habergeon, sword, buckler, bow, sheaf, and knife; and that he who was no bowman should have a good axe or weapon of fence.[6] An

---

[1] 1466, c. 2. A. P. S. vol. ii. c. 86. This act was also repeated, and ordered to be enforced by 1487, c. 13. A. P. S. vol. ii. p. 178. The Act 1503, c. 38, to the same effect, is deleted. A. P. S. vol. ii. p. 245.

[2] 1466, c. 3. A. P. S. vol. ii. p. 86.      [3] 1469, c. 5. A. P. S. vol. ii. p. 95.

[4] 1469, c. 15. A. P. S. vol. ii. p. 97.      [5] 1425, c. 17. A. P. S. vol. ii. p. 10.

[6] 1429, c. 14. A. P. S. vol. ii. p. 18.

act of the same year also prohibited burgesses dwelling in burgh from wearing furs, except aldermen, bailies, and councillors of the town; and their wives were appointed to be arrayed according to the estate of their husbands.[1]  A more specific enactment on this subject is contained in a statute passed on 6th March 1457, to prevent the impoverishment of the country, 'throu sumptuose clething, baith of men and wemen, and in special within burrowis and commonys to landwart.'  By this statute it was enacted that no man in burgh who lived by merchandise, unless he were 'a person constitute in dignity, as alderman, bailie, or other gude worthy men that ar of the council,' and their wives, should wear clothes of silk, or costly scarlet in gowns, or furrings of mertriks.  Merchants in burgh were required to cause their wives and daughters to dress according to their estate, *i.e.* to wear on their heads short curches, with little hoods, such as were used in Flanders, England, and other countries ;[2] and as to their gowns, not to wear mertriks, nor letvise, nor tails of unfitting length, nor furred under, except on holidays.  The same enactment was applied to poor gentlemen without burghs, who were within £40 of old extent, and to their wives.  As regarded the commons, labourers and husbandmen were prohibited from wearing on week days other than grey and white, and on holidays other than light blue, or green, or red.  A similar prohibition was extended to their wives, who were required to wear only curches of their own making, the material not to exceed the price of forty pence the ell.  It was also enacted that no woman should go to kirk or market with her face muffled or covered, so as not to be known, under pain of escheat of her curch.[3]

In 1427 three burgesses were admitted at the following rates :—
James Furde, as in right of his wife, for 6s. 8d.; William Craik for

[1] 1429, c. 9.  A. P. S. vol. ii. p. 18.
[2] This is one of many illustrations of the influence of Continental fashions on the people of Scotland at this early period.
[3] 1457, c. 13.  A. P. S. vol. ii. p. 49.

£3; and Rychart Forrester for 40s.[1]  On 15th February 1473-4
Henry Cant and another, both sons of burgesses, were admitted,
and gave spices and wine.[2]

On 18th February 1473 a seal of cause, granted by the provost,
bailies, and council to the hatmakers, sets forth that the craft had
been allowed to elect a deacon for ' conserving the craft in all good
rules and ordinances;' that a deacon had accordingly been elected,
and certain rules and ordinances had been made, which the council
were asked to confirm.   The seal of cause thereupon confirms these
ordinances, which provide, *inter alia*, that no apprentices should
be taken for a less period than five years, unless the sons of members of the craft, who should be bound only for three years; that
if any stranger of the same craft came to town, he should make
a piece of sufficient work at the sight of the masters before he was
permitted to be fee'd, or to work with any master of the craft;
that thereafter he should remain a year and day in service for
such fee as might be agreed upon; and that if he afterwards desired
to remain and use the craft, he should make two pieces of work
sufficient, and 'make himself frieman of the toun and habill
thairto.' [3]

An act of the Parliament of James III., held on 23d July 1473,
directed that in each town in which goldsmiths were—

' thare be deput and ordanit a wardane and a decane of the craft, that sal
be suorne thairto, and examyne al the werkmanschip that cummys fra thare
handis.' [4]

On 2d December 1474 the craftsmen of the skinners appeared
before the provost, bailies, and council, and complained of various
irregularities practised by many of the craft, for which a remedy
was sought.  The council thereupon issued a seal of cause, which

---

[1] C. R. Ad. Lib. fol. 25.   Extracts C. R. vol. i. p. 26.        [2] Ibid.
[3] Transcript in the archives of the city.   Extracts C. R. vol. i. pp. 26–28.
[4] 1473, c. 17.   A. P. S. vol. ii. p. 105.

contains several regulations for the conduct of the trade, and sup
porting the authority of the deacon.[1]

On 15th October 1475 the provost, bailies, council, dean of guild,
and deacons of the whole craftsmen within the burgh granted to
the masons and wrights (1) the aisle and chapel of St. John
the Evangelist, in the church of St. Giles, to be used by them
as other craftsmen occupied chapels in that church;[2] and (2) a seal
of cause confirming certain rules and regulations made by these
craftsmen for the support of the altar in that chapel, and for the
regulation of their crafts.  By this seal of cause the craftsmen
were authorized to elect four of the best and worthiest persons—
two of each craft—to oversee all work and determine all questions among them.  It also provided that no apprentice should be
taken for less than seven years, and that on the expiration of his
apprenticeship he should be examined by the four overseers, to see
whether he was fit to be a fellow of the craft.  If he was found
sufficient, he was appointed to pay half a merk to the altar, and
to enjoy the privilege of the craft; but if found insufficient, he
had to serve a master until he had learned to be worthy of being
a master himself, after which he had to be made 'frieman and
fallow.'[3]

On 31st January 1475-6 a seal of cause was granted by the
provost, bailies, and council to the websters, in which it was set
forth that the best and worthiest of the craft had presented certain
statutes made by them for confirmation by the council, and that
the council, finding the rules to be reasonable, had confirmed them

[1] Original seal of cause in the possession of the Incorporation of Skinners.
Extracts O. R. vol. i. pp. 28–30.

[2] Register of the Great Seal, Lib. 22, No. 62.  Extracts C. R. vol. i. pp.
30, 31.

[3] Ibid.  It is curious to note, as another illustration of the influence of Continental models, that the two craftsmen elected to be overseers are by this seal
of cause appointed to have 'their placis and rowmes in all general processiouns
lyk as thai haf in the towne of Bruges or siclyke gud townes.'

accordingly. By this seal of cause it was provided—(1) that all 'freemen of the craft that are burgesses,' and none others, should elect a deacon, as other crafts did, to rule and govern the craft ' in all good rules as effeirs;' (2) that no man should occupy the craft as a master until he had been made burgess and freeman, and had been found worthy, and was possessed of 'gude and sufficeand graith and werkloumys' to the satisfaction of four men of the craft, after which he should pay two merks and two pounds of wax to the altar of St. Seuerane in St. Giles; (3) that no apprentice should be taken for a shorter term than five years; (4) that each man or woman that occupied the craft should contribute to the support of the altar and the priest officiating thereat; and (5) that no woman should occupy the craft, as for a master to hold workhouse, unless she were a freeman's wife. [1]

On 29th January 1477–8 Thomas Haliburton was made burgess and guild brother in right of his wife, and gave spices and wine, and paid 20s. for the guild.[2] On 17th October 1481 the provost, great dusane, and deacons ordained that—

'the commoun clark and a seriand with him gather of ilk stallenger pure body that may nocht beir the cost of burgesry, and occupeis the fredome of the towne, ij s. in the yeir, and all stallengeris that may be burges to occupy the fredome as stallengars bot for a yeir and na langer, bot gif he be burges, or ellis devoyde the towne.'[3]

On 10th November 1482[4] or 1492[5] the council ordained that no craftsmen or others resident within the town should occupy the same, or the freedom thereof, 'by intrometting their practike or craft,' whatever it might be, unless they were free burgesses, or lived as stallengers for the year, and paid their duties therefor to

---

[1] Original seal of cause in the possession of the Websters. Extracts C. R. vol. i. pp. 33, 34.

[2] C. R. Ad. Lib. fol. 25.    Extracts C. R. vol. i. p. 36.

[3] C. R. Ad. Lib. fol. 26.    Extracts C. R. vol. i. p. 40.

[4] C. R. vol. i. fol. 31.    Extracts C. R. vol. i. p. 41.

[5] C. R. Ad. Lib. fol. 25.    Extracts C. R. vol. i. p. 65.

the common clerk as effeired, according to the laws of the burgh.[1]
This statute was declared to extend to all manner of unfree persons,
merchants, brewers, bakers, and regratters of fish, butter, cheese,
eggs, wild fowls, and all other things sold and occupied within
burgh.  On 2d May 1483 the provost and bailies, with consent
and advice of the council, granted a seal of cause to the hammermen, in which it is narrated that the head men and masters of the
craft, blacksmiths, goldsmiths, lorimers, saddlers, cutlers, buckle-
makers, armourers, and all others within the burgh, had complained
of various grievances under which they laboured, and for which
they sought a remedy; therefore the council ordained—(1) that
thenceforth no hammerman, master, fee'd-man, servant, or others,
should use more than one craft and live thereby; (2) that no
hammerman's work should be sold in open market except on the
market day, and that searchers should be appointed to search for
and see all work of the craft, and prohibit the sale of such work as
might be found faulty; (3) that all unfree hammermen, booth-
holders, and others who desire to be made masters, should be
previously examined by the masters of the crafts—

'and than he to be maid freman gif he beis fundin sufficient, and do his dewty
to the toun and craft and to the altar as vtharis dois, and set up buith; and gif
he beis sufficient in his craft, and not of powar to mak his expenssis hastely
vpoun his fredome, he sall bruk the priuiledge of a master (?) for ane yeir and
na langer, and all vtharis that ar vnfre, not examinit nor worthy to hald buiths,
sall either be prentis to a maister for certan yeiris, or ellis, gif he be aigit, to
be a feit-man with a maister, and not to labour his awn werk vnto the tyme
that he be habill and worthie to be maister and do his dewtie thairfoir, as
said is.'[2]

On 26th May 1485 Parliament re-enacted the requirement, that
in every burgh in which goldsmiths carried on business, a deacon
and searcher of the craft should be appointed, and that all goldsmiths' work should be marked with the mark of the maker, of the

[1] Antea, p. 7, footnote 6.
[2] C. R. vol. i. fol. 48.   Extracts C. R. vol. i. pp. 47–49.

deacon, and of the town. It was further ordained that no gold-smith should become a master, or hold open booth of the craft, until he had been admitted by the officers and whole body of the craft.[1]

On 13th October 1487, parliament, at the desire of the whole commissioners of burghs, ratified the acts 1424, c. 16; 1457, c. 10; and 1466, c. 3; and also the acts 1466, c. 1, and 1466, c. 2, before referred to.[2] It also ratified the act 1474, c. 12, in regard to the choosing of officers in burgh, and directed the same to be put to execution—

' sa that the electoun of the officiaris micht be of the best and worthiest in-duellaris of the toune, and nocht be parcialite nor masterschip, whilk is vndoing of the borowis whare masterschippis and requestis cummis.' [3]

The Register of Burgesses and Guild Brethren of the city is for-tunately complete since 17th May 1487, in a series of twenty-two volumes. From that register it appears that during the year 1487, subsequent to 17th May, two persons were admitted burgesses, six were admitted guild brethren, having, without doubt, been burgesses previously, and five were admitted burgesses and guild brethren.

On 11th April 1488 the provost, bailies, dean of guild, treasurer, and council granted a seal of cause to the fleshers, whereby they ratified various ordinances made by the deacon and principal masters of the craft, and specially to the effect:—(1) That all unfreemen, lads, and boys using the craft should be expelled therefrom, unless they became apprentices or hired servants, ac-cording to the old acts of the town. The fines for contravention of this regulation were to be applied, two-thirds to the kirk work, and one-third to the reparation of the altar of the fleshers. (2) That any member of the craft who was a freeman, but of small substance, should, ' until God refreshed him,' form a partner-

[1] 1485, c. 15.　A. P. S. vol. ii. p. 172.
[2] 1487, c. 12, 13.　A. P. S. vol. ii. p. 178.
[3] 1487, c. 14.　A. P. S. vol. ii. p. 178.

ship with a master of substance, finding surety to the craft that he
would not bring discredit on them by not paying for the purchases
made by him, and that the officers of the town would not be vexed
by administration of justice.   In this passage the 'freeman of the
craft' is afterwards referred to as a burgess.   (3) That no freeman
of the craft should form a partnership with an unfreeman, or
'colour his goods.'   (4) That no craftsmen, candlemakers or others,
should use the craft, except sons of freemen of the craft, who could
handle it themselves both in slaying and breaking, and had been
learned under a master.   And (5)—

'that ilk prenteis desire of the deykin and maister that lykis to vse the
craft, that first thai desire and obtene the fredome of the toune, and gif he be
fund abill to be ressauit to the craft and to pay his dewteis to the craft and
altar, as efferis.'[1]

In the parliament of James IV., held on 6th October 1488, it
was enacted that all ships belonging to natives or foreigners should
come only to free burghs, and there make their merchandise.
Contravention by strangers of this enactment was appointed to be
punished by 'tynsale and confiscatioun of thar ship and gudes to
the Crown.'[2]   One of the objects of this, as of various other acts
of parliament relative to foreign trade, undoubtedly was to secure
payment of the customs exigible by the Crown; but, as is observed
by the Commissioners on Municipal Corporations, 'the persevering
activity on the part of the burghs in obtaining such frequent re-
enactments of these and other ordinances against unfree traders,
leads to the inference that the interests of the Crown were a
secondary object only, and that it required the utmost efforts of
the Legislature to maintain this monopoly against the general
interests and feelings of the community.'[3]

[1] C. R. vol. i. fol. 51.   Extracts C. R. vol. i. pp. 55, 56.
[2] 1488, c. 12; A. P. S. vol. ii. p. 209: renewed by 1555, c. 37; A. P. S. vol.
ii. p. 499.   1581, c. 27; A. P. S. vol. iii. p. 224.
[3] General Report, p. 74.

In 1488 twenty-one burgesses, four guild brethren, and eleven
burgesses and guild brethren were admitted.[1]

On 6th August 1489 a seal of cause was granted by the provost,
bailies, and council to the coopers, which sets forth that the
masters of that craft had complained of various persons of the
craft, who had refused to conform to the rules made by the council
for the wrights, to which the coopers were conformed, and also of
unfree and incompetent persons practising the trade in burgh;
therefore all masters of the cooper craft were ordained to conform
in all points to the statutes of the wrights, as previously confirmed
by the council. All outlands men were also ordained to desist
from the occupation of the craft in the town, unless they made
residence therein, and paid their duties to the altar of St. John
and the craft, and were received therein by the masters thereof,
and fulfilled the statutes of the wrights.[2]

On 3d February 1489-90 parliament re-enacted, for the protec-
tion of the lieges against the corruption of metal, that there should
be a deacon of the craft of goldsmiths, who should examine all
gold and silver work, and see that it was of the fineness of the new
silver work of Bruges, and thereafter put his mark and sign on
the work so examined by him.[3]

In 1489 one person was admitted a burgess, two were admitted
guild brethren, and five were admitted burgesses and guild brethren.[4]

A memorandum, of date 25th June 1490, refers to the Burghmuir being let, with the consent of the council, deacons (of whom
twelve are referred to), and the community.[5] And about the same
time the council ordained, that whensoever usurpation of the
town's freedom took place at Leith, all neighbours and all deacons,

[1] Register of Burgesses and Guild Brethren.
[2] Register of the Great Seal, Lib. 22, No. 62. Extracts C. R. vol. i. pp.
57, 58.
[3] 1489, c. 13. A. P. S. vol. ii. p. 221.
[4] Register of Burgesses and Guild Brethren.
[5] C. R. Ad. Lib. fol. 94. Extracts C. R. vol. i. p. 58.

with their craftsmen, should be ready, on the summons of the magistrates, to pass with them to Leith, for the holding of the water court, to reform injuries done against their freedom.[1]

On 28th April 1491 parliament ordained that the common good of all burghs should be expended in common and necessary things of the burgh, by advice of the council of the town for the time, and the deacons of the crafts where they existed.[2]

In 1490 and 1491 no entries appear in the Register of Burgesses and Guild Brethren.

On 10th November 1492 it was statuted and ordained by the bailies, council, and community of the burgh—

'that na craiftismen or vtheris, indwelleris within this towne, occupy the fredome of the same be intrometting with thair practik or craft, quhatever it be, bot gif thai be frie burgessis, or leif as stallengeris for the yeir, and pay thair dewteis thairfor to the clerk as effeiris, according to the lawes of the burgh; and this statute to be extendit to all maner of vnfrie folkis, bayth merchants, browsteris, baxteris, and regratouris of fysche, butter, cheise, eggis, wyld fowlis, and all vther thingis sauld and occupeit within burgh.'[3]

In 1492 twenty-five persons were entered as burgesses, twenty as guild brethren, and seventeen as burgesses and guild brethren.[4]

On 8th May 1493 an act of parliament of James IV. prohibited all craftsmen, such as cordiners and others, from levying impositions on men of their own craft coming to market.[5] At the same time, on the preamble that

'it is cleirly vnderstandin to the King's Hienes and his thre Estatis that the vsing of dekynis of men of craft in burrowis is rycht dangerous, and as thay vse the samyn may be the caus of greit troubill in burrowis, and convocatioun and rysing of the Kingis liegis be statutis making contrair the commone proffet, and for thair singulair proffet and avale,'

parliament ordained that all such deacons should cease for a year, and have no power except to examine the fineness of work and

[1] C. R. Ad. Lib. fol. 132.   Extracts C. R. vol. i. p. 59.
[2] 1491, c. 19.   A. P. S. vol. ii. p. 227.
[3] C. R. Ad. Lib. fol. 25.   Extracts C. R. vol. i. p. 65.
[4] Register of Burgesses and Guild Brethren.
[5] 1493, c. 13.   A. P. S. vol. ii. p. 234.

material, and that it was wrought by craftsmen. All makers of statutes, such as those of the masons and wrights, for the payment of wages on holidays; and preventing workmen from finishing work begun by others, were ordered to be indicted as common oppressors of the lieges.[1]

On 13th June 1496 an act of parliament was passed by which, for the remedy of the great hurt and oppression done to the lieges through the exorbitant prices charged by craftsmen and workmen for all kinds of work,—barons, provosts, bailies of burghs, and others having rule in the realm, were required to set prices on victual, bread, ale, and all other necessaries ; to appoint examiners to see that these prices were observed ; and to punish workmen who took exorbitant prices. A third offence was appointed to be visited with deprivation of the craft of the offender, and escheat of the over-charged articles.[2]

By acts of the town council, dated 8th November 1494 and 10th August 1498, 'all and sundry nychtboures and inhabiters of this toune, baith merchandmen and craftismen,' were ordained to have their defensible gear ready beside them in their booths, 'sic as jak, sellat, briggantenis, gluiffis of plait, a handaix or a sword, or at the leist the said ax or sword, with sellat and gluffis of plait,'[3] to come to the aid of the magistrates whenever disturbance arose.

The following entries appear in the Register of Burgesses and Guild Brethren from 1493 to 1500, both inclusive :—[4]

|                              | 1493. | 1494. | 1495–8. | 1499–1500. |
|------------------------------|-------|-------|---------|------------|
| Burgesses,                   | 14    | 49    | 74      | 144        |
| Guild Brethren,              | ...   | ...   | ...     | 43         |
| Burgesses and Guild Brethren,| 1     | 2     | ...     | 2          |

[1] 1493, c. 14.  A. P. S. vol. ii. p. 234.

[2] 1496, c. 5.  A. P. S. vol. ii. p. 238.

[3] C. R. Ad. Lib. fol. 184.  C. R. vol. ii. fol. 32.  Extracts C. R. vol. i. pp. 68, 73.

[4] Register of Burgesses and Guild Brethren.

On 20th August 1500 a seal of cause was granted by the provost,
bailies, and council, to the waulkers and shearers of cloth, by which,
*inter alia*, the following statutes proposed by the craftsmen were
confirmed :—(1) That the craftsmen should have the power, which
other crafts possessed, of annually choosing a kirkmaster of the
altar of Saints Mark, Philip, and Jacob, founded and built by
them in the Collegiate church of St. Giles, and that every freeman
of the craft should pay for the upset of his booth five crowns of
Scots money, his fitness to serve the town and others repairing
thereto having previously been certified by four masters of the
craft :

'and gif he be fundin abill to set up buthe, that he be worth of his awin
substance thre pair of scheris, and of power to pay ane steik of hewit claith,
swa that gif ony falt standis in him he to satefy the party sustenand the scaith.'

(2) That every apprentice should pay at his entry ten shillings to
the sustentation of the altar; and

(3) 'Now becaus the communite of our craft, walkaris and scheraris within
this tovne, walkis wardis extentis, and beris all vthir commoun chargis within
this tovne, and the outland walkaris and scheraris duelland vtouth the fredome
of this burgh takkis the werk of the nichtburis and wynnyn tharof, and beris
na portable chargis within this tovne, that thairfor ilk out walkar or scherar of
claith to landward cumand within this tovne, and takand the stuff thairof till
wyrk sall pay ilk oulk ane penny, quhilk is bot small valour till uphald the
devyne seruice at the said altar of Sanctis Mark, Philip, and Jacob, to be ingatherit be the dekin and kirkmaisters of the saidis crafts for the tyme.'[1]

On 26th August 1500 the provost, bailies, and council granted
a seal of cause to the tailors, whereby, on the supplication of the
kirkmaster and masters of the tailor craft, the council ratified and
approved of certain statutes for the government of the craftsmen,
and, *inter alia*, ordained—(1) That no apprentice should be taken
for less than seven years, and that he should pay ten shillings on
his entry to the altar of St. Ann, in the church of St. Giles.
(2) That no apprentice or other person of the craft should be

[1] Original seal of cause in the possession of the Waulkers. Extracts C. R.
vol. i. pp. 80–82.

allowed to set up booth within the burgh until he had been found
capable and admitted thereto ' be the sworne masters of the
craft, and maid freeman and burgess of the said burgh.' For his
upset the person so admitted had to pay forty shillings towards
the sustentation of the said altar.[1]

On 10th November 1500 the Court of the Four Burghs ordained
that no craftsman should use merchandise in burgh, but only use
his own craft, under the penalties prescribed by the acts of parliament thereanent, and in each burgh searchers were appointed to
be chosen to enforce this enactment. This act also prohibited all
persons from going to Flanders or France with merchandise except
they were burgesses and resident in burgh, or from using merchandise unless they made continual residence in burgh, and paid
the duties that effeired to them therefor. Every burgh was required to enforce this act within its bounds.[2] On 4th December
in the same year, accordingly, the craft of skinners in Edinburgh
was charged not to use merchandise;[3] and on the 8th of the same
month a number of burgesses were ordered to be made—

' for the repairing of the toune, the honour and profit of the kirk, in making
of jowelry, sic-like as the silver candilstekis, silver crowatis, and other anorna-
mentis for the kirk; '

and it was ordered that in future

' the toune be serchit of the personis induelland thairintill that may bere burgesry or gild, that thai be maid in the profit thairof to be warit upon the
honour of the kirk.' [4]

On 8th January 1500–1 the magistrates and customers of Edinburgh were charged to enforce the enactment by the Court of Four
Burghs above referred to.[5]

It would appear that in 1500–1 the provost, bailies, and council

---

[1] Maitland's History of Edinburgh, p. 301. Extracts C. R. vol. i. pp. 82, 84.
[2] C. R. vol. i. fol. 28. Extracts C. R. vol. i. p. 86.
[3] C. R. vol. i. fol. 28. Extracts C. R. vol. i. p. 87.
[4] Register of Burgesses, vol. i. fol. 8. Extracts C. R. vol. i. pp. 87, 88.
[5] C. R. vol. i. fol. 28. Extracts C. R. vol. i. p. 88.

exercised control over the guild court of the burgh, for on 28th
January in that year they granted and consented—

'that the gild court begyn on Fryday next cummis, and swa continow throw
the haill toun, for the commoun proffit and honour of the kirk.'

And they further ordained—

'that quhat persoun beis wairnit to compeir to the gild court be the officer,
and comperis nocht, thai sall pay to the kirk weirk xx s., to be raisit but
fauoris.'[1]

In the parliament of James IV., held on 19th March 1503, an
act was passed ordaining that all officers, provosts, bailies, and
others having office of jurisdiction within burgh should be changed
yearly, and

'that nain haue jurisdictioune within burgh bot gif thai vse merchandice within
the said burgh.'[2]

It was at the same time ordained that the old privileges and freedoms granted to merchants and burghs of Scotland be observed
and kept; and

'that na personis duelland vtouth burrowis vse ony merchandise, nor yit tap
nor sell wyne, walx, silk, nor spicery wad, nor siklike stuf, nor yet stapill
gudis, and that nane pak nor pele[3] in Leitht nor vther placis vtouth the kingis
burrowis vnder the pane of the escheting of the gudis to the kingis vse that
beis tappit, sauld, pakit, or pelit agane this statute.'[4]

---

[1] C. R. vol. i. fol. 29.   Extracts C. R. vol. i. p. 89.

[2] 1503, § 25.   A. P. S. vol. ii. p. 252.

[3] The meaning of the phrase 'packing and peeling' is doubtful.   In the case
of the Duke of Hamilton v. Linlithgow, 4th February 1680, reported by
Fountainhall, 'packing and peeling' were maintained to mean 'loading and
unloading.'   But this interpretation was disputed; and 'packing,' it was
contended, signified 'stowing goods in packs;' while 'peeling' was supposed
by some to mean, 'carrying of goods like a pile of wood' (vol. i. p. 81.
Fountainhall's Historical Notices of Scottish affairs (Bannatyne Club), vol. i. p.
250).   Jamieson suggests that 'peeling' may mean 'to heap', to 'coacervate,'
or to 'pair and adjust to one size,' or to 'guage or measure;' and he adds,
that the phrase is now metaphorically used to denote unfair means of carrying
on trade in an incorporation, as when one who is a freeman allows the use of
his name in trade to another who has not this privilege; voce 'Peiling.'

[4] 1503, c. 29.   A. P. S. vol. ii. p. 252.

On the same day it was also enacted—

'that in tyme to cum na provest, balye, nor aulderman of ony townis, mak burgessis nor gilde brether without the consent of the grete counsale of the toune, and that the proffit that is tane for the making of ilk burges or gilde brether be put to the commoun gude and warit on the common werkis.' [1]

And 'for the weal of merchandice,' officers of towns were appointed to enforce the old acts anent sailors. [2]

On 2d April 1504 an act of council was passed against freemen colouring wool, hides, skins, and such goods belonging to un- freemen, Lombards, and others; and on the same day freemen within the burgh were prohibited from selling any manner of goods or merchandise to strangers or unfreemen free of custom. [3]

By a seal of cause granted to the surgeons and barbers on 1st July 1505, the bailies and council, on the solicitation of the kirk- master and brethren of the craft, authorized the craftsmen to elect yearly a kirkmaster and oversman, and ordained

'that na maner of person occupie nor vse ony poyntis of saidis craftis of surregerie or barbour craft within this burgh bott gif he be first frieman and burgess of the samyn, and that he be worthy and expert in all the poyntis belangand the saidis craftis diligentlie and avysitlie examinit and admittit be the maisters of the said craft.'

They also declared that no one should be admitted freeman and master of the craft who had not been examined and proved in anatomy and other branches of surgical science, of astrology, etc. On such admission every person had to pay for his upset £5 Scots to the reparation and upholding of the altar of St. Mungo in the church of St. Giles, and to give a dinner to the masters of the craft. The sons of masters were relieved from the money pay- ment, but had to give the dinner. [4]

No entries appear in the Register of Burgesses and Guild Brethren from 1501 till 1506, both inclusive.

[1] 1503, c. 31.   A. P. S. vol. ii. p. 252.
[2] 1503, c. 32.  A. P. S. vol. ii. p. 252.
[3] C. R. vol. i. fol. 30.   Extracts C. R. vol. i. p. 99.
[4] C. R. vol. i. fol. 50.   Extracts C. R. vol. i. pp. 101–104.

On 23d March 1507–8 it was enacted by the provost, dean of guild, and councillors, that in

'tyme cuming the priuilegis of burges bairns be observit and kepit in this wis, that the burges eldest son, entrand as air to his fader, sal pay for his burgesry vjs. viijd.; and for gildry entrand be his fader, brother of the gild, xiijs. iiijd. ; and for the second son, his burgesry xiijs. iiijd., and for his gildry xxs.; and siclike the burges doichteris lauchfulle gottin to have the priuilege of the secund son, viz. for the burgesry xiijs. iiijd., and for the gildry xxs. Item, of the vnfremen enterand for his burgesry three li., and for his gildry five li., with the clerkis fee and the vtheris that accordis.' [1]

In 1507 two persons were entered as guild brethren, and three as burgesses and guild brethren.[2]

On 29th March 1508 the provost, bailies, council, and brethren of the guild passed an act against burgesses and guild brethren concealing or colouring unfreemen's goods pertaining either to burgessry or guildry, under pain of losing their burgess-ship or guild-brotherhood.[3]

The following entry, dated 18th July 1508, shows that the freedom of the town and the freedom of a craft were distinct things, but that both were required as a condition of practising a trade:—

' The quhilk day, anent the supplication maid be Thomas Greg, kirkmaister of the flescheour craft and the laif of the masteris of the samyn, that thir personis vnder written, viz. Thomas Harvye, Jhone Glen, David M'Kilwarrand, Will Cristesoun, James Gilry, Jhone Mores, Thomas Robesoun, Jhone Alanesoun, vnfremen of this burgh, Robert Law, Patrik Govanelokis, and Jhone Naper, fre burges, that the vnfremen occupiit the fredome of thair craft, nother havand the fredom of the burgh nor of thair craft, and als that the fremen war nocht vncorporat in thair facultie and fredome, it was ordanit and deliverit be the provest, baillies, and counsall that the said vnfremen be dischairgit fra the operatioun of the flescheour craft except the fre market dayis, Sounday and Monanday, quhill thai obtene thair fredome, and the provest and counsall be further advisit ; and as for the said fremen, thai ar submittit with consent of pairtie to be examit be Thomas Greg, Symon Law, Michel Inche,

---

[1] Register of Burgesses, etc., vol. i. fol. 115.  Extracts C. R. vol. i. pp. 112, 113.

[2] Register of Burgesses and Guild Brethren.

[3] Register of Burgesses, vol. i. fol. 114.  C. R. vol. i. fol. 25.  Extracts C. R. vol. i. p. 113.

and Jhone of Fyfe, sworne thairto in jugement, quhether thai be abile and wirthye be thair practice to be admittit to the occupatioun of the said craft or nocht; and as for thair contributioun of thair vpset, the provest and counsall till auys thairvpon, baith for the honour of thair altar, the proffeit of the toun, and honestie of the craft, and as the said maisteris fyndis in the said examination to schaw the samyn to the toun.'[1]

A portion of the craftsmen of the burgh having, on 29th November 1508, applied to the council to have six or eight members of craft on the daily council of the town, and to have some craftsmen appointed to the office of bailie and other offices, the provost, bailies, and great council, and a part of the craftsmen, answered that no alteration could be made on the existing law without the authority of parliament.[2]

In 1508 one person was admitted a burgess, thirty-one were admitted guild brethren, and seventeen were admitted burgesses and guild brethren.[3]

On 4th February 1509–10 the provost, bailies, and council granted a seal of cause to the cordiners, whereby, on the supplication of the kirkmaster and other masters of that craft, the council confirmed certain statutes for the government of the craft, and specially enacted, *inter alia*—(1) That apprentices should serve for seven years, and pay on entry six and eightpence to the altar of Crispin and Crispiniane in the church of St. Giles. (2) That no apprentice nor other person of the craft should be allowed to set up booth within the burgh until admission to the craft, after examination by the masters, and until 'maid freeman and burgess of the said burgh.' The upset of each person so admitted was declared to be four merks, except the sons of burgesses, who had to pay two merks; and these payments were applicable to the sustentation of the altar.[4]

---

[1] C. R. vol. i. fol. 25.   Extracts C. R. vol. i. pp. 116, 117.

[2] C. R. vol. i. fols. 26, 49.   Extracts C. R. vol. i. pp. 118, 119.

[3] Register of Burgesses and Guild Brethren.

[4] Original seal of cause in the possession of the Incorporation of the Cordiners. Extracts C. R. vol. i. pp. 126–129.

In 1509 one person was admitted as a burgess, and one as a burgess and guild brother. No admissions are recorded in 1510, 1513, and intervening years.[1]

On 30th September 1513 Master Gavin Douglas, provost of the collegiate church of St. Giles, was made a burgess *gratis*, for the common benefit of the town.[2]

A seal of cause granted by the council to the cordiners on 6th December 1513 enacted that no outland folk dwelling beyond the burgh, nor unfreemen, should buy any rough hides or barked leather within the town except on market days.[3]

On 26th October 1514 the kirkmaster and the other masters of the fleshers, described as 'freemen and burgesses within this burgh,' appeared before the president, bailies, and council, and consented that unfreemen fleshers might sell butcher meat on Sunday and Monday, as free market days to them.[4] On 11th August 1515 Hanckyne Thomesoun was declared to have forfeited his burgess-ship because he had hurt his oath 'against the freedom of the toun, in intromitting with strangers in buying and selling, contrary to the statutes of the toun.'[5]

No entries appear in the Register of Burgesses and Guild Brethren for 1514. In 1515 one person was enrolled as a burgess, sixteen were enrolled as guild brethren, and six as burgesses and guild brethren. In 1516 twenty-three were admitted as burgesses, nine as guild brethren, and twenty-eight as burgesses and guild brethren.[6] On 5th September 1517 the provost, bailies, and council granted a seal of cause to the candlemakers, by which, on the supplication of the whole members of that craft, in conformity with 'the awld statutes and privileges that they had of the provost, bailies, and

---

[1] Register of Burgesses and Guild Brethren.
[2] C. R. vol. i. fol. 5.  Extracts C. R. vol. i. p. 144.
[3] C. R. vol. viii. fol. 71.  Extracts C. R. vol. i. p. 145.
[4] C. R. Ad. Lib. fol. 39.  Extracts C. R. vol. i. p. 152.
[5] C. R. vol. i. fol. 7.  Extracts C. R. vol. i. p. 155.
[6] Register of Burgesses and Guild Brethren.

council of before,' the council ordained—(1) That the whole craft should annually choose one of their number, who was 'freman and burgess of the toun,' to be deacon :

(2) 'That na maner of man nor woman occupy the said craft, as to be ane maister and to set up buith, but gif he be ane freman or ellis ane fremanis wife of the said craft allanerlie ; '

and when they set up booth, they had to pay half a merk of silver to St. Giles' work, and half a merk to the sustentation of such altar in St. Giles as the deacon and craftsmen thought most needful, till the craftsmen were furnished with an altar of their own: (3) No apprentice was to be taken for a less term than four years : (4) All women were to be expelled from the craft, except the wives of freemen of the craft, who were bound to obey the deacon and craftsmen.   It was further ordained that—

'quha will nocht be maid freman he sall nocht sett vp nor hald buith, bot to be ane seruand vnder a maister quhill he grow and be reddy thairto, and that nane of the saidis craftsmen, seruands, boyes, nor prenteis, thair termes beand run, mak service to ony vther men except the craftsmen of the said craft, vnto the tyme that thai be reddy to wirk thair awin wark, and to be fremen of the toun.'[1]

On 16th November 1517 an act, reciting that divers and many persons were made burgesses and freemen within the burgh who did not reside within the same, and did not scot, lot, extent, walk, or waird, nor yet bear portable charges within the burgh as they ought to do, and as others neighbours and freemen of the burgh did, required all persons who were made burgesses and freemen to reside and hold their stob and staik therein.[2]

In 1517 eighty-one persons were admitted burgesses, sixty-nine were admitted guild brethren, and twenty-seven were admitted burgesses and guild brethren.[3]

On 10th December 1518 the provost, bailies, council, and com-

[1] C. R. vol. i. fol. 53.   Extracts C. R. vol. i. pp. 170–172.   This seal of cause was confirmed by King James VI. under the Great Seal, of date 4th May 1597.
[2] C. R. Ad. Lib. fol. 25.   Extracts C. R. vol. i. p. 172.
[3] Register of Burgesses and Guild Brethren.

munity granted a seal of cause to the merchants and guild brethren of the burgh, by which, *inter alia*, the grantees and their successors were empowered, ' now at the beginning of the said fraternity,' to choose a master of faculty and such officers and councillors as they might consider proper; and thereafter the master of faculty, councillors, and officers so elected were empowered in all time to come to choose the new master of faculty, councillors, and members of the fraternity, to endure for such space as they might think expedient for the time. One of the duties imposed upon the master, councillors, and officers was—

' to punis alsweill extranearis trespassand within our boundis as induellaris of this burgh, attemptand aganis the privilegis of the burrowis, or aganis the common weill of the merchandis and gild brethir; and to haif power to hald courtis, quhilkis sall be callit courtis of gildry, and to punis the said transgressouris, vnlawis to vplift, rais, and inbring, and gif neid beis to poynd and distrenye thairfor, and the samyn to be disponit to thair commone werkis, as thai think maist expedient.'

The seal of cause also bears that the master of faculty, councillors, and members should have power to make such rules and statutes as they might consider to be expedient for the common weal ' of the haill merchandis of this realm, alsweill beyond the sey as on this syde;' and it declares that—

' it sall nocht be leissum to vse nor to cheis the forsaid maister that sall happen to be for the tyme to beir ony common office of the toun for that yeir, nor to make na maner of persoun burges nor gild without avis and consent of the said maister of faculte and his counsalouris.' [1]

No entries appear in the Register of Burgesses and Guild Brethren for the years 1518 and 1519.

[1] Official transumpt in the archives of the city. Inventory of City Charters, vol. i. fol. 88. No reference occurs to this document in the Records of the Council, but in the volume of extracts from the early records of the city, preserved in the Advocates' Library, a memorandum by the transcriber, dated December 1518, refers to a seal of cause having been granted by the lord provost, president, bailies, council, and community to the fraternity of merchants and guild brethren, conferring on them various privileges. C. R. Ad. Lib. fol. 100. Extracts C. R. vol. i. p. 186.

On 22d September 1520 the provost, bailies, and council granted a seal of cause to the waulkers, shearers, and bonnet-makers, in which the council ratified and confirmed a contract entered into between the masters and brethren of the waulkers and shearers on the one part, and the bonnet-makers on the other, whereby the latter agreed to contribute to the support of the altar of St. Mark in the same way as the former did, and both parties agreed to various regulations for the conduct of their respective businesses as among themselves.[1]

On 27th February 1520–1 the provost, bailies, and council granted a seal of cause to the websters, in the same terms as that dated 31st January 1475–6, with the following exceptions:—(1) Thirty shillings were substituted for two merks as the payment to be made by each person admitted to occupy the craft as a master; and (2) the following clause was inserted:—

'And now becaus the communitie of the wobstaris walkis, wardis, extentis, and beris all other commoun chargis within this toune, and the outland wobstaries duelland vtouth the fredome of this toune takis werk of the nichtbouris and wynning tharof, and beris na chargis within this toone, tharfor that ilk out-wabstar to landwart, cummand within this toune, and takand the stuff tharof till weif, sall pay ilk oulk ane penny, quhilk is bot small valour, to vphald the diuine service at the said altar, situat within the said college kirk of Sanct Geill, to be ingatherit be the dekin and kirkmasteris of the said craft for the tyme, to the vphaldin of diuine service at the said altar.'[2]

In 1520 two persons were admitted burgesses, one was admitted a guild brother, and four were admitted burgesses and guild brethren.[3]

[1] Original seal of cause in the possession of the Incorporation of Bonnet-makers. Extracts C. R. vol. i. pp. 198–201. Among the persons named in the contract as of the craft of bonnet-makers is Agnes Yorstoun, spouse of James Williamson.

[2] Original seal of cause in the possession of the Websters. Extracts C. R. vol. i. pp. 203, 204.

[3] Register of Burgesses and Guild Brethren.

I

On 21st March 1521-2 the dean of guild and six other persons
were ordained to—

'forgather ilk Fryday, and sitt in the tolbuith, or any other place quhair thai
pleis, ane hour, vpoun the materis concerning the common weill of thair kirk,
and avys and mak fremen and gild brether, and to compone with thame as thai
think caus.'[1]

In 1521 one person was admitted to each of the grades of burgess-ship, guild brotherhood, and burgess-ship and guild brotherhood.[2]

On 27th February 1522-3 the bailies and council ordained that
if any neighbour freeman of the town should happen to be present
when any other neighbour bought merchandise in Leith or elsewhere, and desired to have part of the commodity purchased, he
should be entitled to have it on immediate payment of the price
paid for it.[3]

On 20th March 1522-3 the provost, bailies, and council, on the
supplication of the kirkmaster and remainder of the masters of the
craft of baxters, setting forth that—

'the facultie and power they had of before upon the guid guyding and reule of
thair said craft was destroyit, and their seal of cause tane thairfra be negligent
in time of troubill,'

granted a seal of cause to the craft, by which various rules and
ordinances were confirmed, and specially the following :—

(1) 'that na persounes presume them to be maisteris of the said craft to baik
thair awin stuffe to sell without they be first prenteis, syne burges, and thairafter examynit be the maisters of the said craft, fundin able, and admittit
thairto, and syne thairefter till pay thair dewties, as uthir craftis dois within
this burgh ; ' and
(2) 'that they micht have facultie and priviledge yit as of before to mak statuts
and reules for the guyding of thair said craft in honestie, and for the commoun weil of the said toune, accordand till equite and reasoune.'[4]

---

[1] C. R. vol. i. fol. 15.   Extracts C. R. vol. i. p. 208.
[2] Register of Burgesses and Guild Brethren.
[3] C. R. vol. i. fol. 15.   Extracts C. R. vol. i. p. 213.
[4] Print of seal of cause and other documents granted to the Incorporation of
Bakers (1825).   Extracts C. R. vol. i. p. 214, 215.

In 1522 two persons were admitted burgesses, and two burgesses and guild brethren. In 1523 two persons were admitted burgesses and guild brethren.[1]

On 13th August 1524 a flesher or the chaplain of the craft was appointed to pass with an officer of the town among unfreemen of the craft, and if they found them selling on other than market days, to report them for punishment.[2]

In 1524 six guild brethren and three burgesses and guild brethren were admitted.[3]

In 1525 two persons were admitted burgesses and guild brethren.[4]

On 4th May 1526 the council consented and granted to the deacon and masters of the fleshers, that in all extents and other charges within the burgh the candlemakers should extent and bear all portable charges with the fleshers, such having been understood to be the practice in times bygone.[5]

In each of the years 1526 and 1527 only one burgess and guild brother was admitted; and in 1528 two were admitted burgesses, one was entered as guild brother, and three were entered as burgesses and guild brethren.[6]

On 14th April 1529 the Commissioners of Burghs convened at Edinburgh ordained all those who were made burgesses, and that used buying and selling of merchandise, to

'cum and duell within the burgh, and hald stob and stack within the same within forty dais next heirefter,'

under pain of losing their freedom. They also ordained—

'that na outland chapman be maid burges within the burght for vij yeir, except he mary ane burges dochter or wiff, and he be worth ane hundreth lib. of his

---

[1] Register of Burgesses and Guild Brethren.
[2] C. R. vol. i. fol. 46. Extracts C. R. vol. i. p. 218.
[3] Register of Burgesses and Guild Brethren.    [4] Ibid.
[5] C. R. vol. i. fol. 19. Extracts C. R. vol. i. p. 227.
[6] Register of Burgesses and Guild Brethren.

awin gudis, and ane honest persoun till vse merchandise, and that na burges be maid without the provest, bailies, and councill; and this to be keipit vnder the pane of twenty lib., to be tane oup of the provest or bailyeis for every burges that is maid in contrair thairof, and at the commissionaris of burrowis tak cognition quhen the conwein of every brught that brakis this statut, and to raiss the saidis panis, to be disponet as thai sall think expedient.'[1]

On 8th October 1529 the council ordained every merchant and craftsman having a fore-booth to have in his booth 'ane axe or twa or thre, eftir as thai haif seruandis,' and to come incontinent to the provost or bailies, ready to fortify and maintain them, under the pain, for the first fault, of 40s., for the second, if he were a man of substance, of £10 to the common works of the town, and for the third fault, of forfeiture of his freedom. . If the defaulter was not a man of substance, then the penalty was declared to be loss of his freedom for a year and day, and further during the town's pleasure.[2]

In 1529 eleven burgesses, twenty-one guild brethren, and nine-teen burgesses and guild brethren were entered.[3]

On 31st March 1530 the provost, bailies, and council granted a seal of cause to the bonnet-makers, who, as has been seen, were incorporated with the waulkers and shearers, and bound with them to support the altar of St. Mark in the church of St. Giles. By this seal of cause the council ratified and approved of certain rules and statutes submitted to them by the 'bretheris and sisteris of the said craft,'[4] and specially the following:—(1) That an honest man of the craft should be annually chosen, 'be the auise of the provost, bailies, and counsall of the burgh,' to be 'ouerman and ouersear,' and that all the men and women of the craft should obey him at all times; and

[1] Council Records of Aberdeen, vol. xii. pp. 557–562. Convention Records, vol. i. p. 510.

[2] Lib. Stat. Burg. fol. 54, 55. C. R. Ad. Lib. fols. 39, 40, 42, 83, 184. Extracts C. R. vol. ii. p. 7.

[3] Register of Burgesses and Guild Brethren.

[4] Among the names of the members of craft mentioned in the seal of cause are those of 'Jonet Watsoun, Jonet Poilton, and Katran Grame.'

(2) 'At na man nor woman of bonatmakaris vse nor wyrk the said craft of bonatmakyn without at he or scho be first prenteis and ane craftisman or woman of the samyn.'[1]

On 21st June 1530 it was found and ordained by arbiters appointed for the whole body of craftsmen, with the approval of the provost, bailies, deacons, and council, that the shearers, waulkers, and bonnet-makers should pass together under one headman, deacon, or oversman, equally chosen by them, in all processions, conventions, and councils, between the fleshers and barbers, and that the websters should in like manner pass with their deacon in their old place, between the bakers and the tailors.[2] This arrangement appears, however, to have been modified by a subsequent decree arbitral on 19th May 1531, under which the deacon and brethren of the websters were ordained to allow the deacon, oversman, and brethren of the waulkers, shearers, and bonnet-makers to go with them in all processions and gatherings.[3]

In 1530 one burgess and one guild brother were entered.[4]

On 20th October 1531 the provost, bailies, and council granted a seal of cause to the tailors, by which the council confirmed certain rules and statutes proposed by these craftsmen, and, *inter alia*, the following :—(1) That every apprentice should be bound for seven years, and no less, without dispensation of the principal masters of the craft, and specially in favour of the sons of the craft, and should pay 10s. towards the altar of St. Ann, in St. Giles' Church ;

(2) 'That nowthir thir prentisis nor nane vther persoun of the said craft be sufferyt till sett up buyth within this said burgh, nor wyrk of the said craft, bot with ane fre maister of the samyne, without he be sworn maister and fund sufficient, habyll, and worthy thairto in practik and vtherwayis, and admyttyt

---

[1] Original seal of cause in the possession of the Bonnet-makers. Extracts C. R. vol. ii. p. 22.

[2] Notarial instrument in the possession of the Bonnet-makers. Extracts C. R. vol. ii. p. 31.

[3] Extract from Burgh Court book in the possession of the Waulkers. Extracts C. R. vol. ii. pp. 48–50, 56–57.

[4] Register of Burgesses and Guild Brethren.

thairto first be the sworn maisterys of the said craft principall, and maid fre man and burgess of the said burgh, and than for his wpset till pay fyf pundys to the reparatiouns and wphald of dyuyne seruice at thair said altar with an honest dennar to the sworne maisterys thairof; (3) That na maister sall have forman in his buyth till wyrk bot ane allanerly within this fredome.' [1]

On 12th February 1532–3 the candlemakers were ordained by the council to extent and bear all portable charges with the fleshers, until the former obtained discharge 'be sentence that they sould nocht stent with thame, and that without preiudice of onye rycht of the saidis candelmakeris;' and the candlemakers were ordained to pay the fleshers 40s. for their two last extents.[2]  The bonnet-makers were also, on 12th March 1532–3, ordained to pay one-half of the extent to the websters, to help and supply them, and the other half to the waulkers and shearers, and to begin and pay five shillings at that term.[3]

In 1531 twenty guild brethren and seventeen burgesses and guild brethren were entered; and in 1532 two burgesses and one guild brother were enrolled.[4]

On 22d August 1533 the provost, bailies, and council granted a seal of cause to the skinners and furriers, whereby they confirmed to these crafts certain rules and statutes proposed by them, and specially the following:—

'That fra thynefurth na maner of personis of the saidis crafts of skynnaris and furroris be sufferit to set vp buth nor pull skynnis within this burgh without he be first freman and burges of the samyn, fundin sufficient and abill in werkman-schip and vthirwayis, and admittit thairto be the provest, baillies, and counsale, and sworne maisteris of the craftis, and than for his vpsett to pay, gif he be ane skynneris son burges within this burgh, ten schillingis, and gif he be ane vthir mannis son, to pay for thair vpsett the sowme of fyve pundis, vsuall money of Scotland, to the reparatioun and vphalding of divyne seruice at oure said altare.' [5]

---

[1] Printed copy seal of cause in the possession of the Incorporation of Tailors. Extracts C. R. vol. ii. pp. 52–55.

[2] C. R. vol. i. p. 60.   Extracts C. R. vol. ii. p. 60.

[3] C. R. vol. i. fol. 39.   Extracts C. R. vol. ii. p. 60.

[4] Register of Burgesses and Guild Brethren.

[5] Notarial copy seal of cause in the possession of the Incorporation of Skinners and Furriers.  Extracts C. R. vol. ii. pp. 61–4.

On 17th September in the same year the provost, bailies, council, community, and deacons of crafts granted a seal of cause to the cordiners, by which they authorized these craftsmen to levy certain dues on goods belonging to their craft brought from landward to be sold within the burgh; the sums so levied to be applied for upholding their altar of Saint Crispin and Crispiani in the College church of St. Giles.[1]

Eight burgesses, one guild brother, and two burgesses and guild brethren were entered in 1533; and two guild brothers, and one burgess and guild brother were entered in 1534.[2]

On 12th June 1535 parliament ratified and approved of the acts previously made in favour of merchants within burgh;[3] and also the act of King James III., ratified by King James IV., as to merchants passing with merchandise furth of the realm to France, Flanders, and other parts; which act was appointed to be put to execution by the provosts and bailies of burghs.[4] On the same day parliament further passed the following act :—

' *Item*, Becaus all oure Souerane Lordis burrowis are putt to pouertie, waistit and destroyit in thair gudis and polecy, and almaist ruynous, throw falt of vsing of merchandice, and that throw being of outlandis men provest, baillies, and aldermen within burgh for thare awine particular wele in consumyng of the commoun gudis of burrowis grantit to thame be our Souerane Lord and his predecessouris, kingis of Scotland, for the vphald of honeste and polecy within burgh, it is herefore statute and ordanit that na man in tyme cuming be chosin provest, ballies, or aldermen in to burgh bot thai that ar honest and substantious burgessis, merchandis, and induellaris of the said burgh, vnder the pane of tynsale of thare fredome quha dois in the contrar,' etc.[5]

It also statuted and ordained—

' That na man, erle, lord, baroun, or vther of quhateiur degree, about and adiacent nychtbouris to burrowis, molest, truble, nor inquiet the provest, aldermen, ballies, and officiaris of burrowis, and merchandis thairof, in vsing of

---

[1] Original seal of cause in the possession of the Incorporation of Cordiners. Extracts C. R. vol. ii. p. 64.

[2] Register of Burgesses and Guild Brethren.

[3] 1535, c. 31.  A. P. S. vol. ii. p. 348.          [4] 1535, c. 32, Ibid.

[5] 1535, c. 35.  A. P. S. vol. ii. p. 349.

thare franchis, liberties, and priuelegis grantit to thame be oure Souerane Lord and his predecessouris, kingis of Scotland, and in contrair the actis and statutis maid thairupoun, vnder the pane to be callit and accusit as commoun oppressouris of our Souerane Lordis liegis.'[1]

And further ordained as follows :—

'Becaus of the gret oppressioun daile done vpoun our Souerane Lordis liegis be cordonaris, smyths, baxtaris, browstaris, and all vther craftismen, sellaris of vittale and salt, compelland thaim to pay for thair stuff and werkmanschip exhorbitant prices, to the gret scaith of all our Souerane Lordis liegis, bringand silk derth in the cuntre that the samyn may nocht be sustenit ; and for remeid hereof it is statute and ordanit that our Souerane Lord sall gif ane commissioun to certane his lordis and vtheris, quham His Grace plesis best, to sitt, and with thame the provest of Edinburgh, and mak sik statutis and ordinancis as thai sall think maist expedient for the commoun wele, to caus all craftismen within the toune of Edinburgh and vtheris of the realme to mak gud and sufficient stuff, and sell the samin of ane competent price, and to tak competently for thair werkmanschip and labouris gif thai werk ane vther manys stuff and mater, and to make all sellars of vittale or salt to sell the samyn of ane gan and price without derth.  And quha dois in the contrar, to punys thame with all rigour. And the saidis commissaris to do justice vpoune the brekaris of thir ordinances als oft as thai here murmur or complant thairof, and to punis thame in thair gudis as thai find the gretnes of the falt, as efferis.'[2]

On 15th October 1535 the council ordained the acts of parliament in regard to the making of burgesses to be observed and kept in all time to come, so that no burgess should thereafter be made except in the presence of the provost, bailies, and council in judgment; and also ordained all persons previously made burgesses to come and remain personally in town, and hold stob and staik therein, and to bear all portable charges of the burgh, as other neighbours did, within forty days, under pain of losing their freedom.[3]

⟑ On 29th December of the same year the provost, bailies, council, and deacons of crafts ordained that every

'man that beis made burges and freman in this guid towne frae this tyme sall pay to the dene of gild for his fredome and burgesrie the sowm of ten pund,

---

[1] 1535, c. 36.  A. P. S. vol. ii. p. 349.
[2] 1536, c. 43.  A. P. S. vol. ii. p. 351.
[3] C. R. Ad. Lib. fol. 26.  Extracts C. R. vol. ii. p. 71.

vnforgevin, except burges bairnis till bruik thair auld priuelegis; and that euery craftisman that wold be burges to that effect to be maid maister and frie to his craft and nocht ellis, he to pay to the dene of gild the sowm of fyve pund for his fredome, without favouris. And als decernis and ordanis that all thai persouns quhilkis wer maid burges of before and remains furth of the towne contrair the act maid the xv of October last till haif tynt thair fredome because thai come nocht to remayne within the towne after the forme of the said act, and ordanis the customeris of the towne and keperis of the portis of the samyn till tak custome of all guids brocht in be thame within this towne fra this tyme furth as fra ane vnfreman.'[1]

In 1535 ten burgesses, six guild brethren, and fourteen burgesses and guild brethren were entered.[2]

On 22d September 1536 the provost, bailies, council, and community granted a seal of cause to the cordiners, whereby they ratified and confirmed to these craftsmen various rules and statutes and, *inter alia*, the following :—

'All maner of prentesis to be tane to the said craft sall stand in prentischip for the space of sevin yeris and nay les, without dispensatioune of the principall maisteris of the said craft, and speciallie in fauoris of the sonis of the said craft, and ilk prenteis to pay at his entre to the reparatioun and vphalding of devyne seruice at thair said altar twenty schillingis vsuall money of this realme; and that nodir thir prentises nor nane wthir persoune of the said craft be sufferit to set up buith within this said burgh without he be fundin sufficient, habill, and wourthy in practik and wthir ways, and admittit thareto be the kirk-maister and sex maisteris of the craft, and maid burges and freman of the said burgh, and bring his tiket thairupone, and than for his wpset to pay fyve pundis, except burges sonis of this toune to pay fyfty schillingis, to the reparatioun and wphalding of devyne seruice at thare said altar.'[3]

In 1536 six burgesses, one guild brother, and five burgesses and guild brethren were entered; and in 1537 four burgesses, one guild brother, and four burgesses and guild brethren were entered.[4]

On 8th February 1538–9 an act as to having weapons in booths

---

[1] C. R. Ad. Lib. fol. 26. Extracts C. R. vol. ii. pp. 71, 72.

[2] Register of Burgesses and Guild Brethren.

[3] Original seal of cause in the possession of the Incorporation of Cordiners. Extracts C. R. vol. ii. pp. 78–80.

[4] Register of Burgesses and Guild Brethren.

was passed by the council, in terms similar to that of 8th October 1529.[1]

Eight burgesses, seventeen guild brethren, and twenty-nine burgesses and guild brethren were entered in 1538.[2]

On 15th July 1539 the provost, bailies, council, and ' men of gude,' merchants for the time, ordained all persons alleging themselves to be free and comburgesses of the burgh to appear and enter themselves within forty days to remain and make residence within the burgh, scot, lot, ward, and walk with the other comburgesses, under pain, if they failed, of being holden unfreemen.[3]

In 1539 one burgess, two guild brethren, and four burgesses and guild brethren were entered.[4]

By a statute of James v., passed on 14th March 1540–1, the old privileges of burghs were ordained to be kept and observed, conform to the previous statutes and acts of parliament which were ratified and confirmed.[5]   It was also ordained—

'that na persoun vse pakking nor peling of woll, hidis, nor skinnis, loise nor laid outwith fre burgh and priuilege therof.' [6]

And further—

'becaus it is hevely murmurit that all craftismen of this realme and specialie within burrowis vsis sic extorsionis vpoun vtheris oure Souerane Lordis liegis be resoune of thare craftis, and of private actis and constitutionis maid amangis thaim selfis contrar the commoun weill, and in grett hurt, priudice, dampnage, and scaith to all the leigis of this realme : Therefore it is statute and ordanit that in all tymes cuming it salbe lesum to all our Souerane Lordis liegis that hes ony biggingis or reparationis to be maid for making of pollecy in this realme owthir to burgh or to land to cheis gude craftis men, fre men or vtheris, as he thinkis maist expedient, for ordoring, bigging, and ending of all sic werkis.   And giff ony craftis man beginnis the said werk and dilayis to end the samin, that

---

[1] C. R. Ad. Lib. fol. 184.   Extracts C. R. vol. ii. p. 93.
[2] Register of Burgesses and Guild Brethren.
[3] C. R. vol i. fol. 41.   Extracts C. R. vol. ii. p. 94.
[4] Register of Burgesses and Guild Brethren.
[5] 1540, c. 25.   A. P. S. vol. ii. p. 375.
[6] 1540, c. 26.   A. P. S. vol. ii. p. 375.

the persoun that causis to big the said werk or reparatioun forsaid to cheis and tak vtheris in thair placis als oft as neid beis to perfurnis and end furth the said werk for policy of the realme; and that na impediment be maid to sic craftismen vsand thair craft as said is be ony vthir of the said craft within this realm, vnder the pane of tinsale of thair fredome and breking of the actis of parliament. And that the provest and baillies of all burrowis tak inquisitioun herapone, and putt this act to executioun in all punctis.' [1]

The following entries are recorded in 1540, 1545, and intervening years:—in 1540 two guild brethren and seven burgesses and guild brethren; in 1541 one burgess and one burgess and guild brother; in 1542 two burgesses and guild brethren; and in each of 1543 and 1545 one burgess and guild brother. [2]

On 23d March 1544–5 all persons except freemen of the town were prohibited from buying malt in the market. [3]  On 27th February 1545–6 it was ordained that no person should hold open tavern within the burgh but such as were burgesses and guild brethren, and paid duty to St. Anthony's altar.' [4]

Four burgesses and guild brethren were entered in 1546. [5]

On 5th April 1547 the act made on 27th February 1545–6 was ordered to be put to execution. [6]  On 7th November 1548 unfreemen dwelling within or without the burgh, were prohibited from buying on market days or on other days, within the burgh, hides, wool, skins, or such merchandise, except from freemen and burgesses of the burgh, under pain of escheat of the stuff.' [7]  On the 21st of the same month the act of 5th April 1547 was renewed, and the doors of defaulters were ordered to be shut up till they became burgesses and guild brethren. [8]

No entries were made in the Register of Burgesses and Guild

[1] 1540, c. 30.  A. P. S. vol. ii. p. 376.
[2] Register of Burgesses and Guild Brethren.
[3] C. R. Ad. Lib. fol 65.  Extracts C. R. vol. ii. p. 116.
[4] C. R. Ad. Lib. fol. 70.  Extracts C. R. vol. ii. p. 121.
[5] Register of Burgesses and Guild Brethren.
[6] C. R. Ad. Lib. fol. 27.  Extracts C. R. vol. ii. p. 127.
[7] C. R. Ad. Lib. fol. 71.  Extracts C. R. vol. ii. p. 142.
[8] C. R. Ad. Lib. fol. 77.  Extracts C. R. vol. ii. p. 142.

Brethren in 1547; but in 1548 five guild brethren and eight burgesses and guild brethren were entered.[1]

On 13th March 1549–50 James Curle was ordained to have lost his freedom in consequence of his having made a wrong statement against the provost, bailies, and council in an application to the Lords for liberation from the tolbooth, where he was imprisoned by the provost's command.[2]

In 1549 twenty-nine guild brethren and nineteen burgesses and guild brethren were entered.[3]

On 30th July 1550 the following act was passed :—

'The quhilk day, the provest, baillies, and counsall sittand in jugement, for diuers caussis and consideratiouns moving thame, for the weill of this burgh burgessis thairof, hes statut and ordanit that in all tymes cummyng thair be na maner of persoun maid burges nor freman except in jugement, and thair names put in thair lokkit buke, in presens of the dene of gild; and that ilk persoun beand maid burges alanerlie to pay v li., and beand maid burges and gild brother pay xv li., viz. :—v li. for his burgesry, and x li. for his gildrie and fredome thairof, and that to be payit and deliuerit to the said dene of gild ; providing alwys that the said dene of gild pay to the prouest, baillies, and clerkis for the time v li. for ilkane of thair burgesschippis, and thai to mak na burgessis be tham self, bot to be maid as said is, and that na maner of seriandis in tyme cummyng to haif pawer to mak burges nor haif the valour thairof, except alanerlie ane crovne of the sone to be payit be the said dene of gild to ilkane of tham yeirlie ; alsua providing that the fredome of burgessis sonis and dochteris be obseruit and keipit to tham nochtwithstanding this present act.'[4]

On 9th October in the same year persons who sold wine without being guild brethren were called, and found surety to desist under pain of £20.[5] On the 11th of the same month the provost, bailies, and dean of guild, sitting in judgment, ordained—

'that in all tymes cummyng thair be na maner of priuilege obseruit and keipit to burges dochteris lik as hes bene in tymes bygane, conform to the priuilege

[1] Register of Burgesses and Guild Brethren.
[2] C. R. Ad. Lib. fol. 26.    Extracts C. R. vol. ii. p. 147.
[3] Register of Burgesses and Guild Brethren.
[4] Register of Burgesses, etc., vol. i. fol. 29.    Extracts C. R. vol. ii. p. 148.
[5] C. R. Ad. Lib. fol. 77.    Extracts C. R. vol. ii. p. 150.

of the burges secund sone,. without that samyn burges dochter ressaif hir
fredome at hir first marriage; and fra scho be anis maryit, and hir husband
decessand, and scho maryit agane, hir secund husband to pay the rigour, and
to haif na priuilege be hir.'[1]

On 25th February 1550–1 proclamation was made of the act
1535, c. 32, ratifying the acts 1466, c. 3, 1487, c. 12, and 1489, c.
14; and a charge was given to all and sundry that no person should
sail from Leith to France, Flanders, or other parts in merchandise,
unless he had half a last of goods of his own or in governance,
conform to these acts.[2]

In 1550 twenty burgesses, five guild brethren, and fourteen burgesses and guild brethren were entered.[3]

On 26th January 1551–2 the dean of guild was ordered to
shut up the doors of the booths of all persons who were not freemen, and not to allow them to occupy any kind of freedom until
they paid their duty therefor.[4]  On the same day it was also
ordained by the provost, bailies, and council, that the sons, of all
burgesses after marriage should either pay extent with the rest of
the neighbours of the burgh, or pay custom as unfreemen, and
give their oaths upon their goods as unfreemen.[5]

On 1st February 1551–2 an act of parliament of the reign
of Queen Mary, referring to the éxorbitant prices that craftsmen within burgh charged for all such things as belonged to their
crafts, whereby prices were doubled and trebled by many of them,
ordained the provosts and bailies of free burghs with all diligence
to convene the deacons and craftsmen, and to fix reasonable prices
for everything pertaining to craftsmen; which prices were appointed to be reduced to writing and produced to the Lords of the
Articles in the following parliament, and if found reasonable to be
authorized, and if unreasonable to be reformed.  The provosts and

[1] Register of Burgesses, etc., vol. i. fol. 30.   Extracts C. R. vol. ii. p. 150.
[2] C. R. Ad. Lib. fol. 76.   Extracts C. R. vol. ii. pp. 151, 153.
[3] Register of Burgesses and Guild Brethren.
[4] C. R. vol. ii. fol. 4.   Extracts C. R. vol. ii. p. 162.            [5] Ibid.

bailies were also directed to fix the charges of hostellers for dinner and supper, and the sheriff was ordained to cause these prices to be observed to landward.[1] On the same day parliament required the observance of an act of the Privy Council, 'anent the eschewing of derth, and the ordouring of euerie mannis house in his coursis and discheis of meit.' By this act burgesses and other men of substance, spiritual and temporal, were prohibited from having more than four dishes at mess, with one kind of meat in each dish. Contravention of this ordinance inferred a penalty for each offence of twenty merks. Archbishops, bishops, and earls were limited to eight dishes, under a penalty of £100; while abbots, priors, and deans were restricted to six dishes, under a penalty of £40.[2] The acts as to 'paking and peling,' made by James V. and his predecessors, were at the same time ordered to be observed and kept in all points.[3]

During the year 1551 twenty-nine burgesses, two guild brethren, and nineteen burgesses and guild brethren were admitted.[4]

On 4th April 1552 the Commissioners of Burghs, at their convention in Edinburgh, ordered a general proclamation to be made at the market cross of every burgh, requiring such persons as alleged themselves to be free therein to compear within forty days, and hold stob and staik, and watch, ward, and pay extentis and skattis within the burgh conform to their substance, with certification that if they failed, they should be deemed to have lost their freedom and be used thenceforth as unfreemen. Burghs found negligent in the enforcement of this act were appointed to pay £5 for the first fault, £10 for the second, and £20 for the third fault.[5]

On 11th May 1552 all unfreemen, not being burgesses sworn and received, were ordered to pay their customs to the customer

---

[1] 1551, c. 18.  A. P. S. vol. ii. p. 487.     [2] 1551, c. 22.  Ibid., ii. p. 488.
[3] 1551, c. 23.  A. P. S. vol. ii. p. 488.  See the acts 1503, c. 29 ; 1540, c. 26.
[4] Register of Burgesses and Guild Brethren.
[5] Records of Convention, vol. i. pp. 3, 4.

of the wild adventures and other customs.[1]   On 4th March 1552-3 the council, having regard to the great slaughters and 'other cummeris and tulyeis' done in times bygone in the burgh, ordered all merchants, craftsmen, and others occupying booths or chambers on the 'hiegate,' either high or low, to have long weapons therein, such as hand axe, Jedburgh staff, halbert, javelin, and such like long weapons, with 'knaipscawis and jakkis,' and to come therewith, on the ringing of the common bell, to assist the officers of the town for 'stanching thairof,' under the penalty of £10, to be taken of every person failing therein, within eight days thereafter.[2]

During the year 1552 twenty-seven persons were entered as burgesses, two as guild brethren, and six as burgesses and guild brethren.[3]

The accounts of the dean of guild subsequent to Michaelmas 1552 are, with a few exceptions, still extant, and afford some information as to the number of burgesses and guild brethren admitted in each year, and the sums received for their admission. But the numbers as ascertained from the Register of Burgesses apply to the year closing on the 24th of March, while those given in the accounts apply to the year closing at Michaelmas— a difference of six months.

The total dues received by the dean of guild on the entry of thirty-two burgesses and guild brethren for the year from Michaelmas 1552 to Michaelmas 1553, amounted to £251, 6s. 8d. Scots.[4]

On 3d January 1553-4 a sergeant or officer was made burgess *gratis*, because he was made sergeant.[5]   On the 25th of the same month the council ordered the treasurer to pay the dean of guild £5 for the burgess-ship of a servant of the Lord Governor, granted at

---

[1] C. R. vol. ii. fol. 5.   Extracts C. R. vol. ii. p. 163.
[2] C. R. vol. ii. fol. 14.   Extracts C. R. vol. ii. p. 177.
[3] Register of Burgesses and Guild Brethren.
[4] Accounts of the Deans of Guild, vol. i.   Extracts C. R. vol. ii. pp. 331-2.
[5] C. R. vol. ii. fol. 22.   Extracts C. R. vol. ii. p. 186.

his Grace's request, *gratis*.[1]  On the 16th of February a similar
sum was ordered to be paid for a burgess-ship granted at the
request of the provost's wife;[2]  and on the 28th of the same
month a similar sum was ordered to be paid for a burgess-
ship granted at the request of Lord Huntly.[3]  On the same
day also the deacons and craftsmen produced to the provost,
council, and assessors a claim, in which they referred to the
act 1469, c. 5, by virtue of which, they alleged, the deacons of
every craft had taken part in the election of all officers within
the burgh, not only at Michaelmas, but whenever vacancies
arose, down to the present time, when the practice had been
departed from in the election of a sergeant.  They therefore
claimed that the election of the sergeant should be set aside,
and protested that if this were not done, they should be at
liberty to have their rights determined by superior judges.  The
provost, council, and assessors, however, sustained the election
complained of, and thereupon the procurator of the craftsmen
protested, and took instruments.[4]

During the year which ended on 24th March 1553–4 twenty-
eight persons were entered as burgesses, one as a guild brother,
and eight as burgesses and guild brethren.[5]

The accounts of the dean of guild for the year to Michaelmas
1554 show that fourteen burgesses and guild brethren were
entered during that year, and that the dues on their admission
amounted to £72 Scots.[6]

On 2d November 1554 all the neighbours were warned to attend a weapon-shawing on the Burghmuir, and each was required

[1] C. R. vol. ii. fol. 22.   Extracts C. R. vol. ii. p. 187.
[2] C. R. vol. ii. fol. 23.   Extracts C. R. vol. ii. p. 188.
[3] C. R. vol. ii. fol. 24.   Extracts C. R. vol. ii. p. 189.
[4] C. R. vol. ii. fol. 24.   Extracts C. R. vol. ii. p. 189.
[5] Register of Burgesses and Guild Brethren.
[6] Accounts of the Deans of Guild, vol. i.   Extracts C. R. vol. ii. p. 344.

to be provided with long weapons, such as spears, pikes, and culverings.[1]

On 18th January 1554–5 the bailies and council prohibited all burgesses from entering into partnership with indwellers in Leith or Canongate, or other unfreemen, or from making such persons their factors, either within or without the realm, or from freighting ships with them, under penalty of £40.[2] And on the same day they ordered the name of Mr. Robert Glen, who had been made burgess and guild brother *gratis* at the request of Lord Orkney, to be inserted in the locked book of the date on which he was sworn, during the provostship of Francis Tennand.[3] On 1st February 1554–5 the council, at the request of the Queen, directed the duty of the guildry to be given to Robert Lindesay *gratis*.[4]

During the year which ended on 24th March 1554–5 twenty-nine persons were admitted as burgesses, seven as guild brethren, and one as a burgess and guild brother.[5]

On 17th May 1555 the following act of council was passed :—

'The prouest, baillies, and counsall sittand in jugement, understandand that in all tymes bygane this burgh and burgessis thairof hes bene gretumlie defraudit and abusit be the ressauyng burgessis outlandismen, nocht beand maryit, nor haiffand famele nor sufficient substance, and vsand thame self sua vnhonestlie that the haill toun hes been eschamyit thairby : thairfor in tyme cummyng ordanis that na maner of persone be ressauit or admittit burges within this burgh except honest habil qualyfyit men, and that thai be maryit, duelland within the burgh, haiffand sufficient substance, with stob and staik; and that na burgessis be maid except on the counsall dayis, in presens of the prouest, baillies, and counsall.'[6]

On 20th June 1555 parliament

'vnderstandand cleirlie that the estate of burgesses thir mony yeiris bygane be greit trubill of waris hes sustenit infinit skaith baith in thair landis and gudis,

---

[1] C. R. vol. ii. fol. 36.　Extracts C. R. vol. ii. pp. 202, 203.
[2] C. R. vol. ii. fol. 40.　Extracts C. R. vol. ii. p. 207.
[3] C. R. vol. ii. fol. 40.　Extracts C. R. vol. ii. p. 208.　　[4] Ibid.
[5] Register of Burgesses and Guild Brethren.
[6] C. R. vol. ii. fol. 49.　Extracts C. R. vol. ii. p. 216.

and als that thair priuileges grantit to thame be our Souerane Ladyis maist nobill progenitouris and actis of parliament maid thairupone hes not bene obseruit nor keipit to thame as accordis;'

ratified all privileges and acts of parliament granted to burghs, burgesses, and merchants, and ordained them to be put to due execution.[1] Further, on the narrative

'that the chesing of dekinnis and men of craft within burgh hes bene rycht dangerous, and as thay haue vsit thameselfis in tymes bygane hes causit greit troubill in burrowis, commotioun and rysing of the Queenis liegis in diuers partis, and be making of ligges and bandis amangis thameselfis and betuix burgh and burgh, quhilk deseruis greit punischement,'

it was ordained that in time coming no deacons should be chosen in burgh; but the provost, bailies, and council of every burgh were required

'to cheis the maist honest man of craft of guide conscience, ane of euerie craft, to visie thair craft that thay labour sufficientlie, and that the samin be sufficient stuffe and wark; and thir persounis to be callit visitouris of thair craft, and to be electit and chosin yeirlie at Michaelmas.'

The assembling of craftsmen in private convention, and the making by them of acts and statutes, were prohibited, and all craftsmen were appointed to be under the provost, bailies, and council; but the visitors were declared to have the same rights as the deacons had previously enjoyed in the choosing of officers and other things. It was also enacted that no craftsman should

'bruke office in tymes cumming, except twa of thame, maist honest and famous, to be chosen yeirlie vpone the counsall, and thay twa to be ane part of the auditoris yeirlie to the compt of the common gudis, according to the actis of parliament.'

Contraveners of this act were appointed to be punished by imprisonment for a year, loss of the freedom of their burgh, and escheat of a third part of their goods to the Crown; and it was ordained that they should never afterwards be received as freemen until they obtained the favour and benevolence of the provost,

[1] 1555, c. 24.  A. P. S. ii. p. 497.

bailies, and council of the burgh in which the contravention was committed.[1]

The same parliament passed an act to prevent fraud by goldsmiths,[2] and also ordained the act 1488, c. 12, to be put to execution, with the addition—

'that na persoun tak vpone hand to by ony merchandice fra the saidis strangearis, bot fra fremen, at fre portis of the burrowis foirsaidis, vnder the pane of confiscatioun of all the gudis that thay by, togedder with the rest of thair mouabill gudis, to be applyit to our Souerane Ladyis vse, gif thay do in the contrare.'[3]

On 18th September 1555 the Convention of Burghs in Dundee prohibited freemen of every burgh from associating in merchandise with unfreemen, or colouring their goods, under pain of forfeiture of their freedom, and of being otherwise punished by the magistrates of the burgh in which they dwelt, as having violated their oath of burgess-ship.[4]

On 25th September 1555 the council declared that the treasurer had no right to appoint a person to a burgess-ship yearly;[5] but on the 26th of the following month of October the council granted to the provost a freedom of guildry, to be given by him to whomsoever he pleased.[6]

The accounts of the dean of guild for the year to Michaelmas 1555 show that forty-one burgesses and guild brethren were entered during the year, and that their dues amounted in all to £140, 6s. 8d. Scots.[7]

On 27th November 1555 the Queen Regent addressed an order to the provost, bailies, and council, from Falkland, to choose two commissioners, one a merchant and the other a craftsman, to meet with such commissioner as she might appoint, to confer as to

---

[1] 1555, c. 26. A. P. S. ii. p. 498.      [2] 1555, c. 34. Ibid., ii. 499.
[3] 1555, c. 37; A. P. S. ii. 499.
[4] Printed Records of Convention, vol. i. p. 11.
[5] C. R. vol. ii. fol. 57. Extracts C. R. vol. ii. p. 221.
[6] C. R. vol. ii. fol. 59. Extracts C. R. vol. ii. p. 223.
[7] Accounts of the Deans of Guild, vol. i. Extracts C. R. vol. ii. p. 352.

disputes between merchants and craftsmen in sundry burghs, and other matters. In consequence of this order, the council appointed the provost, two merchants, and one craftsman to be commissioners, the treasurer protesting that the election of a craftsman, —being contrary to previous practice,—should not prejudice the town. The visitors of crafts claimed to vote in the election, but the council refused to entertain their claim, and a protest was in consequence taken for remeid. The craftsmen also craved to have two craftsmen elected as well as two merchants.[1]

On 15th January 1555–6 the council made John Finder, a wright, who had been seriously injured in the execution of work of the town, a burgess *gratis;* and on the same day they appointed Alexander Thomson to be burgess and guild brother *gratis,* at the request of Andrew Murray of Blackbarony.[2]

On 24th January 1555–6 the provost, bailies, council, and visitors of the several crafts passed an act, in which they agreed to concur with the other burghs in a general contribution and gift to the Queen, if she would discharge certain acts of the Privy Council in prejudice of burghs, and consent that similar acts should in future be made only by parliament.[3] On the following day the visitors desired that a dispensation from the act 1555, c. 26, made in hurt of the privileges of craftsmen, should also be sought, otherwise they would 'tak the address that thai mycht get for them selffis.'[4]

During the year which ended 24th March 1555–6 forty-seven persons were enrolled as burgesses, three as guild brethren, and fourteen as burgesses and guild brethren.[5]

On 10th April 1556 the council found that Hector Blacader was

[1] C. R. vol. ii. fol. 66.    Extracts C. R. vol. ii. p. 233.
[2] C. R. vol. ii. fol. 65.    Extracts C. R. vol. ii. p. 232.
[3] C. R. vol. ii, fol. 66.    Extracts C. R. vol. ii. p. 235.
[4] C. R. vol. ii. fol. 66.    Extracts C. R. vol. ii. p. 236.
[5] Register of Burgesses and Guild Brethren.

sworn and admitted burgess and guild brother in John Symsoun's time; they therefore ordained his name to be put in the locked book, and directed the treasurer to receive the dues payable at the time of his admission, viz. 33s. 4d. On the same day the council ordained that whenever a person was made burgess or guild brother, the dean of guild should put his name in the book, and answer in his accounts for the dues of admission.[1]

The act 1555, c. 26, was, as might be expected, exceedingly distasteful to the craftsmen, and they seem to have employed all the means they could command to induce the Queen to relax its provisions. In this they succeeded so far as to obtain from her a charter under the great seal restoring their former privileges. This charter is dated at Stirling, on 16th April 1556, and after referring to the privileges which the craftsmen had enjoyed under her predecessors, and to the abatement of those privileges by the act of parliament, sets forth that since the time of that statute she had learned 'that nothing has been done in pursuance of those causes and considerations which had moved our foresaid parliament to pass that measure, nay, that everything is done more carelessly among those craftsmen at this day than formerly;' thereupon, being desirous that the privileges of the craftsmen should not be abridged without urgent and enduring cause, and being desirous also that dissension and contention among the merchants and tradesmen dwelling in her burghs should be prevented, she granted dispensations to all and sundry craftsmen of her burghs and cities in regard to that act of parliament, in so far as the same conflicted with the liberties and privileges which the craftsmen had previously enjoyed, either by royal grant or long and continued use. She further expressly restored to them the power to elect deacons of their several crafts, having vote in the election of officers of burghs, and being auditors of the accounts of the common good; and empowered the craftsmen to meet and make ordinances relat-

[1] C. R. vol. ii. fol. 73.   Extracts C. R. vol. ii. p. 240.

ing to their several crafts, to the preservation of good order among the craftsmen, and the maintenance of divine service. The craftsmen were further empowered to navigate and use and exercise merchandise of all sorts within the kingdom, and beyond the same, as might seem to them to be most advantageous, with all and sundry privileges, liberties, powers, and customs granted and bestowed on them by previous sovereigns, or used and possessed by the craftsmen in times bygone, notwithstanding the provisions of the said act.[1]

On 27th April 1556 a letter from the Queen, dated at Holyrood, was presented to the council, in which she required them, in conformity with her previously expressed wish, to elect John Little to the office of water bailie of Leith. On the presentation of this letter, the visitors of crafts claimed to have the same right of voting as the deacons had previously exercised. At the same time, the provost declared it to be Her Majesty's command that the bailies, assessors, and councillors should vote separately, and in writing, that he might show their votes to her. They, however, refused to give their votes in writing, 'in respect that thai wer ane counsale sworn to gif the best counsale thai culd, and consele the counsale schewne to thame.' Angry communications from the Queen followed; but ultimately Little was appointed, and the councillors who had resisted her mandates were ordered by a royal letter, dated 8th May 1556, to be deprived of their office. Throughout the controversy the craftsmen supported the demands of the Crown.

The accounts of the dean of guild for the year to Michaelmas 1556 show that twenty-six burgesses and guild brethren were admitted during the year, and that their total dues amounted to £102, 6s. 8d. Scots.[2]

[1] M.S. Register of the Great Seal, book 33, No. 192. Printed records of the Convention of Royal Burghs, vol. ii. pp. 469-472.
[2] Accounts of the Deans of Guild, vol. i. Extracts C. R. vol. ii. p. 362.

On 27th November 1556 Alexander Carpenter was made burgess and guild brother *gratis*, at the request of the Queen, on the condition that he should reside within the burgh, and use the freedom thereof within the same, and underlie all charges of the burgh, as others did.[1]   On 2d December, Gilbert Balfour produced an act of council, dated 20th November 1550,[2] and desired in respect thereof, and that divers persons had been made burgesses and guild brethren *gratis*, and without payment to the town, to be repaid the £15 which he had paid for his burgess-ship and guildry.   The demand was refused, and he protested for further remeid.[3]   On the 16th of the same month of December, the council ordained that no person should keep a tavern, or sell wine in great or small, unless he were a free burgess and guild brother, and admitted in the confraternity of St. Anthony.[4]

On 22d January 1556-7 a burgess was deprived of his freedom because he did not dwell within the burgh; he was, moreover, ordained to pay his extents bygone, and to remain in ward till he paid them.[5]   On the 12th of the following month, Janet Richardson, relict of John M'Ane, renounced her freedom of the burgh.[6]

During the year which ended on 24th March 1556-7 twenty-two persons were admitted as burgesses, two as guild brethren, and four as burgesses and guild brethren.[7]

On 17th August 1557 all indwellers within the bounds, liberty, and jurisdiction of the burgh were required to attend a weapon-shawing on the Burgh muir on the following Sunday, ' well bodin, in feir of war, with sufficient armour, long weapons, such as pike,

[1] C. R. vol. ii. fol. 88.   Extracts C. R. vol. ii. p. 256.
[2] The records of the Town Council at this date are not now extant.
[3] C. R. vol. ii. p. 89.   Extracts C. R. vol. ii. p. 257.
[4] C. R. vol. ii. fol. 91.   Extracts C. R. vol. ii. p. 259.
[5] C. R. vol. ii. fol. 92.
[6] C. R. vol. ii. fol. 93.   Extracts C. R. vol. ii. p. 261.
[7] Register of Burgesses and Guild Brethren.

spear, and other fencible long armour, conform to the old custom of the realm.'[1]

The Queen Regent having intimated to the provost, bailies, and council, on 17th September 1557, that if any burghs were exempted from sending their contingent to the army in respect of a commuted money payment, every person dwelling within the burgh should be stented therefor according to his ability and goods, whether he were craftsman or merchant, and not according to the old manner. The craftsmen appeared before the council on the following day, and agreed to be stented in conformity with the Regent's writing, providing always that the same should not hurt their privileges, nor be used as a precedent for stenting them in the same manner in future.[2] On the same day the council ordained (1) that for a year no burgess-ship should be given *gratis* to any person, but that the duty should be uplifted by the dean of guild unforgiven;[3] and (2) that all manner of persons, merchants, craftsmen, and others, having booths or dwelling-houses on the foregait, should be sufficiently provided with long weapons, such as axes, halberts, and Jedburgh staves, for stopping of tulzie, according to the former ordinance, and under pain of £40 to be taken from each defaulter.[4]

The accounts of the dean of guild for the year to Michaelmas 1557 show that sixteen burgesses and guild brethren were admitted during the year, and that their total dues amounted to £67, 13s. 4d. Scots.[5]

On 12th November 1557 the lord provost, at the request of the Earl of Glencairn and other courtiers, asked the bailies and council for a burgess-ship to a person whose name is not given. They

[1] C. R. vol. ii. fol. 98.   Extracts C. R. vol. iii. p. 9.
[2] C. R. vol. ii. fol. 103.   Extracts C. R. vol. iii. p. 10.
[3] C. R. vol. ii. fol. 103.
[4] C. R. vol. ii. fol. 105.   Extracts C. R. vol. iii. p. 12.
[5] Accounts of the Deans of Guild, vol. i.

replied, however, that they were under oath to grant no burgess-ship for a year to come,

'except to men of fame, honestie, and sufficient substance, quhilkis had or schortlie suld have stob and staik within this toune, and that man pay their dewtie the tyme of thair admissioun, and thairfore prayit his lordship be nocht offendit with thame, to the quhilk he alswa condisendit.' [1]

The following act of the council, dated 26th November in the same year, explains what were regarded as privileges of the sons of burgesses at this time :—

'Efter ressonyng vpoun the complaynt gevin in before thame be William Fowlar, Alexander Vddert, and vtheris, in name and behalf of the haill young men burgessis sonnis of this burgh, makand mentioun that thai wer hevely hurt in this last taxt of xij* lib. rasit for licence grantit to the inhabitanttis of this burgh to remane and abyde at hame fra our Souerane Ladeyis hoist and armye ordanit to convene vpoun Fawlay Mure the        day of        last by-past for the assault of Wark, etc., in sa far as thai wer ordanit be the settaris of the said taxt to pay ane pairt thairof, expres contrair to the laudabill ws and obseruit priuilegis grantit and obseruit to burges sonis nocht mareit, as at mair lenth is contenit in thair said complaint ; quhilk being considerit, as my lord prouest, ballies, and counsall foresaid fand the samyn to be ane noveltye, and to the gret hurt of thair barnis, and expres contrar to the actis, statutis, and priuilegis grantit and obseruit to burges barnis past memour of man, as said is, concludis, decernis all in ane voce that na burges sonn within this burgh salbe haldin to pay taxt, stent, walk or waird, in ony tyme cumin, nocht haffing stob nor staik, and being vnmareit, bot sall bruke and joyse the priuilege of the actis maid in thair fauoris of before, prouyding always thai pay the sowmes to the quhilk thai wer sett in the extent aboue writin.' [2]

During the year which ended on 24th March 1557–8 sixteen persons were entered as burgesses, two as guild brethren, and four as burgesses and guild brethren.[3]

On 16th April 1558 the president, bailies, and council ordained—

'in all tymes cuming, quhen ony taxtis, stenttis, or otheris portabill chargis sall happin to cum vpoun this burgh, that all manner of personis that hanttis, vsis, or exersis the libertie and privielege of merchandis or fre burgessis of the same, that is to say, the venting of wyne or onye other kynd of mer-

---

[1] C. R. vol. ii. fol. 110.    Extracts C. R. vol. iii. p. 13.

[2] C. R. vol. ii. fol. 113.    Extracts C. R. vol. iii. pp. 13, 14.

[3] Register of Burgesses and Guild Brethren.

chandice, quhatsumeuer stait thai be, men of law, scribe, or other priueliegit persoun, nochtwithstanding thair saidis priueliegis, in all tymes cuming, thay stent, scait, lott, and beir chargis, walk and waird with the saidis merchandis sa lang as thai vse thair libertie or onye pairt thairof.'[1]

On the 27th of the same month Thomas Henderson, residing in Tranent, was ordered by the president, bailies, and council to come, with his wife, bairns, family, and household, and make their dwelling and remaining within the town at Whitsunday, under pain of ' tynsale of his fredome.'[2]

The arrangements made in 1558 for resisting the threatened invasion by the English indicate the relative numbers of merchants and craftsmen, and the force that they could raise for the defence of the town. On 27th May the deacon of each craft was ordered to consult and advise with the 'remanent of the freemen of his occupation' as to the number of men they could enrol, and to give in the names to the bailies and council.[3] Then on 5th June all the neighbours, merchants, craftsmen, and others were ordered to be convened in the tolbooth, and ' thair, be thair awin avise, counsale, and consent, to heir and se euery ane of thame to be set to samonye men as his substance may sustene, weill prouidit in armour and wappynnis.' And on the same day the merchants voluntarily undertook to furnish 736 men well provided in armour and weapons, and more if necessary.[4] On the 10th of the same month the craftsmen in like manner undertook to provide 717 ' abill men of craftis, well provided, and more if necessary. Of these, the skinners agreed to furnish 63 men, of whom 42 were to be masters and 21 servants; the furriers 9; the websters 26, of whom 13 were to be masters and 13 servants; the tailors 178, of whom 81 were to be ' freemen,' 72 were to be servants, and 25 were to be ' in mer-

[1] C. R. vol. iii. p. 121.   Extracts C. R. vol. iii. pp. 18, 19.
[2] C. R. vol. ii. fol. 122.
[3] C. R. vol. ii. fol. 125.   Extracts C. R. vol. iii. p. 22.
[4] C. R. vol. ii. pp. 126–31.   Extracts C. R. vol. iii. pp. 23, 24.

chant housis and up and down the toun in hole and bore;' the
bonnet-makers 53, of whom 14 were to be masters and 39 servants; the barbers 25; the hammermen 151, of whom 66 were to
be masters and 85 servants; the goldsmiths 20, of whom 14 were
to be masters and 6 servants; the waulkers 43, of whom 24 were
to be masters and servants within the town, and 19 outwith the
West Port; the baxters 100, of whom 45 were to be masters and
55 servants; and the cordiners 49.[1]

On 10th June the president, bailies, and council, taking into
consideration a complaint by ~the skinners that unfreemen
from St. Johnston and other parts sold 'maid work' of their craft,
not only in wholesale but in small, on the High Street daily,
prohibited such sale in future, except on the market day and
during proclaimed fairs, under pain of escheat of the goods.[2]
A similar act was passed on 23d June on the complaint of the
bonnet-makers.[3]

The accounts of the dean of guild for the year to Michaelmas
1558 show that fourteen burgesses and guild brethren were entered
during the year, and that their dues amounted in all to £32, 13s.
4d. Scots.[4]  During the year which ended on 25th March 1558–9
twenty-five persons were admitted burgesses, and seven burgesses
and guild brethren.[5]

On 26th May 1559 it was found by the council, that the free
burgesses were greatly hurt, and the common profit overlooked, by
the dean of guild improperly permitting a great number of merchants and craftsmen to occupy the liberty of free merchants
within the burgh, though they were not burgesses.  To remedy
this state of matters the dean was ordained in future to hold

[1] C. R. vol. ii. pp. 131–6.   Extracts C. R. vol. iii. pp. 24, 25.
[2] C. R. vol. ii. fol. 131.   Extracts C. R. vol. iii. p. 24.
[3] C. R. vol. ii. fol. 132.   Extracts C. R. vol. iii. p. 25.
[4] Accounts of the Deans of Guild.
[5] Register of Burgesses and Guild Brethren.

guild courts twice a week for calling such unfreemen to order. To aid him in doing so, he was appointed to be furnished with a copy of the stent rolls, and he was ordained to call the unfreemen occupiers of merchandise first. The deacons of the crafts were also required to give in to the dean the names of all persons occupying crafts, that he might proceed in like manner against the unfree craftsmen.[1]

On 20th September in the same year the provost, bailies, dean of guild, councillors, treasurer, and assessors, being present for the election of the new council, the deacons of crafts presented a letter from the Queen Regent, dated Holyrood, September 1559, in which she stated that although, since the restitution of the craftsmen of burghs to their liberties three years previously, the deacons of Edinburgh had annually offered to take part in the election of the new council, the provost, bailies, and councillors had refused to receive their votes. The magistrates and councillors were therefore charged, under the pain of disobedience, to allow the deacons to vote in the election of the council leets and all other officers of the burgh. The bailies and councillors, with their assessors, nevertheless refused to allow the deacons to vote in the election of the new council, or in choosing leets, in respect they had never been in use to do so, and that the restitution of the deacons referred to in the Queen Regent's letter had only reference to the liberties enjoyed by them previous to the passing of the act 1555, c. 26. A similar demand was made by the deacons two days later, when the council met to choose leets for offices, but the demand was refused on the same ground, and the deacons protested.[2]

The accounts of the dean of guild for the year to Michaelmas 1559 are awanting; but the Register of Burgesses and Guild Brethren shows that during the year which ended on 24th March

[1] C. R. vol. iii. p. 15.   Extracts C. R. vol. iii. p. 39.
[2] C. R. vol. iii. fols. 22-5.   Extracts C. R. vol. iii. pp. 52-56.

1559–60, seventeen persons were admitted as burgesses, one as a guild brother, and four as burgesses and guild brethren.[1]

On 1st August 1560 the dean of guild complained that divers persons occupied the liberty of free merchants and free craftsmen without being free burgesses, to the great hurt of merchants and craftsmen and of the common weal of the burgh if remeid were not provided; whereupon the council ordained the dean and one of the bailies, accompanied by such number of officers as they might consider necessary, to pass through the town, and search for un-freemen occupiers of the liberties of merchants, and compel them to become free, otherwise to imprison them until they found caution to desist. At the same time the deacons of crafts were ordained to give up the names of all the masters of crafts who were unfree, that such order might be taken with them touching their freedom as with the others; but it was provided, that if any of these craftsmen had occupied the liberty of free burgess for a long time, and were not able at the time ' to satifye according to the present use, or otherwise may nocht be povertie,' such persons should be considered by the council, and used according to their power.[2]

On the 30th of the same month, burgesses and guild brethren were ordained to receive, along with their ticket of burgess-ship or guildry, the form of the oath which they took on admission.[3]

On 5th September the provost, bailies, councillors, and deacons, having regard to tumults that had taken place, and the deforce-ment of the bailies and officers of the town, renewed the act requiring the keeping of long weapons in forehouses and booths, and ordering all indwellers to support the magistrates in main-taining the peace of the town.[4] On the 16th of the same

[1] Register of Burgesses and Guild Brethren.
[2] C. R. vol. iii. fol. 43.   Extracts C. R. vol. iii. p. 72.
[3] C. R. vol. iii. fol. 45.   Extracts C. R. vol. iii. p. 75.
[4] C. R. vol. iii. fols. 46, 47.   Extracts C. R. vol. iii. p. 77.

month the provost, bailies, council, and deacons ordained the
deacon of the fleshers to admit John Johnston to be freeman of the
craft, in respect he was first apprentice and then burgess, and
offered all duties to the craft that was in use to be demanded.[1]
On the 26th of the same month the provost, bailies, council, and
deacons ordained—

'that in all tyme cuming at the election of the new counsaill, the electaris
thairof sall cheis the twa craftismen quhilkis sould be thairvpone furthe of the
sax personis to be presentit to thame be the dekynnis of craftis, providing
alwayis that gif the saidis electaris sall nocht think the saidis personis nor ony
twa of thame to be presentit sufficient meet nor hable to be vpone the counsaill,
the saidis dekynnis sall present vther sax personis in ane vther tikkat to the
saidis electaris, and fra thyne furthe vther sax in cais tha be nocht satefeit, ay
and quhill the saidis ij craftismen of the counsaill be electit.'[2]

On 14th October it was ordained that none but freemen, freemen's wives, widows and relicts of freemen, should brew within
the burgh.[3]  And on the 30th of the same month the council,
considering that sundry persons who had been made burgesses
and freemen of the burgh did not dwell within the same, nor
scot, lot, extent, walk or ward, nor bear any portable charges
within the burgh as they ought to do, and as other neighbours
and freemen of the burgh did, 'incontrair the auld statutis maid
thairvpoun,' ordained proclamation to be made that all burgesses
and freemen should become resident in the town within forty days,
and that such as failed to do so should 'bruik na maner of fredome
within the samyne, conform to the auld statutis maid thairupoun.'[4]
On the same day the old act as to having weapons in booths was
re-enacted.[5]

The accounts of the dean of guild for the year to Michaelmas

[1] C. R. vol. iii. fol. 48.    Extracts C. R. vol. iii. p. 82.
[2] C. R. vol. iii. fol. 50.    Extracts C. R. vol. iii. p. 83.
[3] C. R. vol. iii. fol. 51.    Extracts C. R. vol. iii. p. 84.
[4] C. R. vol. iii. fol. 56.    Extracts C. R. vol. iii. p. 87.
[5] C. R. vol. iii. fols. 55–57.   Extracts C. R. vol. iii. p. 87.

1560 show that the dues of the burgesses and guild brethren admitted during the year amounted, in all to £122, 13s. 4d. Scots; but the number of persons admitted is not given.[1]

On the 20th of the following month of November the council ordered a search to be made for all persons, sellers of staple goods, such as velvets, silks, fine cloth, or similar costly wares, and to prohibit them trafficking therein unless they were both burgesses and guild brethren, and failing their compliance, to shut up the doors of their booths until they became guild brethren, 'nochtwithstanding thai be free burgesses ellis.'[2] On 6th December in the same year the council appointed the bailies to compel all traffickers within the burgh who were not free burgesses or guild brethren, and had the requisite means, to acquire the freedom of the burgh, and also to compel all sellers of wine, wax, velvets, silk, and fine cloth, who were only burgesses, to become guild brethren, or else to desist from selling such merchandise, under the pain of imprisonment or such other punishment as might be thought most expedient.[3]

On 3d January 1560–1 the bailies and council ordained the dean of guild—

'to ressaue sic nychtbouris of this burgh as is knawyn, or salbe thocht be the said counsall or ballies, nocht of puissance to pay thair haill burges or gyldschipps in hand, actit for the half of thair dewitie, and to ressaue reddy payment of the other half.'[4]

During the year which ended on 24th March 1560–1 sixty-six persons were enrolled as burgesses, twenty-eight as guild brethren, and twenty-four as burgesses and guild brethren.[5]

On 24th September 1561 the provost, bailies, and council,

[1] Accounts of the Deans of Guild, vol. i.
[2] C. R. vol. iii. p. 60.   Extracts C. R. vol. iii. p. 89.
[3] C. R. vol. iii. p. 63.   Extracts C. R. vol. iii. p. 96.
[4] C. R. vol. iii. fol. 68.   Extracts C. R. vol. iii. p. 97.
[5] Register of Burgesses and Guild Brethren.

being convened to elect a new council, one of the deacons, in name of all, presented a list of six craftsmen, of whom he required two to be chosen on the council for the year to come. The council thereupon required a list of other six, in terms of the act of council dated 26th September 1560; but this was refused, and it was protested for the crafts that, in so far as the six persons proposed were honest men, they ought not to be objected to, notwithstanding any act to the contrary. It was thereupon protested for the council that the refusal by the deacons left the council free to choose whom they pleased out of the crafts.[1] The council appear then to have elected a craftsman not on the list, and a protest was taken against his election on the 26th of the same month. On that day also one of the deacons presented an act of James III., together with a copy of a writing by the Queen Regent, granting certain privileges to the craftsmen of the burgh; and he claimed that the deacons should vote in the choosing of all leets to offices. The council, however, found that no privileges were granted to the crafts by these writs other than a vote in the election of sergeants, and they refused to concede further privileges concerning the leets.[2]

The accounts of the dean of guild for the year to Michaelmas 1561 show that the dues of the burgesses and guild brethren entered during the year amounted to £740, 6s. 8d. Scots; but the number of persons admitted is not stated.[3] During the year which ended on 24th March 1561-2 sixty-six persons were admitted as burgesses, twenty-three as guild brethren, and eighteen as burgesses and guild brethren.[4]

On 27th August 1562 the council granted Alexander Weyland,

---

[1] C. R. vol. iv. fol. 15.   Extracts C. R. vol. iii. p. 122.
[2] C. R. vol. iv. fol. 15.   Extracts C. R. vol. iii. p. 124.   See similar proceedings on 6th October 1562.   C. R. vol. iii. p. 150.
[3] Accounts of the Deans of Guilds, vol. i.
[4] Register of Burgesses and Guild Brethren.

lorimer, a 'guildship' free, in respect of the injuries he had sustained from the French the time of their 'raig' within the burgh, and of the services rendered by him to the town.[1]

On a complaint by the bonnet-makers that divers craftsmen, such as fleshers, wrights, slaters, cordiners, and others within the burgh had drawn from them their servants and apprentices, unfree persons, and caused them to execute the work pertaining to their crafts, the council on 18th September declared that no craftsman should be served by servants or apprentices who had their beginning under the deacon and masters of the bonnet-makers, and further, that the servants and apprentices of that craft should be prohibited from working with other unfreemen.[2]

One hundred and eleven burgesses and guild brethren were entered in the accounts of the dean of guild for the year to Michaelmas 1562, and the total dues paid on their admission amounted to £513, 13s. 4d. Scots.[3]

On 8th December 1562 the council ordained that all burgesses who failed to make their residence within burgh previous to Martinmas thereafter should lose their freedom.[4]

On 27th January 1562–3 the Queen ordered the magistrates to see that every cordiner and man exercising that craft had sufficient leather and other stuff to work and labour for furnishing of the lieges upon the prices fixed by the magistrates; and if any of these craftsmen were destitute thereof, that the magistrates deprive them from all using of their craft, and enjoying of any freedom within the burgh in time coming. Proclamation was accordingly made in terms of the Queen's order.[5]

[1] C. R. vol. iv. fol. 41.    Extracts C. R. vol. iii. p. 147.

[2] C. R. vol. iv. fol. 42.    Extracts C. R. vol. iii. p. 148.

[3] Accounts of the Deans of Guild, vol. i.    These accounts show the rates of admission to have been as follows :—eight at 6s. 8d., twelve at 13s. 4d., eight at £1, nine at £1, 13s. 4d., fifty-nine at £5, eight at £10, and seven at £15 each.

[4] C. R. vol. iv. fol. 53.

[5] C. R. vol. iv. fol. 58.    Extracts C. R. vol. iii. pp. 155–6.

During the year which ended on 24th March 1562–3 sixty-eight persons were admitted as burgesses, six as guild brethren, and six as burgesses and guild brethren.[1]

On 23d April 1563 John Paterson, deacon of the masons, represented to the council that he had served truly and diligently at the work of the new tolbooth to the ending thereof, and that other masons not so qualified as he was had obtained their burgess-ships for their bounty; he therefore supplicated the council to make him a guild brother. To this application, however, it was answered,

‘ that thay have nocht bene in vse to grant ony sic libertie or privilege to men unmariet; and thairfoir, quhen it sould happen the said dekyn to have ane lauchful wyfe and mariit according to the ordour of the Kirk now present vpoun his gude behavour and service he sould be considerit in this his desyre and satifeit to his plesour.’[2]

On 4th June parliament ratified and approved all acts of parliament, statutes, privileges, and immunities granted by Queen Mary or her predecessors in favour of the burghs, and of the provosts, aldermen, bailies, communities, and indwellers within the same.[3]

On 27th September a burgess was deprived of his freedom and liberty of burgess-ship for refusing to attend an assize held by the water bailie of Leith.[4]

Sixty-seven burgesses and guild brethren were entered in the accounts of the dean of guild for the year to Michaelmas 1563, and the total dues paid on their admission amounted to £289 Scots.[5]

On 24th December 1563 William Abercrummy, taverner, was made burgess and guild brother *gratis*, at the request of the abbot of St. Colme’s Inch. But on the same day the council ordained that no burgess-ship or guild-brothership should be given *gratis* for a year

---

[1] Register of Burgesses and Guild Brethren.
[2] C. R. vol. iv. fol. 68.   Extracts from C. R. vol. iii. p. 159.
[3] 1563, c. 24.   A. P. S. vol. ii. p. 543.          [4] C. R. vol. iv. fol. 79.
[5] Accounts of the Deans of Guild, vol. i.   There appear to have been five ‘ gratis entries ’ during this year.

thereafter, under the penalty of £10, to be taken of the consenter and giver without favour.[1]

During the year which ended on 24th March 1563–4 fifty-four persons were enrolled as burgesses, six as guild brethren, and fourteen as burgesses and guild brethren.[2]

At the election of the new council on 20th September 1564, the council declined to accept any of the six craftsmen submitted to them with a view to their being elected upon the council, and they required the names of other six to be given in. Against this requisition the craftsmen protested. On the 27th of the same month the council declared that they would elect their council and officers conform to the act of parliament of James III. touching the election of officers within burgh:

'Quhilk is ane law that thay dar na wayis pretend to alter, quhairintill is speciallie contenit that the auld counsale sall cheis the new without mention of ony dekyn to haue voit or entres thairintill, and thairfor gyf thay wald nocht gyf in vther tikettis thay wald proceed according to the said act.'

The deacons protested against this deliverance, and this matter seems to have formed the subject of a complaint to the Privy Council, who, however, ordained them to present before the town council other new tickets, and to observe the said act of parliament. On 30th September, accordingly, a new ticket, containing the names of other six persons, was given in by the craftsmen under protest that their old liberty should not be thereby prejudiced. On the same day the deacons desired that the deacon of the candlemakers might have a voice with them in electing officers, in respect of their seal of cause; but the council refused, on the ground that the occupation of candlemakers was not worthy of a deacon.[3]

During the year ending Michaelmas 1564 sixty-four burgesses and guild brethren were entered in the accounts of the dean of

[1] C. R. vol. iv. fol. 88.   Extracts C. R. vol. iii. p. 175.
[2] Register of Burgesses and Guild Brethren.
[3] C. R. vol. iv. pp. 111, 112.   Extracts C. R. pp. 185, 186.

guild, and the dues of their admission amounted to £270, 13s. 4d. Scots.[1]

On 3d November 1564 the council ordained that no man or woman within burgh engage in dyeing, ' bot sic as be burgessis and fremen,' and complied with the other conditions therein set forth.[2]

On the 8th of the same month the following act was passed as to the admission of burgesses and guild brethren :—

' The prouest, baillies, dene of gild, counsale, and dekynnis, for certane caussis and consideratiounis moving thame, statutis and ordanis that fra this day furth all sic personis as salhappin to be maid burges and freman of this burgh pay to the dene of gild present and for the tyme the sowme of xx li. for thair said burgesschip allanerlie, and for thair gildrie the sowme of xl li.; and this act to indure without preiudice of the richtis granttit to burges barnis contenit in the actis maid of befoir ; and siclike concerning prenteissis quhilkis hes bene or sal happin to be heirefter prenteis and bound seruand to merchand or fre craftisman in tymes bygane or to cum, nocht burges barnis, for the space of sevin or five yeiris at the leist, thai to pay for thair burgeschip five pund allanerlie, and for thair gildrie, being wordie thairfoir, ten pound allanerlie, the clerkis dewtie except. Providing the saidis prentissis bring with thame the testificatioun of thair maister quhome thai seruit for the said tyme, togidder with thair part of the indentour made betuix thame and thair said master, and witnes to appreve thair seruice all the tyme thairin contenit befoir the prouest or baillies as said is, and vtherwayis nocht to be resaueit nor admittit.' [3]

On 2d January 1564–5, the council and whole deacons being convened, the deacon of the tailors, for himself and the other crafts,

' oblist him and thame to sustene the hale pure of all occupatiounis within this burgh, sic as craftismen, craftismenis wyffis, seruandis, and wedois, vpoun thair awin proper chargeis fra this day furth, sua that the gude toun nor nane resortand thairto salbe trublit with thair purys; and siclike qubatsomever ordour salbe found gude be the prouest, baillies, and counsale foirsaid for sustenying of the ministerris that thay sall gladlie beyr and deburse thair ressonabill pairt thairof at thair sychtis.' [4]

[1] Accounts of the Deans of Guild, vol. i. During this year five ' gratis entries ' appear.
[2] C. R. vol. iv. pp. 111, 112. Extracts C. R. vol. iii. p. 188.
[3] C. R. vol. iv. fol. 115. Extracts C. R. vol. iii. p. 188.
[4] C. R. vol. iv. fol. 123. Extracts C. R. vol. iii. p. 193.

On the 6th of the same month the council, at the request of Alexander Guthrie, common clerk, received an Englishman, arrow-maker, as a burgess, 'to gif him occacioune to remane in the toun for instructing vtheris his occupation.'[1]

On 1st March 1564–5 Queen Mary, by a charter under her great seal, dated at Edinburgh, on a narrative similar to that contained in her charter of 16th April 1556, and on the further narrative that she had then attained her lawful and perfect age of twenty-one years, renewed the same, and granted the several dispensations and privileges to the craftsmen of all the burghs and cities of the kingdom as were set forth in that charter.[2]

During the year which ended on 24th March 1564–5 fifty-six persons were enrolled as burgesses, three as guild brethren, and twelve as burgesses and guild brethren.[3]

On 30th June 1565 the council ordered the bailies and officers to visit all dwelling-houses within the burgh, and see that every fencible person inhabiting the same was sufficiently provided with armour and weapons, and to enrol the names of such persons, with their weapons.[4]

During the year ending Michaelmas 1565 thirty-four burgesses and guild brethren were entered in the accounts of the dean of guild, and the dues of their admission amounted to £121 Scots.[5] In the following year forty-one burgesses and guild brethren were entered, and the dues of their admission amounted to £180 Scots.[6]

During the year which ended on 24th March 1565–6 thirty-nine

---

[1] C. R. vol. iv. fol. 123.  Extracts C. R. vol. iii. p. 193.

[2] MS. Register of the Great Seal, book 33, No. 195.  Printed Records of Convention, vol. ii. pp. 473–476.

[3] Register of Burgesses and Guild Brethren.

[4] C. R. vol. iv. fol. 130.  Extracts C. R. vol. iii. p. 198.

[5] Accounts of the Deans of Guild, vol. i.  Eleven 'gratis entries' appear this year.

[6] Ibid.  Seventeen 'gratis entries' appear during this year.

persons were entered as burgesses, one as a guild brother, and three as burgesses and guild brethren.[1]

On 14th October 1566 the act passed on 8th December 1562, above referred to, was renewed.[2]

During the year which ended on 24th March 1566–7 forty persons were elected as burgesses, six as guild brethren, and twelve as burgesses and guild brethren.[3]

On 18th June 1567 the following act was passed :—

'The quhilk day the prouest, baillies, and counsall, vnderstanding the grit skayth and dampnage sustenit be the inhabitantis fremen of this burgh be making of outlandis men, having nother wyf, barnis, familie, stob nor staik within the samyn, burgessis of the said burgh, nochttheles the saidis outlandis burgessis duellis outwith the burgh, and passis throu the cuntre foirstallis skyn, hyde, and other merchandice, and traffectis in selling, bying, and saling, nochtwithstanding the quhilkis thai eschap fra taxtis, stentis, and all otheris portable chargis, and can nocht be apprehendit nor caussit pay nor do the samyn be ressoun thai haif nother stob nor staik as said is, in contrair the commoun weill of the samyn ; and inlykwys considdering the gret skaithe and dampnage sustenit be the craftismen of the said burgh be making of other townis prentesis and seruandis alyke fre as gif thai had bene prenteis within this burgh, quhilk is the gret hurt of the said fremen and thair prentesis, and contrair the commoun weill of burrowis ; for remeid of the quhilkis the prowest, baillies, and counsall, with consent and awys of the dekynnis of crafts, statutis and ordanis that in tyme cuming na maner of outlandis men be maid burges or fremen of this burgh vnto he be mariit and haif stob and staik within the samyn, sua that he may be apprehendit and compellit to paye taxt and stent, and bere his pairt of sic portable chargis as otheris fremen induellaris within the samyn, and that na craftisman be ressauit freman within this burgh bot onelie thai that hes bene prentis within the samyn, and thair prenteschip fullelie outroun ; providing allwayis that this act preiudge nocht fremenis bairnis nor prentesis being fullelie outrun within this burgh, bot thai sall be ressauit but stop or impediment conforme to the ald vse ; and this act to haif strenthe, force, and effect induring the will of the saidis provest and baillies.'[4]

On 20th August the provost, bailies, and council,

' vnderstanding the hale ipoticaris of this burgh to be the principal ventaris and

---

[1] Register of Burgesses and Guild Brethren.
[2] C. R. vol. iv. fol. 163.   Extracts C. R. vol. iii. p. 222.
[3] Register of Burgesses and Guild Brethren.
[4] C. R. vol. iv. fol. 191.   Extracts C. R. vol. iii. pp. 231, 232.

sellaris of spices, quhilk apertenis principallie to the bretheriog of gild and nane vtheris, quharfoir thay ordane Maister Johnn Prestoun, dene of gild, to caus all the ipoticaris of this burgh to desist and ceis fra venting of spices in commoun, vtherwise than in thair medicinis, failing heirof to close and lok vp thair durris, ay and quhill thay becum fre burgessis and gild brether.'[1]

During the year ended Michaelmas 1567 twenty-five burgesses and guild brethren were entered in the accounts of the dean of guild, and the dues of their admission amounted to £72, 13s. 4d. Scots.[2]

On 20th November 1567 Charles Studeman, cook, having paid £10 for his freedom, was made guild brother, under the obligation—

' that fra this day furth he sall nocht be sene vpoun the calsay, as the remanent commoun kukis, with meitt to sell in commoun houssis, bot sáll caus his seruandis pas with the samyn, and that he sall hald his taverne on the hie gaitt fra Witsonday furth nixtt, and behaif him selff honestlie in all tymes cumyn, vnder the pane of escheitt of his wynes.'[3]

On 20th December parliament ratified all the privileges formerly granted to the burghs and burgesses of the realm ;[4] and on the same day it enacted that—

' thair be na dekin of craft of maltmen outher to burgh or land, or ony vther pairt within this realme.'

It also annulled any writing, gift, or privilege to the contrary—

' sua that it salbe never lesum to ony of the maltmen of this realme to haue dekennis, bot to be repute na craft.'[5]

On 24th December the town council ordained—

' that euerye man at the making of him burges sall obleis him self to haif jak, speir, swerd, buklar, and steill bonet, for serving of the baillies and gude toun quhen thai haif ado, and to keip the wappinschawing with the nychtbouris, vnder sic panis as may be laid to thar charge.'[6]

---

[1] C. R. vol. iv. fol. 199.   Extracts C. R. vol. iii. p. 240.

[2] Accounts of the Deans of Guild, vol. i.   Nineteen ' gratis entries' appear during this year.

[3] C. R. Ad. Lib. fol. 32.   C. R. vol. iv. fol. 209.

[4] 1567, c. 33.   A. P. S. vol. iii. p. 33.

[5] 1567, c. 37.   A. P. S. vol. iii. p. 33.

[6] C. R. vol. iv. fol. 212.   Extracts C. R. vol. iii. pp. 244, 245.

During the year which ended on 24th March 1567–8 twenty-seven persons were enrolled as burgesses, two as guild brethren, and thirteen as burgesses and guild brethren.[1]

On 20th April 1568 Andro Hagye was made burgess and guild brother *gratis*, at the request of the Earl of Mar.[2]  On 4th June William Leich, one of the grooms of the Lord Regent, was made burgess and guild brother, and the duty thereof was given him *gratis*, at the request of the Lord Regent.[3]  On 11th August the council ordained the whole deacons to convene their crafts, masters, taskmen, apprentices, and servants, and take inquisition, by their oaths, what part they would take in the present troubles, to enrol their names, and report their depositions on the following day.[4]

The accounts of the dean òf guild from Michaelmas 1567 to Michaelmas 1568 are awanting, so that the number of burgesses and guild brethren entered during the year, and the amount of their admission dues, cannot be ascertained.

On 21st October 1568 all non-resident burgesses were required to come and make their 'remanyng' in the burgh within forty days, under pain of losing their freedom.[5]

During the year which ended on 24th March 1568–9 twenty-nine persons were enrolled as burgesses, four as guild brethren, and two as burgesses and guild brethren.[6]

On 23d September 1569,

' the baillies and counsale being convenit for electing of the new counsale for the yeir to cum, compeerit Walter Wauhane, dekyn of the tailyouris, with certane vtheris deaconis, togither with James Young and Dauid Kinloch, pro-

---

[1] Register of Burgesses and Guild Brethren.
[2] C. R. vol. iv. fol. 217.   Extracts C. R. vol. iii. p. 248.
[3] C. R. vol. iv. fol. 219.   Extracts C. R. vol. iii. p. 249.
[4] C. R. vol. iv. fol. 221.   Extracts C. R. vol. iii. p. 251.
[5] C. R. vol. iv. fol. 226.   Extracts C. R. vol. iii. p. 256.
[6] Register of Burgesses and Guild Brethren.

locutouris for the hale craftis, and desyrit to be hard to resoun for the saidis
craftis concernyng the tua craftisman that suld be vpoun the counsale for the
said yeir, quhilk wes grantit, and efter lang resonyng it was desyrit be the
saidis prolocutouris that the said David Kinloch, baxter, and sic vtheris as
thai wald joyne to him, to quhome it was ansuerit that nane sic as of thair
occupatioun, sic as baxteris, fleschouris, maltmen, quhilkis had the handling
of mennis sustentatioun, had bene vpoun the counsale of the toun in ony
tyme bypast, nather aucht nor suld be, becaus thai mycht woit and persuade
to thair awin particular commoditie, to the greit hurt of the kingis liegis,
and siclyke that na cordineris, nor littistaris, nor vtheris of sic rude occupatioun, aucht to be vpoun the counsale, nouther wald thay admit nor resave
ony sic ; and thairfoir ordanit the saidis dekynnis and thair prolocutouris to
geve in ane new tiket of sic vtheris occupatiounis as had bene vpoun the
counsale of befoir, with certificatioun and thai failyeit thai wald chuse sic as
thai thocht expedient incontinent but langer delay ; and the saidis prolocutouris protestit for licence to avyse with thair brethrene and suld report
ansuer, quha being remouit and raenterit thai gaif in ane new tikket out of
the quhilk was chosen James Norwell and William Harlaw, saidler, coun-
sallouris for the said yeir to cum.'[1]

During the year ended Michaelmas 1569 eighteen burgesses and guild brethren were entered in the accounts of the
dean of guild, and the dues of their admission amounted to
£75, 13s. 4d. Scots.[2]

On 2nd December the deacons of crafts gave in a supplication
in favour of the candlemakers, reviving a claim made in 1564,[3]
and asking that the deacon of that craft should have vote with
the other deacons in the causes of the commonweal, but the town
council declined the request because it had not been proved that
there had ever been a deacon of the candlemakers.[4]

On 20th January 1569-70

'the baillies, counsale and dekynnis, efter lang ressonyng vpoun the
commoun effaris, and in speciall vpoun sic thingis as war hurtfull to the
commoun weill and fredome of this burgh, thay haue found amangis vther
inconvenienttis that the making of monye burgessis, and in speciall of sic as

---

[1] C. R. vol. iv. fol. 246.    Extracts C. R. vol. iii. p. 263.
[2] Accounts of the Deans of Guild.
[3] Antea, p. 99.
[4] C. R. vol. iv. fol. 249.    Extracts C. R. vol. iii. p. 266.

ar na burges bairnys and procuris thair fredome and libertie be way of court,
or vtherwayis gratis and payis na dewtie thairfor to the commoun gude;
quhairfor it is statute and ordanyt that the bairnys of all sic as gettis thair
fredome gratis in maner forsaid sall nocht haue the libertie of ane fre burges
bairne, and this ordinance to indure but reuocatioun.' [1]

During the year which ended on 24th March 1569–70 thirty-
one persons were enrolled as burgesses, and eleven as burgesses
and guild brethren.[2]

Edinburgh had been erected with all the privileges of a free
burgh to the bounds of the freedom of Haddington on the east,
Almond Water on the west, the sea on the north, and the
extremity of the sheriffdom on the south; and in the year 1398
the haven and shore of Leith was acquired from Robert Logane
of Restalrig, knight,

'quha alswa for him and his airis and assignayis perpetuallie ventit the
taverning and selling of wyne, the bakyng of breid to sell, the halding and
keiping of marchand buithis, girnelling of quheit, and all uther thingis that
wer contrair the libertie and consuetude of the said fre burgh of Edinburgh,
swa that nother he his airis nor assignais, nor na vtheris in his name or on
his pairt sould hald venting and selling of wyne, baking of breid to sell,
marchand buithis, girnellis of quheit, be thameselfis nor na vtheris within
the toun and landis of Leyth or thairabout nor yit thole the samyn in ony
tyme thaireftir to be haldin.'

These facts are set forth in an action brought before the bailies
and council of the burgh by the treasurer, who farther states that
'the cheif libertie and fredome of ane fre burgh of ryaltie consistes
in twa thingis, the ane in vsing of marchandice, the vther in vsing
of craftes, resaving of fremen thairto, chesing of dekynnis of craftis,
for examinatioun of thame that ar admitted thairto that thai be
qualifeit, swa that the leigis of the realme be nocht dissauit of
thair occupationes.'  Notwithstanding all this, the treasurer was
now informed that certain inhabitants of the town of Leith had
usurped the offices of deacons of crafts of the smiths, coopers,

---

[1] C. R. vol. iv. fol. 252.  Extracts C. R. vol. iii. p. 267.
[2] Register of Burgesses and Guild Brethren.

tailors, baxters, cordiners, fleshers and websters, and he having appeared by his procurator on 12th July 1570, 'and the saidis defenderis alswa comperand in jugement to heir sentence gewin, the saidis baillies and counsall, with awys of thair assessouris, decernis and ordanis the saidis persones and euerye ane of them to desist and ceis fra the vsurping of the saidis names and offices and vsing thairof in ony tyme cuming within the said toun of Leyth or barronye of Restalrig.' This decree was followed by another pronounced on 6th December in an action at the instance of the treasurer and procurator fiscal 'aganis the craftismen and vnfremen occupyaris and induellaris within the vnfre toun of Leyth,' when the bailies and council discharged them 'of all using of the said artificiall crafts in tyme cuming within the said vnfre toun of Leyth, and gif ony of thame will vse the samyn to draw thame to ane fre toun and burghe to the vsing thairof to beir portabill chargis as the rest of the vsaris of thai craftis dois.'[1]

The deacons of the crafts having consulted their brethren as to what 'of thair benevolence' each craft would give for support of the ministry, reported on 1st November that the following sums would be given by the respective crafts :—skinners, £20; wrights and masons, £10; tailors, £16; goldsmiths, £6, 13s. 4d.; barbers, £3; John Wilson, smith, 20 merks; baxters, 20 merks; cordiners, £8; fleshers, £10; websters, 20s.; bonnet-makers, 20s. The furriers are mentioned, but their contribution is left blank.[2]

Among a number of statutes passed by the convention of burghs, on 5th January 1570-1, for 'remeid of the greitt hurte and manifold dampnages' sustained by the burghs from past negligence is the following :—

'Item, becaus the saidis commissaris thinkis thameselves greitlie hurt be the multitude of the burgesses and gild brether, and for certane causis moving

---

[1] C. R. vol. iv. fols. 259, 269.  Extracts C. R. vol. iii. pp. 273-4, 281.
[2] C. R. vol. iv. fol. 266.  Extracts C. R. vol. iii. p. 278.

thame they haif statute and ordanit that nane be gild brether within burgh
fra this day furth without the payment of xl pundis to the dene of gild, to
be applyitt to the commoun gude; and gif it salhappin the provest, baillies
and counsall of ony burgh to consent and give ony burgeschippis or gildries
gratis, for requeistis of greitt men or vtheris occasionis quhatsumeuir, the
consentaris thairto to be haldin to refound the said soume of xl pundis to
the commoun gude, sa oft as itt salhappin thame to do the contrair the
tenour of this present ordinance: And becaus itt has bene in vse in tymes
past, the provest, baillies, and vtheris officiaris of the burgh hes had granttit
to thame be rycht of thair offices certane burgeschippis, quhilkis thai disponit at thair plesour, it is found be the saidis commisaris, that the saidis
officiaris sall haif na farther [claim] for the dewties of the saidis burgeschipp
and gildries, nor thai had befoir the making of the saidis ordinances, nouther
sall it be lesum to thame to dispone to vtheris than to men of gude fame and
honestie; provyding alwayis this present ordinance be nocht prejudiciall to
the barnis of frie merchantis and frie craftismen.'[1]

It was probably in consequence of this resolution that on the
7th of the following month a dissent on behalf of the deacons of
crafts was intimated to the town council of Edinburgh against
any alteration on the admission dues of burgess-ship or guildry,
'or ony hiear prices nor hes bene usit of befor'; but the bailies and
council directed the dean of guild 'to execute the auld statutis
and hieast prices vpoun burgeschippis and gildreis to be made
conforme to the auld ordinances in all tymes cuming, nochtwithstanding onye protestatioun in the contrair.'[2]

During the year which ended on 24th March 1570–1 forty-two
persons were enrolled as burgesses, twenty-two as guild brethren,
and thirteen as burgesses and guild brethren. In the following
year the Register, which has no entries between 3rd April 1571
and 22nd August 1572, contains the names of only one guild
brother and three burgesses and guild brethren. During the
period of the year from 22nd August to 24th March 1572–3
eleven persons were enrolled as burgesses, and thirteen as burgesses and guild brethren.[3]

[1] Convention Records, i. p. 20.
[2] C. R. vol. iv. fols. 271-2.  Extracts C. R. vol. iii. pp. 282-3.
[3] Register of Burgesses and Guild Brethren.

Between 1st May 1571 and 13th November 1573, a troublous
time throughout the country, and specially in the capital with
its besieged citadel, no records of the town council of Edinburgh are in existence. Legal proceedings, which during this
period had been raised as to the privileges of the burgh of
Canongate,[1] are referred to on 30th April 1574, when 'efter
lang resonyng vpoun the greitt hurtis thay daylie sustenis be
non calling of thair actioun befoir the Loirdis aganis the
unfriemen of the Canogait,' certain persons, by monthly rota-
tion, were appointed to expedite--the cause.  On 3rd June
following the town council discharged all agreements made
between them and the craftsmen of Leith and all claims
'prejudicial to the fredom and libertie of this burgh'; and at
the same time 'ordainis the baillies to close vp all the duris
in Leyth on, this syde of the brig of all sic as occupeis
craftis or merchandises or ventis wynes, [and to] mak oppin
all gyrnell durris for seruyng oure Souerane Lordis liegis of
wittalis.'[2]

During the year ended 24th March 1573-4 fifty-seven persons
were enrolled as burgesses, six as guild brethren, and nineteen as
burgesses and guild brethren.[3]

On the supplication of the deacon of the fleshers 'bering that
his craft was sa depauperat that thay war nocht abill to pay
taxationis according to the auld rollis,' and after consultation
with all the deacons, who desired the bailies and council, in any
alteration of the extent rolls, 'to considder the craftis dekayitt,
and deduce of the auld extent according to gude conscience
and lay the samyn vpoun the craftis enrichitt, quhairat thay

---

[1] See Privy Council Register, ii. pp. 220, 260.

[2] C. R. vol. v. fols. 17-9.  Extracts C. R. vol. iv. pp. 13-5.

[3] Register of Burgesses and Guild Brethren.  On 6th January 1573-4,
Thomas Weir was made burgess 'at the requeist of George Douglas, capitane
of the castell of Edinburgh, and the dewtie gevin gratis at the said capitanis
requeist' (Extracts C. R. vol. iv. p. 9).

bynd and obleis thame to abyde,' the new roll was, on 15th
September 1574, fixed as follows:—

| | Of every hundreth pundis. | |
| | Of auld. | Now of new. |
| | £ s. d. | £ s. d. |
| Skynnaris and furrouris . . . . . | 18 0 0 | 20 1 6 |
| Tailyouris . . . . . . . | 14 5 4 | 18 1 6 |
| Baxters . . . . . . . . | 17 12 6 | 13 0 4 |
| Hammermen, without alteratioun . . . | 13 5 6 | 13 5 6 |
| Fleschouris . . . . . . . | 13 2 4 | 9 0 0 |
| Cordinaris, without alteratioun . . . | 6 13 4 | 6 13 4 |
| Goldsmyths . . . . . . . | 4 11 3 | 6 0 0 |
| Wobstaris, walkeris and bonetmakeris, with-out alteratioun . . . . . | 2 13 4 | 2 13 4 |
| Barbouris, without alteratioun . . . | 3 1 3 | 3 1 3 |
| Wrychtis and masons . . . . . | 7 2 9 | 8 3 4 [1] |

During the year ended Michaelmas 1574 sixty-seven burgesses
and guild brethren were entered in the accounts of the dean of
guild, and the dues of their admission amounted to £325.[2]

On 24th December the deacons of crafts gave in a series of
'articles,' relating to their privileges, 'desyring the samyn articles
to be considerit for ane gude ordour to be obseruit in this
commoun weill in tyme cumyng.' [3]   The bailies and council
promised to give an answer, and in the meantime directed the
articles to be registered:—

'In the first, that the act and ordinance to be maid anent the burgessis
toward the rasing of thair burgeschip to xx lib. and gildry to xl lib., that it
be maid be ane minute to be gevin be the deaconis as the saidis provest and
counsall desyrit thame to do, the quhilk minute was gevin in to Alexander
Guthre, commoun clark, twa syndry tymes, desyring thairfoir that the act to
be maid heirefter thairanent be maid according to the minute, vtherwayes
that na burgesschippis nor gildrie be raisit heichar nor thai war of befoir.

'Secundlie, desyris that thair be na vote nor electioun in the chesing of the
provest, baillies, dene of gild, thesaurer, nor vther officiar and member of

---

[1] C. R. vol. v. fols. 26, 29, 30.   Extracts, vol. iv. pp. 21, 23–4.

[2] Accounts of the Deans of Guild.   The accounts for the years 1570–3,
inclusive, are wanting.

[3] C. R. vol. v. fols. 39, 40.   Extracts, vol. iv. p. 32.

court bot sa mony as is ordanit be the act of parliament, as alsua be the act and ordinance maid be the commissionaris of burrowis thairanent, haldin at Edinburgh the feird day of Aprile the yeire of God $j^m$ $v^c$ fyfty twa zeris, and we to have ane vote ilk ane of us alsweill in the electing as in the lyting according to the act of parliament maid be King James the second or at the leist ane of euery craft quhilk wil be ma in nomber nor the dekynis swa that your assissouris be na law nor resoun that is knawin aucht to haif ony vote thairin.

'Thridlie, quhairas euery zeir thair is chosin twelf lytes to be baillies, and thair efter ardevydit in foure pairtis quhilk is thrie in every pairt of foure, desyris that they may be chosin as apperandlie aucht to be, that is of the haill twelf ane, off aleven ane vther, off ten the thrid, and of the nynt and rest the feird, and nocht ane of every thrie, be the quhilk ordour thay wil be gottin maist qualefeitt and abill in that maner.

'Feirdlie, desyris that at the nominatioun and electing of the commissionaris of this burgh in tyme cuming, that we may be wairnit and have vote thairintill sen we are ane pairt of the commoun weill of this burgh, and mon sustene oure pairt of the burding and all portabill chargis thairintill as vtheris nychtbouris dois, and that thairby we may knaw the cause quhairfoir the comissioun is gevin, alsweill in the begynning as quhat succedis and happynis to be done thairefter.

'Fifthly, that thair be na officiaris within this burgh nor na collectour chosin for ingaddering of the annuelles quhilkis pertanit to the freiris, chaiplanis, and vtheris commoun rentis within this burgh, bot the advyse and consent of the counsall and ws had thairto, and we to haif vote thairintill and to be wairnit be the officer of counsall to that effect lyke as has bene vsit towardis vtheris officiaris, quhilk ordour as we vnderstand hes nocht bene obseruit, alsua that as quhen ony office or benefice happynis to vaik, that oure votis may be haid towardis the dispositioun thairof.

'Sextlie, desyris that thair be na dispositioun nor away putting of ony the commoun gude of the tovne without the avyse and consent of ws, and that the compte of the same commoun gude be sene and considerit zeirlie that it may be knawin gif the samyn be bestouit for the commoun weill of the burgh or nocht, and to that effect wairnyng to be made zeirlie that all they that plesis and aucht to cum for examenyng of the saidis comptes may be present at the hering thairof that thay may resoun thairvpoun and as neid beis to impugne and object aganis the samyn that thairby all murmour and occasioun thairof may ceis, and gude ordour continew for the commoun weill of this burgh in tyme cuming, alsua desyris that the comptes of the thesaurary of this burgh the zeiris lxxij and lxxiij as alsua of all vtheris restand awand to the tovne may be veseit, sene and examinat and perfyte compte to be haid thairof as efferis.

'And that the ordour quhilk sould haif bene maid anent the premissis may be resonit and put in forme, subscryvit and registrat, and we to haif the

authentik copy thairof subscryvit with us in keping, in respect your wisdomes
ar ane pairt of the contractaris and we the vther.

'Desyring your wisdomes richt hertlie to considder the articles foirsaidis
aggreabill to resoun and gude conscience and to give ansueir thairto in sic
maner as ane gude ordour may be obseruit in this commoun weill and all
murmour and occasioun thairof stayitt in tyme cumyng.'[1]

It appears that Cuthbert Thomson, deacon of the fleshers, had
raised an action against the town council before the privy council,
and the treasurer and procurator fiscal, on 2nd March 1574,
'protestit for sic remeid as he micht incur of the law for trubling
of his lauchfull magistrats contrair his aith.' The deacon, however, asserted 'he had done na thing in that case bot for the
weill and defence of his craft, without the assistance or concurrance of the dekynnis or ony vtheris and sua had done na
wrang.'[2]

During the year ended 24th March 1574–5 fifty-six persons
were enrolled as burgesses, three as guild brethren and six as
burgesses, and six as burgesses and guild brethren.[3]

During the year ended Michaelmas 1575 forty-four burgesses and guild brethren were entered in the accounts of the
dean of guild, and the dues of their admission amounted to
£280, 13s. 4d. Scots.[4]

On 11th October 1575 the bailies and council consented
that the crafts should not be 'extentit' for the ministry from
Martinmas following till new order was taken, and the collector of
the annuals had made up his account so that it might be ascertained what the annuals amounted to.[5]

During the year ended 24th March 1575–6 twenty-four persons
were enrolled as burgesses, one as a guild brother and six as burgesses and guild brethren.[6]

[1] C. R. vol. v. fols. 39, 40.  Extracts, vol. iv. pp. 32–4.
[2] C. R. vol. v. fol. 43.  Extracts, vol. iv. p. 36.
[3] Register of Burgesses and Guild Brethren.
[4] Accounts of the Deans of Guild.
[5] C. R. vol. v. fol. 54.  Extracts, vol. iv. p. 44.
[6] Register of Burgesses and Guild Brethren.

On 7th June the council, after reasoning with John Murdo, deacon of the tailors, as to making a person named Fischer, who was alleged to have been an apprentice, a burgess, enacted

'that na craftisman sal be admyttit burges that bringis nocht with him his indentour of prentischip, with testificatioun of his gude and trew seruice all the tyme he wes boundin prentis ; and the said Murdo allegeand the said Fischerris name to be in thair craft buke, and thairfor aucht nocht to be refusit; and the saidis baillies and counsale fand na fayth to be gevin to thair bukis in the caussis of the commoun weill, the samyn havand na autoritie bot sic as thay had vsurpit and taikin at thair awin handis.' [1]

Thirty-one one burgesses and guild brethren were entered in the accounts of the dean of guild for the year to Michaelmas 1576, and the total dues paid for their admission amounted to £194, 3s. 8d. Scots.[2]

On 9th November in the same year the council ordained that all such persons as were burgesses before the act of the commissioners of burghs 'beand wourth,' pass guild brother for £20.[3]

· The following act, of date 11th January 1576-7, shows that the town council controlled the deacons of crafts in the exercise of their authority :—

'The provest, baillies, [and council,] being convenit in the counsallhous for resoning vpoun the commoun effaires, and vnderstanding that the dekynnis of craftis, being personallie present, had deposit Jhonn Hendersoun, dekyn of the fleschouris, of his office and dekynrie within the yeir, na falt being knawin to the juges committed be him, and that thay had input at thair awin handis John Robesoun, fleschour, in his place, for avancing of thair particulairis for subscryving of bandis with thame, contrair the commoun weill and autorite of the juges foirsaidis, thay, all in ane voce, dischargis the said John Robesoun of his vsurpit and pretendit office, and neuer to bruik the lyke in tymes cuming, and restoiris and reponis the said John Hendersoun, and commandis him to vse his said office of dekynrie, and nane vtheris to haif vote thairintill vnto the lawfull tyme vsit and wont, except sum notorious offence be committed be him and

---

[1] C. R. Ad. Lib. fol. 30.    C. R. vol. v. fol. 63.    Extracts C. R. vol. iv. p. 49.

[2] Accounts of the Deans of Guild.    Five 'gratis entries' occur during this year.

[3] C. R. vol. v. fol. 69.

knawin to the saidis juges, and inlykemaner dischargis the saidis dekynnis of all sic ordour of prosceding at thair awin handis in tymes cuming, vnder the payne of tynsall of thair fredomes.' [1]

On 6th March in the same year, John Couper, tailor, and Henry Blyth, surgeon, appeared before the provost, bailies, and council, and consigned each ten shillings; Patrick Turner, son of Patrick Turner, skinner, also appeared and consigned thirteen shillings and fourpence, and all of them desired to be made guild brethren, in conformity, as they alleged, with the old acts, in respect they had been apprentices within the burgh. The consignation was not accepted by the council, who refused to admit the applicants as guild brethren unless they 'refusit thair craftis and bure burding with the merchantis.' The applicants thereupon protested for remeid,[2] and proceedings appear to have been taken before the Privy Council on a complaint presented by the craftsmen, burgesses, and guild brethren, against the town council, in respect of their refusal to receive Blyth as a guild brother. The Privy Council ordained ' that the said Henry sould not be stoppit to be ressauit in gild brother, except they wald schaw him ressonabill cause on the contrair.' It was then averred by the town council that the act alleged to have been made by them, and in virtue of which Blyth claimed to be admitted, was ' fals, fenzeit, and disconform to the original register,' and they were allowed to disprove the act before the Lords of Council and Session.[3] The issue of the proceedings is not known.

During the year which ended on 24th March 1576-7 forty-four persons were enrolled as burgesses, seven as guild brethren, and seven as burgesses and guild brethren.[4]

On 16th April 1577 the following entry exhibits the town

[1] C. R. vol. v. fol. 73.  Extracts C. R. vol. iv. p. 56.
[2] C. R. vol. v. fol. 75.  Extracts C. R. vol. iv. pp. 57, 58.
[3] Printed Register of Privy Council, 12th March 1576, vol. ii. pp. 597-8, 601-2.  C. R. vol. v. fol. 76.
[4] Register of Burgesses and Guild Brethren.

council as interfering to prevent exorbitant prices being demanded by workmen :—

' The provest, baillies, and counsall, vnderstanding that the wrychtis and masonis of thair pretendit maner had stoppit certan masonis, vnfriemen, to big ane cone in Grayes clois becaus the baxteris wald nocht geve thame sic exhorbitant prices as thay desyrit ; for remeid quhairof the provest, baillies, and counsall foirsaidis hes statute and ordanit that the saidis vnfrie masones, conforme to the Act of Parliament, sall compleit and end the said wark, and nane vtheris ; and commandis this ordour to be kepit in all tymes cuming quhen wrychtis or masonis becumis vnresonabill in thair prices.' [1]

On 10th July in the same year the bailies and council ordained

' the vnfree bonnet makkeris to be seperatat fra the burgessis and fremen of the samin, and to haif thair stand be thamselfis vpon the mercat day allanerlie beneth the auld fische mercat, vpone the north syde of the Hie Streit of this burgh, induring the said bailyeis and counsellis willis.' [2]

On 6th January 1577–8 the council assigned Wednesday next to give answer to the desires of the deacons ' tuiching thair gilderis.' [3]

The accounts of the dean of guild for the year to Michaelmas 1577 are awanting. During the year which ended on 24th March 1577–8, forty-eight persons were enrolled as burgesses, fifteen as guild brethren, and fifteen as burgesses and guild brethren.[4]

On 28th March 1578 the town council found that ' fremen sall pay na customes.' [5]

On 25th July, in the same year, Parliament confirmed the privileges of burghs, and empowered the burghs to convene four times in the year, in such burgh as might be considered most expedient, to deliberate on such matters as concerned their estate.[6]

[1] C. R. vol. v. fol. 77.   Extracts C. R. vol. iv. p. 58.
[2] C. R. vol. v. fol. 78.   Extracts C. R. vol. iv. p. 59.
[3] C. R. vol. v. fol. 85.   Extracts C. R. vol. iv. p. 62.
[4] Register of Burgesses and Guild Brethren.
[5] C. R. vol. v. fol. 91.   Extracts C. R. vol. iv. p. 68.
[6] 1578, c. 11, A. P. S. vol. iii. p. 102.

On 8th October in the same year the council required a person who had been made burgess and guild brother, and who had only paid £30 to the dean of guild, to pay £10 more, ' it being statuit that nane sall pass the said dignitie vnder the soume of fourtie pund at lest.' They further ordained that none should be made burgess or guild brother in future unless he were admitted in presence of the provost, bailies, and council, or a majority of them.[1]

On 11th October two of the Lord Provost's servants were made burgesses, and the duties given them,—one by right of the provost's office, and the other at his request.[2]

The accounts of the dean of guild for the year to Michaelmas 1578 show that the total dues paid for the admission of burgesses and guild brethren during the year amounted to £304, 13s. 4d. Scots, but furnish no details.[3]

On the 1st November 1578 the convention of burghs, at Dundee, ratified their former act requiring outland burgesses to ' resoirt to the tovne thay are maid friemen' of, within forty days after being charged, under pain of losing their freedom, and ordained the act to be put to execution immediately.[4] At the same time they ratified their former act against freemen colouring unfreemen's goods. Frequent acts of the town council of Edinburgh enforcing this enactment occur.

In February 1578–9 the convention of burghs, at Cupar, enacted, (1.) that every merchant of the realm, before sailing in merchandise, should produce to the magistrates of the burgh from which he intended to sail a ticket signed by the dean of guild, bailie, or common clerk of the burgh to which he belonged, certifying the fact of his being a free burgess, guild brother, and indweller therein; and (2.) that no persons should be eligible as commis-

[1] C. R. vol. v. fol. 110.
[2] Register of Burgesses and Guild Brethren. Extracts C. R. vol. iv. p. 87.
[3] Accounts of the Deans of Guild.
[4] Printed Records of Convention, vol. i. p. 75.

sioners to Parliament or convention except free merchants and guild brethren. The convention also renewed their former act against freemen entering into partnership with unfreemen, or colouring unfreemen's goods.[1] On 6th March 1578–9 two of the provost's servants were made burgesses 'be the said provestis rycht.'[2]

During the year which ended on 24th March 1578–9 forty-eight persons were enrolled as burgesses, and eleven as burgesses and guild brethren.[3]

On 7th May 1579 the deacons of crafts-engaged to furnish one hundred and fifty men, good soldiers, to pass to Hamilton upon their charges, 'for whom thay oblis thame to ansuer to await vpoun my lord provest, at his remanyng fra Hamyltoun for keeping of the gude toun, and to have iij s. on the day.'[4]

On 13th July 1579 the following act of council was passed:—

'Maister Johne Prestoun, Johne Johnstoun, Alexander Clark, Alexander Vddart, Williame Littill, efter ressoning with the deaconis, being personallie present, findis that it hes bene hurtfull and aganis the commoun weill the passing of craftismen to haue libertie or fredome within this burgh befoir thai be first presenttit be the supplicatioun desiring to be maid burges conforme to the auld ordour, quhilk the saidis deakynnis grantit and thoucht maist ressonabill, and thairfoir consentit, in cace that ony craftman vse the fredome of ane freman befoir his admissioun in maner foirsaid, thai ar content to tyne thair seill of caus, previlegis, and fredomis thairof.'[5]

On 23d September 1579 an act is recorded relative to a dispute with the deacons of the crafts as to the mode of selecting the two craftsmen who were to be on the council.[6] It is unnecessary, however, to refer to the details of the frequent and bitter contentions between the merchants and craftsmen, the latter claiming on all

[1] Printed Records of Convention, vol. i. p. 75.
[2] C. R. vol. v. fol. 134.
[3] Register of Burgesses and Guild Brethren.
[4] C. R. vol. v. fol. 142.　Extracts C. R. vol. iv. p. 108.
[5] C. R. vol. v. fol. 147.　Extracts C. R vol. iv. p. 110.
[6] C. R. vol. v. fol. 163.　Extracts C. R. vol. iv. p. 119.

occasions to have a larger share in the municipal government of the city, and the former maintaining with equal pertinacity the exclusive privileges which they possessed.[1]

The accounts of the dean of guild for the year to Michaelmas 1579 show that the total dues paid for the admission of burgesses and guild brethren during the year amounted to £383 Scots, but furnish no details.[2]

On 11th November in the same year Parliament again confirmed the privileges of burghs;[3] and on the same day it enacted

'that na vnfreman hant or vse the trafficque of merchandize in tyme cuming, speciallie in the Law Cuntries vndir the King of Spayne's dominion, vndir the pane of confiscatioun of all thair gudis doand in the contrair.'[4]

On 4th December in the same year Nicol Udart, merchant, appeared before the council, and renounced his burgess-ship and guildry, with every 'fredom he had thairby in this burgh,' on the ground that

'he was sa extraordinarly extented in all extentis bygane, and in speciall in this last extent maid to the kingis entry, being extentit thairin to ane hundreth merkis, quhilk he was content to pay, as he culd nocht sustene the samyn, and protested that heirefter he suld nocht be subiect to any portabill chairges within this burgh in respect of this his ouergeving of his burgeschip and gildrie and renunciatioun thairof, and heirvpoun askit instrumentis.'

But the council refused to accept his renunciation, and 'altogether halelie disassented thairto.'[5]   On the 23d of the same month Cuthbert Mathieson was deprived of his freedom for deforcement;

---

[1] It may be mentioned, as illustrative of the position and claims of the merchant class in the Scottish burghs at this time, that in a dispute between Dundee and Perth for precedency, in 1581, Dundee put forward in a supplication to Parliament as one of the grounds of its claim to have the first place in parliaments, conventions, and assemblies, that the estate of the burgh was 'governit be the merchandis, excluding the craftismen fra all office of governament within the samyn.'—1581, c. 47, A. P. S. vol. iii. fol. 232.

[2] Accounts of the Deans of Guild.      [3] 1579, c. 23, A. P. S. vol. iii. p. 145.

[4] 1579, c. 35, A. P. S. vol. iii. p. 152.

[5] C. R. vol. v. fol. 183.   Extracts C. R. vol. iv. p. 129.

and five days later he found caution to cease from using merchandise.[1]

On 6th January 1579–80 the council passed the following act:—

‘The provest, baillies, and counsall, vnderstanding that to the provestis of
the yeris past, and in speciall to George Douglas of Parkheid and Archibald
Stewart, provestis for the tyme, thair hes bene granted twa burgesses by and
attour the sovme of ten lib., express contrair the actis, quhairas of auld dewtie
thay aucht onlie to have the benefite of twa burgesses or ten lib. thairfoir, and
thatt allowance hes bene gevin to the denis of gild of the yeris past thairof ;
and willing that the samyn be remeditt in tyme cuming, concludis and decernis
that in all tymes cuming the provestis tocum have na farther benefite than hes
bene granted to thair predecessouris, to witt, outher the admissioun of twa
burgessis or ellis ten pundis thairfoir, and nocht to bruke the benefite of
baith ; and ordanis thatt be the auditouris of dene of gildis comptes thair be
na farther allowance gevin than of the ane thairof, becaus be the granting of
baith they have found thair liberties gretumlie preiugit and the commoun
proffeit of the burgh hinderit thairby.’[2]

They further ordained

‘ thatt fra this day furth thair be na burgessis nor gildis resauit, suorn, or
admitted bott at foure seuerall tymes in the yeir, viz. the four heid courtis,
and thatt in presens of the provest, baillies, and counsall for the tyme, and na
vtherwyes ; and to the effectt this thair ordinance may the better be obseruit,
ordanis thatt the lokkitt gild buke be putt vp in the chairterhous, nochtt to be
removitt furth thairoff quhill twa dayes befoir the saidis heidis courttis, to the
effect the extract of the names of sic as ar insertt thairin may be delyuerit to
thame that sutis to bruke the previlege of burgesschippis and gildries be thair
fatheris richtis vpoun thair resonabill expenssis.’[2]

On 13th January 1579–80 the council, after advising a complaint by Hugh Westoun, eldest son to umquhile John Westoun,
burgess and guild brother of the burgh, wherein he craved that the
officers of the burgh should be ordained to desist from troubling
him for payment of bygone extents, ‘insafar as the samyn was
contrair the privilege granted be thair lordships predecessouris to
burges bairns,’ found that the complainer should be ‘exemit and
fred fra payment of bygane extentis, and that in tyme cuming, insa-

[1] C. R. vol. v. fols. 194, 198.
[2] C. R. vol. v. fol. 206.   Extracts C. R. vol. iv. p. 140.

far as he is admitted thair frie burges and gild, that he be subiect to all portabill chargis within this burgh according to the ordour.'[1]

On the 15th of the same month the council ordained Thomas Ros, second son to James Ros, merchant, to pay extents with the merchants, although he alleged that he had paid them with the skinners, ' becaus he traffecquid with merchandise and vsis nocht the skynner craft.'[2] On the 20th of the same month Alexander Achesoun of Goffurde and Thomas Marioribankis of Rathow appealed against ' the daylie extentis laid vpoun thame,' on the ground that they used no manner of traffic within or without the burgh, and had only the title and name of burgesses, doing their observance to the good town in all their affairs according to their power ; and they craved that in future they should only be extented with the rest of the neighbours of the burgh, according to their ability, whenever any raid occurred, or when the extent was laid on lands within burgh. The council sustained the appeal, and ordered accordingly, ' except it sall happin thame to traffique in merchandise or vse ony forther tred within this burgh nor they do now presentlie at the making heirof.'[3]

On 23d March 1579–80 the deacons of the crafts of skinners, chirurgeons, hammermen, baxters, tailors, fleshers, cordiners, goldsmiths, and weavers, to whom it was assigned to give their answer and resolution anent the order to be taken for sustaining the poor of the burgh conform to the acts of the last parliament made thereanent, undertook for themselves, and in name of the whole crafts of the burgh, ' to tak and sufficientlie sustene and vphald from begging thair awin puir, sic as ar faillit craftismen, with thair wyffes, bairnis, and seruandis.'[4]

During the year which ended on 24th March 1579–80 thirty-

---

[1] C. R. vol. vi. fol. 1.   Extracts C. R. vol. iv. p. 141.
[2] C. R. vol. vi. fol. 2.   Extracts C. R. vol. iv. p. 143.
[3] C. R. vol. vi. fol. 3.   Extracts C. R. fol. iv. p. 144.
[4] C. R. vol. vi. fol. 27.   Extracts C. R. vol. iv. p. 154.

nine persons were enrolled as burgesses, four as guild brethren, and fifteen as burgesses and guild brethren.[1]

* On 1st June 1580 the deacons of the crafts appeared before the provost, bailies, and council, to give their final answer as to the order to be taken for sustaining the poor of the burgh and keeping them from begging, conform to the last Act of Parliament, and offered

' to sustene and hald fra begging vpoun the chairges of the craftes thair awin puir and all decayit and faylit persounes als weill frie as vnfrie that hes bene of any craft, with thair wyffes, bairnis, and seruandes, and disassentit to all contributionis to be vniuersallie vpliftet of all the nychtbouris of this burgh owerheid for susteining of the haill puir thairof in general, and to any vther ordour to be tane for thair pairt except as is before rehersit and offerit be thame.' [2]

In July 1580 the commissioners of burghs assembled in Aberdeen renewed the act against non-resident burgesses and guild brethren, and ordained each burgh to report its diligence to the next convention, under pain of £40.[3]

On 31st August 1580 the town council ordered proclamation to be made, prohibiting

' all burges and fremen thairof to pas and tak or resaue wedges of any maner of persoun in debaitt of thair priuate querrellis and controuerseis without special licence of the guid toun, under the payne of tynsale of thair fredome for euir.' [4]

The object of this ordinance, as appears more plainly from the rubric on the margin, was to prevent burgesses or freemen from taking pay as soldiers from subjects of the Crown to fight in any private quarrel.

On 28th September 1580 the following act of council occurs :—

' Anent the supplicatioun gevin in before thame be Jhonn Gibsoun and Robert Lekpreuik, buikbinders, burgessis of this burgh, bering in effect that

---

[1] Register of Burgesses and Guild Brethren.
[2] C. R. vol. vi. fol. 48.   Extracts C. R. vol. iv. p. 164.
[3] Printed Records of Convention, vol. i. p. 98.
[4] C. R. vol. vi. fol. 68.   Extracts C. R. vol. iv. p. 176.

Robert Wodhous, Inglisman, being ane forane straynger and vnfrieman, hes this lang tym bygane vsurpitt vpoun him the priuilege of ane frie burges be selling and bynding of all kynd of buikis within the fredome of this burgh, to the greitt hurt and preiudice of the saidis compleners, quha ar burgessis and friemen, quha stents, watches, and wairdes, and beris all vther portabill chairges with the nychtbouris of this burgh, quhilk thai ar nocht abill to do heirafter gif the said Robert be sufferit to continew in the said tred, and thairfor desyring him to be dischairget of the samyn,—the said Robert Wodhous and Jhone Gibsoun comperand personally, thair ressonis and allegatiouns hard and considerit, the saidis prouest, baillies, and counsale dischairges the said Robert Wodhous frome binding of any kynd of buikis within the fredome of this burgh fra the xiiij day of October nixt, vnder the payne of confiscatioun of the saidis buikis quhaireuir thai may be apprehendet.' [1]

The accounts of the dean of guild for the year to Michaelmas 1580 show that the dues paid for the admission of burgesses and guild brethren during the year amounted to £759, 6s. 8d. Scots, but furnish no details.[2]

During the year which ended on 24th March 1580–1 seventy-five persons were enrolled as burgesses, and twenty-two as burgesses and guild brethren.[3]

At the convention of burghs held at Edinburgh on 18th April 1581, the commissioners of Edinburgh declared that they had no outland burgesses exercising traffic or doing contrary to the liberty of the burgh, but that they had nevertheless ordained, in the general, that those who failed to repair to the burgh within forty days and bear ordinary charges should forfeit their freedom.[4] And on the 20th of the same month the convention, ' for suppressing of the multitude of vnfrie traffiquers,' ordained each burgh to use its privileges and execute the Acts of Parliament thereanent, or otherwise to send the names of such unfree traffickers, as well those within the burgh as in the shire in which the burgh is situated, to Edinburgh, that the town council thereof might deliver the names

---

[1] C. R. vol. vi. fol. 74. Extracts C. R. vol. iv. p. 177.
[2] Accounts of the Deans of Guild.
[3] Register of Burgesses and Guild Brethren.
[4] Printed Records of Convention, vol. i. p. 111.

to the King's treasurer, searcher, or other officers, for execution of
the Acts of Parliament and privileges of burghs against such
persons ; and that under the pain of £10 to be taken from the
burgh failing therein.[1]  On the following day, it being desired by
the commissioners of Perth that

> ' sum remeid mycht be fund and devysitt againis the vnfrie craftismen werking
> and dwelling in the suburbs of thair burch, and dyuers vtheris burrowes of the
> realme, to the greit hurt of the frie craftismen berand chairges within the
> burch,'

the convention appointed the matter to. be remembered in the
articles to be given in to the next Parliament, and to the convention
which should be held before the assembling of Parliament ; and
in the meantime ordained each burgh to be diligent in withstanding
' this greit enormity.'[2]

On 31st May 1581 the provost, bailies, and council, at the
request of James, Earl of Arran, granted licence to John Reid,
servitor to the Earl, to

> ' exerce the tred of ane gild brother within the fredome of this burgh, nocht-
> withstanding that he be nocht admitted, bot onelie fre burges, and further
> promesis sua sone as he sall be mareit to admit him frie gild brother for the
> requeist of the said earle.'[3]

On 22d July 1581 King James VI., by a charter under the Great
Seal, which proceeds on a narrative similar to that of the charter
by Queen Mary dated 1st March 1564, dispensed with all the provisions of the Act of 1555, which obstructed the liberties and
privileges of craftsmen in burghs.  The charter thereafter proceeds
as follows :—

> ' And we restore to them the privilege of enjoying and having deacons of
> crafts, who shall have suffrages and votes in electing the officers of the burghs,
> and there shall be elected craftsmen of every craft within the burgh, who shall
> enjoy and exercise the same, provided they be found suitable for it ; and they
> shall audit the accounts of the common good of the burghs, and shall be part of

---

[1] Printed Records of Convention, vol. i. p. 115.    [2] Ibid. vol. i. pp. 116, 117.
[3] C. R. vol. vi. fol. 137.   Extracts C. R. vol. iv. p. 209.

the auditors of the same, and shall meet and make lawful statutes and regulations anent their own crafts, for the preservation of good order among the
craftsmen and the maintenance of divine service ; and they shall navigate and
enjoy and trade in merchandise of all sorts within our said kingdom and beyond
the same, as shall appear to them most advantageous, with all and sundry
privileges, liberties, powers, and customs granted and conceded to them by our
most noble ancestors, and held by them by use and possession of the same in
times bygone, notwithstanding the said Act of Parliament, or any penalties
whatsoever in the same contained, as to which with them we, by these presents,
dispense.' [1]

The accounts of the dean of guild for the year to Michaelmas
1581 show that thirty-eight persons were entered as burgesses and
guild brethren, and that the total dues paid on their admission
amounted to £252, 13s. 4d. Scots.[2]

At the convention of burghs held at Edinburgh on 21st October
in the same year, each burgh was ordained to call before it all
outland burgesses by their names in particular, and to deprive
them of their liberty, and to report the decreet of court containing
the names of the persons so deprived as unfreemen, that they
might be known to each burgh and be used thereafter as unfreemen.[3]

On 29th November 1581 Parliament confirmed the Act 1488, c.
12, and decerned the same to have full effect in time coming, with
an addition applicable to ships and others repairing to the west
parts of the realm, and to the west and north isles thereof.[4]

During the year which ended on 24th March 1581–2 twenty-
two persons were entered as burgesses, and three as burgesses and
guild brethren.[5]

On 4th April 1582 the following act of council was passed :—

[1] Register of the Great Seal, book 35, No. 420. Printed Records of Convention, vol. ii. p. 476.
[2] Accounts of the Deans of Guild. Thirteen ' gratis entries ' are stated in this
account.
[3] Printed Records of Convention, vol. i. p. 122.
[4] 1581, c. 27, A. P. S. vol. iii. p. 224.
[5] Register of Burgesses and Guild Brethren.

' John Moresoun, baillie, Jhonn Harwod, dene of gild, Jhonn Robertsoun, thesaurer, [and the council,] anent the supplicatioun gevin in before thame be Henry Charteris, baillie, Jhonn Gibsoun, buikbinder, for thame selffis and in name of the remanend nychtbouris, burgessis, and fremen of the burgh, leivand be the trafficque of selling and binding of buikis, vpoun Mr. Jhonn Cowper, seruand to Thomas Vantrollier, prenter and straynger, makand mentioun that quhair it is nocht only provydit be ancient lawes, customes, and priuileges, maid in favouris of burgessis and fremen of burrowis, and for vphalding of thair estaitt, but als be speciall acts and statutes of this burgh, with continuall possessioun followand thairvpoun, that na strayngeris or vnfremen may top or sell in smallis within the fredome of the burgh ony kynd of merchandice or wairis, vtherwayes it wer nocht possibill to frie burgessis to leif and ber chairges within the burgh ; and better-it wer to be vnfrie than frie, for gritter is thair skayth and gritter is the vnfremenis commodity than vtheris. And it is of verity, that Thomas Vantrollier, prenter, beand ane straynger and vnfrieman, hes thir dyuers yeiris bygane, be him selff and his seruandis, and speciallie be the said Maister Jhonn, quha is lykewayes ane vnfreman, toppitt and sald within this burgh all maner of buikis in smallis, and lykwayes bindis the sam, contrair to the priueleges of the burgh, and to our intollerabill damnage, quha hes na vther tred quhairby we and our famelies are sustenit, he bering na charges whateuer, and we watcheing, wairding, and extenting at all tymes, as at lenth is contenit in the said supplicatioun,—the said Henry Charteris and Jhonn Gibson on the ane pairt, and the said Maister Jhonn Cowper on the vther pairt, comperand personally in jugement, thair ressonis and allegatiouns hard and vnderstand,—the saidis baillies, dene of gild, thesaurer, and counsall decernis and ordanis the said Maister Jhonn Cowper to desist and ceiss fra all topping and selling in smallis of ony maner of buikis in tymes cuming within this burgh and fredome thairof, becaus the said Maister Jhonn culd show na ressonabill caus in the contrair.' [1]

At the convention of burghs held at Perth on 23d June 1582, a supplication was appointed to be given in to the King and the Privy Council ' that ordour may be tane anent sic as ar unfriemen and vsis merchandise,' and anent merchants, freemen, who coloured unfreemen's goods.[2]

On 26th September 1582 the town council, in consideration of the good service done to the town by umquhile Alexander King, advocate, and sometime clerk-depute of the burgh, and understanding that he was both burgess and guild brother, although his

---

[1] C. R. vol. vi. fol. 182.   Extracts C. R. vol. iv. p. 233.
[2] Printed Records of Convention, vol. i. p. 136.

name was not inserted in the locked books, granted to ' his airis and bairnes the richt and priuelege of the bairnis of ane burgess and gild brother, to be admittit thairto for the sam dewty, and thair names insert in the gild buik quhen thai requyre the sam.'[1]

The accounts of the dean of guild for the year to Michaelmas 1582 show that fifty-nine burgesses and guild brethren were entered during the year, and that the total dues paid on their admission amounted to £469 Scots.[2]

The disputes between the merchants and craftsmen relative to the right of the latter to a larger share in the government of the city seem to have culminated on the occasion of the election of the magistrates on 2d October 1582. On that occasion the assessors of the city were prevented by a tumultuous assembly from entering the council-house and voting, as they had done for many years previously; whereupon, and notwithstanding the protests of the craftsmen, the bailies and councillors elected three persons to vote in name of the assessors. Against this step the craftsmen renewed their protest, urging that it was contrary both to the Acts of Parliament and the constitution of the royal burghs for the assessors who were not members of the council to vote. The protest was, however, disregarded; whereupon a number of the craftsmen forced their way into the council chamber, with a view to intimidate the council from receiving the votes of the assessors. The intruders having been ejected, the deacons of crafts were called on to vote, but they declined to do so unless the assessors were removed. The council refused to comply with this demand, and proceeded with the election; but this step so infuriated the craftsmen that they again invaded the chamber, and threatened to destroy the books and records.[3] These acts of violence, and the popular irritation, induced the Privy Council to interfere. They by an act

[1] C. R. vol. vi. fol. 206. Extracts C. R. vol. iv. p. 247.
[2] Accounts of the Deans of Guild. Four ' gratis entries' appear during this year.
[3] C. R. vol. vi. fols. 208–210. Extracts C. R. vol. iv. pp. 250–255.

dated 2d, and proclaimed at the market cross on 13th October 1582,[1] ordained the election to stand, but required both the merchants and craftsmen to submit their differences to twenty-four arbitrators, to be chosen by both parties, with the King as oversman.  The arbitrators having been appointed, proceeded to deal with the questions at issue, and, after much deliberation, issued an award which the merchants were prepared to accept.  The craftsmen, however, objected to it; whereupon the King ordered both the parties to appear before him, and recommitted the whole subjects in dispute to the same arbitrators, and to himself as umpire.[2]  The decree-arbitral following on this submission, and afterwards known as the ' Set of the City,' is dated 22d April 1583, was recorded in the books of Council and Session at Edinburgh on 19th June 1583,[3] and was ratified by Parliament on 22d August 1584.[4]  It ordained the

[1] C. R. vol. iv. fol. 210.   Extracts C. R. vol. iv. p. 255.

[2] C. R. vol. vi. fol. 228.   Extracts C. R. vol. iv. p. 264.

[3] Mr. John Scherp, Mr. Thomas Craig, and Mr. John Prestoun, assessors, and Mr. John Skene, procurator-fiscal, or any two of them, were, on 25th May 1583, appointed procurators to appear before the Lords of Council and Session, and consent to the registration (C. R. vol. vii. fol. 1.   Extracts C. R. vol. iv. p. 276).

[4] 1584, c. 25.   A. P. S. vol. iii. pp. 360–364.   The pleadings in the case of Kinloch, Johnston, and others against Sir Andrew Ramsay, Lord Abbotshall, Lord Provost, 7th February 1673, fully reported by Fountainhall, contain the following statement as to the origin of this decree-arbitral: —' The true occasion and originall of the said sett was, that there being ane ancient custome of the toune counsell of Edinburgh to have always three able lawyers their assessors, with whom they advised in their affairs; and these lawyers being men usually of great parts and abilities, they did, by little and little, creep in and insinuat themselfes unto a share of the government of the burgh, even to that lenth that they came to sit with them in their councell and vote in their leittings and elections and in all other affairs of the burgh; and being able men, procured themselfes sometymes to be chosen provosts, and of this kind were Mr. James M'Gill of Rankeillor, and Mr. Thomas M'Caulay of Cliftonhall, who were at first the tounes assessors only; and which abuse in the government being considered by the neighbours of the toun, and especially the trades (for the assessors oft syded with the merchands and magistrates against them), gave rise to the submission and decreet following theiron; for at the election of 1582, the three lawyers assessors, coming to councell to vote at the election, they were violently debarred by some craftesmen

the magistrates and officemen—such as the provost, bailies, dean of
guild, and treasurer—to be, in all time coming, of the estate and
calling of merchants, conform to the Acts of Parliament; and if
any craftsman exercising merchandise was for his good qualities
promoted thereto, he was required in that case to leave his craft,
and not to occupy it by himself or his servants during the time
of his office, nor to return to it at any time thereafter without
the special leave of the provost, bailies, and council. The decree
also ordained that the council should consist of the officemen of
the year, viz. the provost, the four bailies, dean of guild, and
treasurer, and eighteen other persons, of whom ten were to be
merchants and eight were to be craftsmen. Of the ten merchants,
the old provost, four old bailies, dean of guild, and treasurer of the
immediately preceding year were to form seven, and three were to
be chosen yearly to them. The eight craftsmen were to consist of
six deacons and two other craftsmen. The decree further declared
that no one should be elected provost, bailie, dean of guild, or
treasurer, though a burgess and able for the office, unless he had
been in the council for a year or two previously; and it ordained

'the awld maner of gevin in of tikketis be the deykins, owt of the quhilk the
twa craftismen wer yeirlie chosin, to be abrogatt, ceise and expyre in all
tymes cuming, swa that the saids twa craftismen sall be chosin yeirlie, without ony ingevin of tikkets, indifferentlie, of the best and worthiest of the craftis,
be the saids provest, bailyeis, dene of gild, thesaurer, and counsale allanarlie;
and nane to be on the counsale abone twa yeir togidder, except thai be officemen, or be vertew of thair offices be on the counsale. Sicklyke anent the lyttis
of the bailyeis, thay sall nocht be deuydet nor cassin in four ranks, thre to
euerie rank, as thai were wont to be, bot to be chosin indifferentlie, ane out of

out of the councell-house, and after that never more had vote, for much tumult
and uproar was about it; and the flam still increasing between merchands and
trade, that wise and politique prince, our peaceable James, forced them to
compromit all their differences to so many gentlemen, adjacent heritors to the
towne, on ather syde, and himself umpire and oversman, and who, after very
much paynes and travell in it, gave furth his decreett-arbitral and award, as we
all know.'—*Historical Notices of Scottish Affairs* (Bannatyne Club), vol. i. pp.
53–81.

the twelff lyttis, ane vther owt of alleven lyttis, the thrid owt of ten, and the fourt out of nyne lyttes.  Anent the deykins, that nane be electit deykin except he that hes bene ane maister of his craft twa yeir at the leist; and that nane of thame be continewit in thair offices of deykinschip aboue twa yeir togidder.  Last, in generall, that nane haif vote in lytting, voiting, or electing of the provest, bailyeis, counsale, deykins, dene of gild, or thesaurer, but the personis heirafter following in maner after specified.'

It thereafter provided for the election of the fourteen deacons of crafts, and of the six deacons, three merchants, and two craftsmen who were to be upon the council, and of the provost, bailies, dean of guild, and treasurer, and declared as follows :—

' The saids provest, baillies, dene of gild, thesaurer, and counsale, electit as said is, makand in the haill twenty-fyve personis, thay onlie, and na vtheris, sall haif the full government and administratioun of the haill commoun-weill of this burgh in all things, as the provest, baillies, and counsale thairof, or of any vther burgh had of before, or may have heirafter, be the lawes or consuetude of this realm, infeftments and priveleges grantit to this toun be our Souerane Lordis maist nobill progenitouris ; exceptand always thir cawssis following, in the quhilks the haill fourtene deykins of craftis sall be callit and adioynit with thame to gif thair speciall vote and consultatioun tharinto, to witt, in electioun of the provest, baillies, dene of gild, and thesaurer, as said is ; in setting of fewis, or ony maner of taks, attoure the yeirlie rowping on Mairtymes evin ; in gevin of benefices and vther offices in burgh ; in granting of extents, contributiouns, emprwnts, and siclyke ; bigging of commoun warks ; and in disponing of commoun guid aboue the sowm of twenty pund togidder.
 . . . And to avoyde all suspitioun that hes rissin in tymes past throw the particulare assemblies and conventiouns and convocations contrer to the Acts of Parliament, and to the trubill of the quyett estaitt of this burgh, it is agreit and concludit that nather the merchants amang thameselffis, nather the craftis and thair deykins or visitouris, sall haif or mak ony particulare or generall conventiouns, as deykins with deykins, deykins with thair craftis, or craftis amang thameselffis, far les to mak privat lawes or statutes, poind and destreyngyie at thair awin handis for transgressiouns, by the avyse and consent of the provest, bailyeis, and counsale.  Exceptand alwayes, that the dene of gild may assembill his brether and counsall in thair gild cowrts, conform to the ancient lawes of the gildry and priveleges thairof ; and that ony ane craft may convene togidder amang thameselffis for the chesing of thair deykin at the time appoyntit thairto and in maner befoir expressit, making of maisteris, and tryell of thair handiewark allanerlie ; and gif ony brether or deykins of craftis sall find owt or devyse ony guid heids that may tend to the weill of thair craft, thay sall propone the sam to the maiestrats, quha sall sett fordwart ane act or

R

statute thairvpoun, and interpone thair authority thairto, as it bees fund reasonable.

' Item, as twicheing the commissioners in parliament, generall counsall, and commissioneris in conventioun of burrowes, it is thocht guid be the commonaris, that in all tymes coming the ane of the saids commissioneris for the burgh of Edinburgh sall be chosin be the said provest and baillies, furth of the number and calling of the craftismen, and that persoun to be an burges and gild-brother of the burgh, of the best expert, and wise, and of honest conversatioun.

' Item, it is agreit, that the auditouris of all the townis comptis sall heirafter be chosen of equall number of merchants and craftismen, be the provest, bailyeis, and counsall.

' Item, toward the lang controuerseis for the gildrie, it is fynallie, with commoun consent, appoyntit, agreit, and concludit, that als weill craftismen as merchants sall be resauet and admittit gild-brether, and the ane nocht to be refusit or secludet thairfra mair nor the vther, thay being burgessis of the burgh, als meit and qualefeit thairfore; and that gild brother to haif libertie to use merchandice. Thair admissioun and tryell of thair qualificatioun to be in the power and handis of the provest, bailyeis, thesaurer, and counsall, with the dene of gild and his counsall, quhilk sall consist in equall number of merchants and craftismen, gild brether, nocht exceiding the number of sex persouns, by the dene of gild himselff; and that na persoun, of quhat facultie soeuir he be, sall bruik the benefice of ane gild-brother, without he be resauet and admittit thairto as said is.

' Item, that na maner of persoun be sufferit to vse merchandice, or occupy the handiewark of ane frie craft within this burgh, or yitt to exerce the libertie and priviledge of the said burgh, without he be burges and frieman of the sam.

' Item, becaus the merchants and craftismen of this burgh ar now to be incorporat in ane societie, and to mak ane haill toun and ane commoun weill, it is thocht expedient, and concludit to abrogatt the former custome of devyding and setting of extents, quhairin the merchants payet foure pairts, and the craftis the fyft part: and thairfore it is agreit, that as thai watche and waird togidder, swa in all extents, emprunts, contributiouns, and the like subsideis to be imposit upon the burgh, merchants and craftismen to beir the burding and chairge thairof indifferentlie owerheid, according to thair habilitie and sub-stance, throw the hail quarteris of the toun, without diuisioun of the rollis in merchants and craftismen in ony time cuming. The extentouris sall be of equall number of merchants and craftismen, aucht personis of the ane calling and aucht personis of the vther, to be electit, sworne, and resauit be the provest, bailyeis, and counsale, owt of the maist discreit and skilfull of all the town, voyde of all partiall affectioun and haitrand; and that na persoun vsand the tred of merchant or craftismen, and occupeand the fredome of the burgh, and habill to pay ony extent, nocht beirand the office of provest or bailyeis in the meane tyme, sall be ony wayis exemit fra the reall and actuall payment thairof.

‘ Item, as the haill body of the towne, consistand of merchants and craftismen, dois beir ane commoun burding of watcheing, wairding, extenting, and
of the lyke publict chairges, haiffing ane commoun guid proper to nane, swa
neidfull it is for making ane equall vnitie, and cheritabill concord, that thair be
in the haill toun but ane collectioun, and ane purse, nocht peculiar to any bot
commoun to all, of the haill dewteis and casualiteis, callit the entres syluer of
prenteissis, upsettis, owlklie-penneis, unlawes, and siclyke, to be collectit in
all tymes cuming, and resauit baith of merchants and craftismen, and put in ane
commoun purse ; and to that effect the merchants to tak and haif prenteisses
als well as craftismen, and to be astrictit and oblist thairto, and na prenteisses
alwayes to be resauit of ather of thame for schorter tyme nor the space of fyve
yeir compleitt.   And for the better knawlege to be had heirof, and for
obseruing ane guid ordour in collectioun- of the sam, that thair be ane commoun buik maid, and keipit be the commoun clerk of this burgh present and
to cum, quhairin the names of all prenteisses to merchants and craftismen, the
name of their maister, day of thair entres, and space of their prenteischip, sall
be insert and buiket ; for the quhilk the clark sall haif at thair buiking of ilk
persoun sex penneis, and for the owtdrawcht twelf penneis ; quhilk buik sall
be to the prenteis ane sufficient probatioun of his entres and ane chairge to
the collectowris of the said dewteis.   Gif ony man be ane prenteis heirafter,
and nocht putt in the said buik, his prenteischip sall be to him of na effect.
Alswa, be ressun euerie industrie is nocht of lyke valour and substance, it is
declairit quhat ilk rank or degrie of prenteissis sall pay, to witt, the merchant
prenteis, and sic kynd of peple as wer wont to extent with thame, and ar
nocht vnder ane of the said fourtene craftis, to pay at his entrie the day of
his buiking to the said collectioun threttie schillings, and at his vpsett, or end
of his prenteisschip, fyve pund.   The prenteis to ane skynner, chirurgeane, gold-
smyth, flescheour, cordiner, tailyeour, baxter, and hammerman, at thair entrie
and buiking, to the said collectioun twenty schilling, and for thair upset fyve
pund.   The prenteis to ane masoun and wricht at his entrie threttein schillings
foure penneis, and his vpsett thre pund sex schilling aucht penneis.   The
prenteis to ane wobster, walker, bonetmaker, furrour, at his entrie ten
schillings, and for his vpsett fiftie schillings.   And thir dewties to be tane by
thair owlklie penneis, and dewteis of thair burgesschips.   And to caus all
persouns to be mair willing to enter thamselffis in prenteisschip with the
burgessis and friemen of the burgh, this priveledge is grantit to the saids
prenteissis, that thai sal pay na mair for thair burgesschip to the dene of gild,
but fyve punds by the dewteis foresaids.   And in augmentatioun of the said
collectioun, quhen ony persouns sall happin to be maid burgessis of this burgh,
quha wes na prenteis to ane merchant or craftisman, frie burges of the said
burgh, or hes nocht compleitt his prenteisschip, sall pay to the said collectioun
at his admissioun the doubull of the haill prenteis or entres syluer, vpsett and
buiking, by the dewtie payet to the dene of gild for his burgesschip or gildrie,
quhilk is twenty punds for his burgesschip, and fourtie pund for his gildric ;

the privilege alwayes of the bairnis of burgessis and gild brether nocht beand preiugeit heirby, quha sall pay the awld and accustomat dewtie to the dene of gild allanerlie.   Thir dewties and collectiouns, or casualiteis of entres syluer, vpsetts, owlklie penneis, vnlawes, and siclyke, to be resauet in all tymes cuming, of all merchants and craftismen indifferentlie, putt in the said commoun purse, and imployet be the advyse and command of the provest, bailyeis, and counsall, for support and releif of the failyeit and decayet burgesses, merchants, and craftismen, thair wyffes, bairnis, and awld seruands, and vther puir indwellaris of the towne.   The provest, bailyeis, counsall, and haill deykins, euerie yeir after electioun of the maiestrats, sall cheise the collectoures of the said dewteis and casualiteis, of equall number of merchants and craftismen, and to devyse and sett down sic guid ordour as thai sall find meitt and expedient for the perfyte and reddie inbringing thairof.   And last, the said collectouris sall make yeirlie compts of their intromissioun thairwith, at the tyme of making of the townis compts; and sall find sufficient cawtioun at thair admissioun, for compt, rekning, and payment.'[1]

During the year which ended on 24th March 1582–3 sixty-three persons were enrolled as burgesses, and two as burgesses and guild brethren.[2]

### On 4th June 1583,

'The foresaidis baillies, counsall, and deykins of craftis being of guid will and mynd to obey and fulfill the sentence and decreitt arbitrall gevin be our souerane lord the Kings Maiestie and the juges arbitratouris chosin betuix the merchants and craftismen of this burgh, after consideratioun of sic heidis and articles contenit in the said decreit as aucht and suld be putt to present executioun without delay, hes devyset and sett down for the better obedience of the sam the ordour following, quhilk thai ordane and commands to be obseruit and keipit be the haill inhabitants of the said burgh.   First, anent the article of the gildrie, to bring and reduce the said gildrie to the first institution thairof, swa far as may be, after swa lang confusioun of all things, and to mak distinctioun batuix ane gild brother and vther singill burgessis quha are nocht callit to that estaitt and honour within burgh, it is declairit, statute, and ordanet that na maner of persouns bot thai that ar swa resauet and admittit in the societie of the gild brether, top or sell in smallis any maner of wyne, walx, wad, spycereis of all sortis, clayth of silk, gold, syluer, or ony forane or owtlandis clayth of woll (exceptand alwayes thir claythis following, to witt, lynning, freis, kelt, Yorkschyre clayth, cairsayes, and all sort of schrynking clayth, quhilkis sall be commoun to all burgessis), dischairging and inhibiting all per-

---

[1] C. R. vol. vii. fols. 37–41.   Extracts C. R. vol. iv. pp. 265–275.

[2] Register of Burgesses and Guild Brethren.

souns sempill burgessis and vtheris quhilk are nocht gild brether to tred, occupy, exchaynge, top, or sell in smallis fra this day furth the wairis and merchandice before writtin (exceptand as said is) vnder the payne of escheitt thairof, and that na gild brether vse the tred of topping and selling in smallis of sic grof waires as efferis nocht to the honestie of ane gild brother, bot specially of thir wairis following, to wit, oylie, saip, butter, fruitt, fegs, raisins, plowmdames, eggis, fische, vinagar, or sicklyke, vnder the payne of fyve pund swa oft as thai failyie. And for the better knawlege to be had of sic persouns as ar nather gild brether nor burgessis, and yit vsurpis the liberty and privileges of this burgh, it is thocht guid, statute, and ordanet that the baillies be thair quarteris, with the dene of gild and four of the counsell adioynet with thame, sall call in before thame the haill inhabitants of this burgh to schaw and produce thair tikketts of burgesschip and gildrie, and sic as ar nocht frie to be discharget of all vsing of the liberteis of this burgh in tyme cuming quhill thai be maid frie, vnder the payne of twenty pund swa aft as thai failyie, and that thai fynd cawtioun heirvpoun.

'Item, anent the article concerning the owlklie penneis, vnlawes, vpsetts, entres syluer, and siclyke, it is thocht guid, statute, and ordanet that all gild brether vsand the tred thairof sall pay four penneis owlklie; all burgessis vsand merchandice with the gild brether that vsis nocht the tred of gildrie to pay owlklie twa penneis, and all craftismen levand be thair handiewark allanarlie, and all vtheris of lawer calling to pay owlklie ane penny; and thir owlklie penneis to be collectit, tayne, and vpliftet quarterlie, begynnand the first quarter at Lambes nixt, and to be imployit for sustening of the faillit and decayet burgessis and fremen, thair wyffes, bairnis, seruands, and vther puir of the town, conform to the said decreitt.

'Anent the vnlawes of this burgh quhatsumeuir, it is thocht guid that vpoun the counsall dayes, Wedinsday and Fryday, at counsale tyme, ilk baillie sall be his quarter gif in the names of sic persouns as he hes vnlawet, the sowm of the vnlaw, and caus thairof, to be insert in ane buik ordanet for that purpose, and according to the chairge of the said buik sall delyuer to the collectour of the vnlawes other the vnlaw, or a sufficient poynd thairfore; and gif the baillies failyie, to pay the sam of thair awin purse.

'Item, becaus it is speciallie provydit in the said decreitt that nane sall occupy the liberty of the burgh bot sic as ar frie burgessis, and vnderstanding that the greitt multitude of jurnaymen or taskmen of the craftis are na thing ellis bot idill vagabund persouns, bund to na maister, trublers of the quyet estaitt of this commoun weill, polluting the sam with all wikketnes, and beris na burding with the towne, bot ar verray hurtfull to the honest nichtbouris burgessis and frie craftismen of the sam; thairfore the saidis prouest, baillies, counsale, and deykins of craftis commandis and chairges, in our Souerane Lords name and thairis, that na sic persouns remayne within this burgh, bot depesche thame selffis furth thairof vnder the payne of pvneissing of thair bodeis as vagabunds, conform to the acts of parliament. Siclyke, it is statute that na maner of persouns mareit or vnmareit quhilkis ar nocht frie burgessis occupy ony craft within this burgh without thai be bund to ane maister as ane feyit seruand for meitt and fie for yeir or half yeir quha sall ansuer for him to the magestrats as law will, with certificatioun to the saidis persouns, and thai failyie, thai sall be tayne and putt in wairde, thair to remayne vpoun thair awin expenssis ay and quhill thai find cawtioun other to enter thame selffis bund as said is to ane maister within xxiiij houris, or ellis to desist and ceis and nocht to be fund within this toun vnder the payne foresaid and payment of ane pecuniar payne at the will of the magestrats.

'Item, anent the prenteissis, it is statute and ordanit for the better executioun of the said decreitt, that na persouns tak or resaue ony prenteissis to be bund to thame without thai enter thair names in the townis prenteis buik and pay the dewteis of ane prenteis, vnder the payne of fyve pund to the maister resaver and that sic prenteissis sall nocht bruik the privelege of ane prenteis in his burgesschip.' [1]

On 14th June the council, at the request of the King, admitted Phinlaw Tailyeour, 'laquay to His Majestie,' to be a burges gratis.[2]

On 28th June the council, with advice of the deacons,

' for the better knawlege to be had of all maner of persouns admittet to any craft as frieman thairof, that he may pay his vpsett to the collectouris appointet thairto, hes agreit, statute, and ordanet that in all tymes cuming, sen the gevin of the decreitt arbitrall, ilk deykin of craft bring and produce with him before the counsall all persouns admittet friemen to their craft, gif vp thair names to be insert in the common buik for payment of thair vpsett, and this to be done the nixt counsell day after thair said admissioun, vnder the payne of payment of the vpsett be the deykins failyeing heirinto of thair awin proper purse, with als mekill for thair vnlaw in brekking of this present ordinance.' [3]

On 19th July 1583 the following act was passed :—

' The sam day at afternone, the prouest, Andro Sclater, bailie, Maister Jhonn Prestoun, dene of gild, Mungo Russell, thesaurer, John Robertsoun, Jhonn Jhonestoun, William Inglis, Jhonn Mayne, Alexander Naper ; the deykins, Jhonn Wat, smyth, Edward Galbrayth, skynner, Gilbert Primrose, chirurgeane, James Nicolsoun, tailzeour, for the better explanatioun of the act contenit in the gild buik, maid anent burges dochteris quha ar commoun or notorious huiris, fyndes, declairis, statutes, and ordanis, that na burges dochter quha ather is ane commoun or notorious harlott, or quha sall anes defyle hir body

---

[1] C. R. vol. vii. fols. 3, 4. Extracts C. R. vol. iv. pp. 277–279. This act was proclaimed at the market cross on 10th June 1583.

[2] C. R. vol. vii. fol. 5. Extracts C. R. vol. iv. p. 280.

[3] C. R. vol. vii. fols. 6, 7. Extracts C. R. vol. iv. p. 280.

with fornicatioun, and is nocht at the tyme of the solemnizatioun of hir mariage ane clene virgine swa repute and haldin, sall in ony tyme cuming bruik the priuelege of ane burges dochter to mak hir husband burges or gild brother be hir richt for the dewty vsit to be tayne of ane that mareis ane burges dochter, bot *ipso facto* to haif forfaltit and tint the said liberty for euir.'[1]

The accounts of the dean of guild for the year to Michaelmas 1583 show that one hundred and eight burgesses and guild brethren were entered during the year, and that the total dues on their admission amounted to £350 Scots.[2]

On 9th November 1583 the council passed the following act :—

' After lang resoning vpoun the richts and privileges of the prenteisses to burgessis and friemen of this burgh, vpoun consideratioun of the consuetude of burgh, certane acts and statutes maid heirtofoir, and of the effect and meyning of the decreitt arbitrall, and for guid ressonis moving thame, thay haif declairit, statute, and ordanet that quhen any maner of persoun sall be lawfullie bund prenteis to ane burges and frieman of this burgh, and sall compleitt his prenteisschip, and fulfill the poynts of his indentour, and beand fund qualefeit and worthie in honestie and substance to be admittet in the societie of the gild brether of this burgh, quhidder his maister wes gild brother or nocht, he sall pay na mair to the dene of gild for his gildrie bot the sowm of ten pund allanerlie, for the quhilk he sal be maid gild brother, and this likewayes to be extendet to thame that wes prenteissis befor the making of this present act.'[3]

On 21st February 1583–4 the council passed the following act :—

' The sam day, etc., forswamekill as thair is ane greitt number of burges sones within this burgh quha exerceis all kynd of trafficque and merchandice with thair awin proper guidis, quhairby thai ar become mair welthy and habill nor sindry vther nichtbouris and craftismen to extent, watche, wairde, and beir all portabill chairges, and neuirtheles refuissis to do the sam, importunes daylie the counsall with thair supplicatiouns, pretending for thair excuis ane act of counsall sett furth the xxvj of Nouember 1557, quhilk tuik na effect at the making thairof, bot wes maid at the instance of certaine particulare persones without rype avisement and sufficient cognitioun of the caus, bot now, in respect of the alteratioun of the tyme and greitt chairges daylie falling vpoun the town, intollerabill to ane few number, quhilk of all guid equitie awcht to be equallie born of all that hes thair lyfe and tred within the burgh, according to thair habilitie, and conform to the laitt decreitt gevin betuix the merchants and

---

[1] C. R. vol. vii. fol. 9.  Extracts C. R. vol. iv. p. 284.

[2] Accounts of the Deans of Guild.  Four 'gratis entries' appear in the account for this year.

C. R. vol. vii. fol. 45.  Extracts C. R. vol. iv. p. 306.

craftismen : Thairfore the said provest, bailyeis, counsall, and deykins of craftis, efter consideratioun of the premissis, with dyuers vthers greitt and wechtie ressonis moving thame, rescindis, cassis, annullis, and dischairges the said act, haill strenth, force, and effect thairof, in all tyme cuming, and for thame and thair successouris, fyndis, declairis, and als statuts and ordanis all the lawfull sones of the burgessis of this burgh quha hes ony tred or trafficque of merchandice be thame selffis with thair awin proper guids, and wynnis thair leving be thair awin industrie, quhidder thai be at thair fatheris or motheris tabillis or nocht, and mareit or vnmareit, and quhidder thair said fatheris or motheris be deid or on lyfe, to extent, watche, waird, and beir all portabill chairges with the rest of the nichtbouris, according to thair habilitie and substance, nochtwithstanding ony acts, privelegeis, or exemptiounis quhilk thai can pretend in the contrair ; for the quhilk it is grantet to thame to pay na vnfremenis customes and to haif thair burgesschip and gildschip of the awld pryce, quhairas the sam is greitlie rayset vpoun vtheris ; quhilk being considerit, thai haif na just caus to compleyne.' [1]

On 28th February the council passed the following act :—

' Becaus it is lattin thame to vnderstand that sindry of the brether of the craftis and certane vthers ar nocht content to pay to thar owlklie penneis, conform to the act maid thairvpoun the fourt of June last, quhilk is four penneis of the gild, twa penneis of the merchant, and ane penny of the sempill craftismen, as at lenth is mentionat in the said act, bot murmuris and grudgeis at the same, allegeing that the said act is in that pairt contrer to the decreitt arbitrall, thairfore to satisfie all parteis, statuts and ordanis that thair be bot ane owlklie penny to be tane indifferently of the haill nichtbouris, merchants and craftismen, be the collectouris nominat thairto, and imployet according to the decreitt arbitrall, and in that pairt cassis, rescyndis, and discharges the said act before mentionat.' [2]

On 13th March William Logane, messenger, having been accused of circumventing the town by obtaining his bastard son to be made a burgess as if he had been his lawful son, and having admitted the charge, the council deprived the son of his burgess - ship, ordained the burgess ticket to be taken from him, and ordered his name to be deleted from the guild book. At the same time the council ordained Cudbert Murray ' to be wairnet and accusit for the cawsing of his guidsone to be maid burges be rycht of his bastard dochter.' [3]

[1] C. R. vol. vii. fol. 72.    Extracts C. R. vol. iv. pp. 325, 326.
[2] C. R. vol. vii. fol. 73.    Extracts C. R. vol. iv. p. 326.
[3] C. R. vol. vii. fol. 77.    Extracts C. R. vol. iv. p. 328.

During the year which ended on 24th March 1583–4, seventy-six persons were enrolled as burgesses, two as guild brethren, and thirty-five as burgesses and guild brethren.[1]

Notwithstanding the act that the children of persons made bur-guesses *gratis* should not receive the privilege which was accorded to the children of burgesses who had paid the full fees, the council in special cases modified their act, and admitted the children of *gratis* burgesses on easy terms. Of this there is an illustration under date 13th May 1584, when the council,

'at the requeist and solistatioun of Thomas Murray, furrour to the Kings Maiestie, and vpoun howpe of the guid behaviour in tyme cuming of Dauid Corsbie, skynner, and in consideratioun of the multitude of his bairnis, havcand bot small substance to susteyne thaime, hes grantet and promittit that albeit the said Dauid be maid burges onelie gratis, neuirtheles to admitt and resave his sones and the husbands of his dochteris to be burgessis of this burgh vpoun ane resonabill modificatioun of the dewtie to be payet to the dene of gild for the sam at the discretioun of the counsall, and nocht to be chairget with the extreme dewte, bot to be considerit according to thair substance and honest conversatioun.'[2]

On 22d August Parliament ratified and confirmed the liberties and privileges granted to the estate of burghs, and ordained them to have full force and effect in all respects;[3] and also ratified and confirmed the decree arbitral in all points.[4]

On 16th September the council passed the following act:—

'For the weill of the estaitts of free burrowes, ordanis ane article to be gevin in to this present parliament aganes all craftsmen quha remaynis in the suburbs of burghs and places thair about; and Henry Nisbet, bailyie, and William Fairlie, to caus the said article be formet and gevin in to the lordis of articles.'[5]

Forty-four burgesses and guild brethren were entered in the accounts of the deans of guild for the year from Michaelmas 1583

---

1 Register of Burgesses and Guild Brethren.
2 C. R. vol. vii. fol. 88.  See also on 26th Sept. 1582, *antea* pp. 125-6.
3 A. P. S. vol. iii. p. 354.
4 A. P. S. vol. iii. p. 363.
5 C. R. vol. vii. fol. 108.  Extracts C. R. vol. iv. p. 350.

to Michaelmas 1584, and the total dues paid on their admission amounted to £294, 6s. 8d. Scots.[1]

On 11th November the council ratified the following heads and articles proposed by the deacon of the tailors and others, freemen of that craft and burgesses of the burgh :—

'In the first.' Forswamekill as it is complenit be the said deykin and brether that thai are heavelie hurt and damnefeit be ane greit number of vnfremen dwelland within this burgh, als weill mareit as vnmareit, quha ar nawayes vnder subiectioun of ony maisteris nor yitt subiect to ony stenting, watcheing, wairding, or vther portabill chairges with the friemen of the said craft, bot levis licentiouslie and workis all maner of wark that thai may purches, in privie howssis, lofts and chalmeris, and takkis payment thairfore as thai wer admittet to thair friedome, and thairby hinders and preiuges the frie brether of the said craft quha ar subiect to all portabill chairges of thair commoditie and proffeitt ; for remeid thairfore that gif onie sic vnfrie persouns of the said craft quha makis daylie residence within the toun beis apprehendit within this burgh, ather vpoun the Hie gaitt, privie howssis, loftis, chalmeris or vther streittis in tyme cuming, nocht subiect to ane frie maister aither for meitt, fie, or owlklie waige, and his conditioun of seruice maid before the deykin and foure maisteris that thai sall be tayne and put in waird quhair euir thay may be apprehendit, and gif thai be ony sic houssis that officeris of this burgh maks oppin durris quhill thai be apprehendit and mak payment of the sowm of fourtie schillings als oft as thai be apprehendit furth of the seruice of ane frie maister, viz. the twa pairt of the said sowm to the vse of the hospitall and the thrid pairt to the apprehendaris at the distributioun of the said deykin and maisteris being for the tyme. *Item*, Becaus the said deikin and brethir complenit that thai ar havelie hurt and damnefeit be sindrie persouns of the said craft, nocht beand friemen of this burgh, duelland in the Cannogait, Potterraw, and West Port, and vther suburbs of the said burgh, quha daylie cumis within the fredome of the samyn and takis furth wark, schaipin and vnschaipin, pertening to the burgessis and friemen of this burgh, and wirkis the samyn in thair awin fredomis, and thairafter inbringis the said wark agane to this burgh to the awner thairof, and takis thair pryce thairfore, and thairby also grittumlie hurtis the said deykin and brether of thair commoditie and proffeitt quhilk thai wald obtene of the said wark gif thai wer stoppet to vsurp thair fredome and libertie. For remeid thairof, the said provest, bailyeis, counsall, and deykins, hes statute and ordanit that gif ony sic vnfrie persouns, dwelland outwith the said fredome, nocht beand burgessis and friemen of the samyn burgh, beis apprehendit with ony sic wark in tyme cuming, ather

---

[1] Accounts of the Deans of Guild. Six 'gratis entries' occur during this year.

schaipin or vnschaipin, in the owttaking or inbringing within this burgh, that it sall be lesum to the said deykin and maisteris, or ony of thame, with the concurrance of ane officer, to tak and intromett with the said wark fra the haver thairof quhaireuir the sam may be apprehendit within the fredome of this burgh, and to keip and retene the samyn quhill payment be maid of the soum of fourtie schillings be the warkman that wirkis sic wark and as thai be fund and apprehendit committing the said falt, the twa pairt of the said sowmes to the vse of the hospitalitie and the thrid pairt to the apprehendaris at the distributioun of the said deykin and maisteris being for the tyme. *Item*, Becaus the said deykin and brether havelie complenis that thai ar grittumlie hurt of thair commoditie and proffeit be sindrie of thair awin brethrein, burgessis and friemen of this burgh, quha vnder cullour and pretence of ane seruand takis, resavis and resettis, within thair buithis, vnfriemen, nather being thair seruands nor prenteissis, and sufferris and permittis thame to wirk and inbring within thair buithis to thair awin behuiff and profeitt all maner of wark that thai may purches and obtene and to tak pryce thairfore and to dispone thairvpoun at thair plesure and to vse all vther liberteis of the said craft as the said frie maister micht do himselff, for granting of the quhilk pretendit libertie the said vnfrie personis ar bund and oblist for payment to the maisteris of craft that resettis and resauis thame of ane certane sowm of money, to the greitt abuse of the said craft and preiudice of the liberteis of the samyn ; for remeid quhairof, the provest, bailyeis, counsall, and deykins of craftis, hes statute and ordanit that na frie maister of the said craft sall be sufferit to hald, resett, nor resaue ony sic vnfrie persouns to wirk within thair buithis in tyme cuming, nor yitt to hald nor resaue any seruand of the said craft in thair seruice with-out he be bund for certane yeiris to remayne in his said maisteris seruice for meitt and fie as his maister and he can agrie, and the condition of seruice to be maid before the said deykin and foure sworne frie maisters being for the tyme ; and gif it be fund verefeit and provin that ony frie maister of the said craft sall happin to do in the contrare, or that the said maister and seruand sall happin to mak any collusion betuix thame to the hurt of the said craft, vtherwayis nor beis in thair appoyntment to be maid before the said deykin and brether, the said maister and seruand sall pay euerie ane of thame swa oft as thai failyie heirin the sowm of fourty schillings money, the twa pairt to the hospitalitie and the thrid thairof to the apprehenderis at the sicht and distributioun of the said deykin and brether. *Item*, To the effect that the nichtbouris of this burgh be nocht hurt nor preuigeit be debarring of the vnfriemen to mak or mend thair claythis in thair howssis, it is thairfore agriet, statute and ordanet, that the deykin and brether of the said craft sall, be thameselffis or thair seruands, mak the said nichtbouris als guid and reddie seruice within and without thair howssis as thai wer wont to haif be the said vnfriemen ; and thairfore quha swa wirks thair nichtbouris claythis sall at all tymes quhen he is requyret, vpoun xxiiij houris wairning, appoint ane of his seruandis for quhome he sall ansuer to pas to the nichtbouris dwelling hous for mending and repairing of sic ornaments and clething as ar to be mendit of all sorts without exceptioun.  And the said seruand to enter to wark at five houris in the morning, vngangand· owt without leiff quhile nyne houris at evin, and to haif thairfore ilk day twelf pennies and his meitt ; and quhair any maister of the said occupatioun failyeis to do as said is sall pay ane vnlaw of xl s. to be applyet as said is.  *Item*, That na prenteis be maid frieman quhill he. serue his maister fyve yeir during his prenteischip and thairafter with him or with ony vther frie maister thre yeir for meitt and fie quhilk will mak of the haill awcht yeiris or he be maid frie, and na vther to be made frie except he marie ane friemanis dochter of the said craft or haif bene ane prenteis as said is.  *Item*, Gif any frie maister of the said craft in ony tyme heirafter sall happin to procure in favouris of ony prenteis or seruand to be maid frieman of the said craft, after the owtrynning of his prenteisschip or of his seruice, without the said prenteis haif seruet ane frie maister of this burgh thre yeiris after the owtrynning of his prenteisschip for meitt and fie, or that the said seruand that beis procureit and requeistet for haif mareit or is to marie ane frie manis dochter of the said craft, the said maister or maisters that sall mak the said requeist or procuratioun sall pay thairfore the sowm of ten pund money to be bestowet to the puir at the discretioun of the counsall.  *Fynallie*, Quhen any difference sall aryse betuix ane of the nichtbouris of the toun and ane frieman of the said craft anent the pryce of anye maid wark, or vpoun the insufficiencie of the warkmanschip, or vpoun any fraude or deceitt committet, bayth the said pairteis sall abyde and vnderly the tryell and in-quisitioun and als fulfill the jugement and will of ane bailyie, the deykin of the craft, with twa of the counsall of the towne, the ane beand ane merchant the vther ane craftisman, to be chosin be the said bailyie.  And for the mair securitie, fayth and authoritie to be gevin heirto, ordanis the seill of caus of the said burgh to be appendet to the extract of this present act and ordinance, to be subscryuet be the provest and bailyeis and be thair commoun clerk.' [1]

On 27th November the council passed the following act :—

'Forswamekill as the deykin and brether of the wobsteris and walkeris of this burgh havelie lamentit and complenit that thai beand burgessis of the said burgh and friemen of thair craftis, watcheing, wairding, and bering all portabill chairges within the samyn, and lykewayes habill to serue all oure Souerane Lordis lieges thairof in all poynts belånging to thair occupatiouns, als weill and easelie bayth in wark and pryce as any vtheris within this realme having the lyke cair burding and chairges.  Nochttheles the haill inhabitants of this burgh, at the leist the maist pairt, movet be solistatioun, acquentance, and dyuers vther meanis and wayis vnknawin to the said brether, daylie puts thair wark in the hands of the vnfriemen dwelland to landward and in the suburbs of this burgh, personis be that way greitlie incressit in number and substance, leving

in all securitie frie from ony burding and subiectioun of lawis, quha fynding
sic immunitie as na frie burges can haif ar gadderit from all pairts reteining
thame selffis furth of the jurisdictioun of frie burghs at thair verray durris,
eitting thair breid furth of thair mowthis, and now hes begun to tak prenteissis,
cheise deykins and quarter maisteris, mak contributiouns, and swa erect ane
monopole amangs thameselffis, doing all things and mair than to ony frieman
is lesum and tolerabill to do, contrair the ancient lawis of the realme and
priuilege of burrowis, and to the greitt hurt and preiudice of the said friemen
quha ar alluterlie decayet in thair number and depauperat in substance and na
mair habill to beir burdein within the toun bot will be constraynet to withdraw
thame selffis, and with tyme to adioyne to the said vnfriemen.   And albeit the
exampill of this evill and dayngerous preparatiue be begun at thame, yitt it is
apperand nocht to end schortlie, but with continuall consuetude growing in
ane law is habill to pas throw all sorts and degreis within the burgh, bayth
merchants and craftismen, and swa at lenth to bring the estaitt of burrowis in
ane confusioun, and last to ane vtter decay and submersioun gif this owersicht
and negligence be nocht preventit in tyme, ather be seiking redres in parliament, be putting the ancient lawis and liberteis of burgh to spedie executioun,
or ellis be inhibiting sic persouns within the burgh on quhome the jurisdictioun
thairof cheiflie hes place, to gif occasioun of swa greitt inconvenients, with
scherp executioun and pvnisement to be vset vpoun the doares thairof.   With
the quhilk the said bailyeis, counsall and deykins, being rypelie avyset, and
fynding the sam to be of veritie, thairfore, at this present, quhill farther remeid
may be had and provydet thairto, hes thocht expedient, statute, and ordanet
that na maner of persouns, burgessis and indwellers of this burgh, be thame
selffis, their wyffis, seruandis, or vtheris in thair names in tyme cuming, tak
vpoun hand to carie, send, or delyuer thair yairne, clayth, webbis, or vther
stufe, belanging to the said occupatiouns, to be wrocht, maid, or dressit be ony
wobsteris or walkeris, vnfriemen, dwelland within the Cannogaitt, Potterraw,
owtwith the West Port, and in the suburbs of this burgh, or within halff ane
myle to the toun wallis, inhibiting and dischairgeing thame of the samyn be
thir presents, vnder the payne of escheitt of the said stufe quhen euir the samyn
sall be apprehendit passand to the saidis plaices or cumand fra the samyn, the
twa pairt thairof to the hospitall and puir and the thrid to the apprehendares.
And to the effect that the nichtbouris of this burgh may be the better movet to
put thair wark in the hands of the friemen of the said craft and na vtheris, it
is lykewayes statute and ordanit that gif thair wark sall be misuset and spilt,
or yitt retardit and haldin bak and nocht depescheit and wrocht with all
possibill diligence, in that case the deykin and quarter-maisters of the wobsters,
coniunctlie and seuerallie, for thair craft, and thair successouris respectiue, sall
refound, content, and pay to the awneris of the said stufe all damnage and
entres to be sustenit be thame thairthrow and mak satisfactioun and contenta-
tioun to the said saidis awneris for thair slak seruice, besyde ane vnlaw to the
toun and puir, at the arbitrament, sicht, and discretioun of ane bailyie or any

aucht of the counsall, quhais will and jugement thai sall vnderly and fulfill, bot
ony proces of law, quhidder the principall offender be callit and convict or
nocht.  And Johnn Moyses, deykin of the walkeris, and William Cowts, Jhonn
Fairlie, William Robesoun, Gilbert Eddislaw, Leonard Phillip, quarter maisteris
thairof, and Jhonn Stevinsoun, deykin of the wobsteris, Leonard Thomesoun,
Thomas Wricht, Rychart Dalgleische, James Melros, quarter maisteris of the
samyn, comperand personallie for thame selffis and thair successouris, deykins
and quarter maisteris of thair said craft, agreit and consentit heirto and oblist
thame respectiue, coniunctlie and seuerallie, and thair foresaids, for obseruing,
keping and fulfilling heirof in maner abone writtin.  And the said provest,
bailyeis, counsall and deykins ordanet publicatioun to be maid of this present
act and ordinance that nane pretend ignorance of the samyn.'[1]

On 16th December in the same year the doors of all taverners
who sold wine without being guild brethren were ordered to be
closed up.[2]

On the 23d of the same month the council prohibited unfreemen
who were not burgesses and guild brethren from retailing wines,
under the penalty of £40 Scots each person weekly, and appointed

'sic as hes presentlie vsurpet the fredome of this burgh and layet in thair
wynes, that thai denude thair hands thairof and sell the samyn in greitt to
friemen betuix this and the first day of Januar nixttocum, bot forther delay,
vnder the payne of xl li. ilk persoun.'[3]

On 6th January 1584-5 the following act was passed to define
the conditions of admission as burgesses and guild brethren :—

'The quhilk day, etc., the foresaid bailyeis, counsall and deykins fyndis
expedient, statutes, and ordanis that nane sall be resauet gild brether within
this burgh, nother the gild brether bairnis nor vtheris, except thai be of honest,
discreitt, and guid conversatioun, swa tryet and fund be the provest, bailyeis,
and counsall for the tyme ; and the said gild brether bairnis and the prenteissis
to friemen within this burgh, being found sic as said is, sall be resauet, paying
onelie the awld dewtie, that is to say, the eldest lawfull sone, for his gildrie,
threttein schilling foure penneis, the rest of the lawfull bairnis twenty schillings,
. . . and sic as hes bene prenteissis dewlie according to the law, for his gildrie,
ten pund, and all vtheris that sall happin to be resauet to pay the dewtie of

[1] C. R. vol. vii. fol. 136-8.   Extracts C. R. vol. iv. pp. 374-376.
[2] C. R. vol. vii. fol. 141.   Extracts C. R. vol. iv. p. 378.
[3] C. R. vol. vii. fol. 144-5.   Extracts C. R. vol. iv. p. 381.

fourtie pund to the dene of gild, without preiudice of vther dewteis, and
nane to be resauet gild brother in tymes cuming bot sic as sall haif the
qualiteis aboue writtin; and he that sall be of the merchant vocatioun sall be
estemit in movabill guids worth ane thowsand merkis of frie geir, and the
handie lawborer vsing his craft in movabill guids to be estemet worth fyve
hundredth merkis of frie geir by his craft, and quhatevir he be that vsis
nocht the craft sall be worth ane thowsand merk of frie movebill geir;
quhilkis haill gild brother sall be subiect to vnderly and obey the particulare
lawes and statutes contenit in the forme of the gildrie sett owt be the provest,
bailyies, counsall, and communitie.'[1]

On the 8th of the same month the council elected the dean of
guild's council, consisting of three merchants and three craftsmen,
in terms of the decree arbitral:—

'And thai with the dene of gild to trye the qualeficatioun of all persouns
quha ar to be admittet burgessis and gild brether, and to devyse and sett doun
in writt lawes and statutes for the weill of the burgessis and gild brether of this
burgh to be sene and allowet be the counsall of the town, and to vplift the
vnlawes and peñalties thairof to be bestowet the ane half be the greitt counsall
of the toun and the vther half to the said gild counsall.'[2]

On the 3d of the following month of February the following
oath was appointed to be administered to all burgesses who might
be afterwards admitted:—

'I sall be leill and trew to oure Soverane lord and to his hienes successoures,
to the provest and bailyeis of this burgh. I sall vnderly and keip the lawis and
statutes of this burgh. I sall obey the officeris of the burgh, fortefie and men-
teyne thame in executioun of thair offices with my body and my guidis. I sall
nocht cullour vnfriemenis guidis vnder cullour of my awin. I sall nocht purches
lordschips nor authoriteis contrare the fredome of the burgh. In all taxatiouns,
watcheing, wairding, and all vther chairges to be layet vpoun the burgh, I sall
willinglie beir my pairt of the commoun burding thairof with the rest of the
nichtbouris of the burgh as I am commandet thairto be the maiestratis and
officeris of the burgh, and sall nocht purches exemptiouns, privelegeis, nor
immuniteis to be frie of the sam, renunceand the benefite thairof for evir.
Fynallie, I sall attemp or do nathing hurtfull or preiudiciall to the libertie and
commoun weill of this burgh. And swa oft as I sall brek any poynt or article
heirof, I obleis me, my aires, executoris, and assignayes, to pay to the commoun warkis of this burgh the soum of ane hundreth pundis as ane interest

---

[1] C. R. vol. vii. fol. 148.  Extracts C. R. vol. iv. p. 383.
[2] C. R. vol. vii. fol. 149.  Extracts C. R. vol. iv. p. 384.

and damnage liquidat, and sall remayne in waird quhill I mak payment of the samyn. Swa help me God, and be God himselff, etc.'[1]

On the 3d of March 1584–5 the rights and privileges of the dean of guild and his council in regard to burgesses and guild brethren were defined by the provost, bailies, and council in the following act :—

'Having hard and considerit the articles vnderwrittin concerning the dene of gild and his counsall, after resouning vpoun euerie poynt thairof, fyndis the sam to agrie with the ancient liberteis of the burgh and priveleges grantet to the gild brether for the singulare weill and commoditeis of the commoun weill of this burgh and haill inhabitantis and fremen thairof, als weill craftismen as merchantis, and ratefeis, appreveis, and authorizeis the said articles, and interponing thair authority thairto, decernis and ordanis the samyn to be obseruet and keipet in all tymes cuming. Followes the saidis articles :—

' Item, the said dene of gild and his counsall to dischairge, pvneis, and vnlaw all persouns vnfriemen vsand the libertie of ane burges gild brother or friedome of craftis as thai sall fynd guid, ay and quhill the said vnfriemen be put of the toun or ellis maid frie with the toun, and thair craftis ; siclyke persew before the juges competent all persouns dwelland without the burgh and vsurpand the libertie and fredome thairof, obtene decreitis againis thame, and caus the sam be put to speidie executioun.

' Item, na burgessis nor gild brether to be maid nor prenteissis buiket bot in presens of the dene of gild and his counsall ; and gif any beis vtherwayes maid or buikit, the sam to be of na effect to the resaver, quha sall lykewayis lose his money gevin thairfore.

' Item, the dene of gild and his counsall to haif power to raise taxatiouns vpoun the gild brether for the weilfair and mayntenance of thair estaitt and the help of thair failyeit brether, thair wyffes, children, and seruandis ; and quha refuissis to pay the said taxte be vnlawet in the soum of xl s. swa oft as thai failyie, provyding the sam exceid nocht the soum of ane hundreth pund at anes.'[2]

On the 10th of the same month the council empowered the dean of guild and his counsel, upon payment of a reasonable duty, at their discretion, to receive and admit to be burgesses and freemen such persons as had ' bene awld seruandis within the toun.'[3]

---

[1] C. R. vol. vii. fol. 155.    Extracts C. R. vol. iv. p. 387.
[2] C. R. vol. vii. fol. 162.    Extracts C. R. vol. iv. pp. 395-398.
[3] C. R. vol. vii. fol. 165.    Extracts C. R. vol. iv. p. 399.

On 17th March the council ordained

'that na maner of persouns quha ar nocht burgessis and friemen of this burgh tak vpoun hand fra this day furth to vse the libertie of ane burges and frieman thairof, vnder the payne of fyve pund the first falt, ten pund the second, and banisement of this burgh for the thrid. Sicklyke that na vnfrie persouns or syngill burgessis vse the libertie of ane gild brother, vnder the payne of x li. the first falt, twenty pund the secund falt, and fourty pund the thrid falt.' [1]

On 19th March Nicol Vddert, dean of guild, was empowered to receive and admit the unfree websters and walkers dwelling at the West Port, and other unfree persons of those crafts, to be burgesses and freemen of the burgh, and to agree with them for the duties both of their burgess-ship and upsets, taking security that they should come, remain, and dwell in the burgh at Whitsunday then next.[2]

During the year which ended on 24th March 1584–5 forty-five persons were enrolled as burgesses, eleven as guild brethren, and two as burgesses and guild brethren.[3]

On 28th April 1585 the council passed the following important act :—

·'The sam day, it wes proponet be Nicoll Vddert, dene of gild, and certane of his counsall, that sindrie persouns hes comperit befoir thame and desyrit to be resauet burgessis and gild brether of this burgh, thair resultet some difficulteis thairvpoun, quhairof thai culd nocht be resoluet of thameselffis without avyse and consent of the greit counsall, and the said difficulteis beand put in articles, and proponet and schawin, desyrit the said bailyeis, counsall, and deykins to set doun in writt thair will, consent, and command quhat way he sall follow thairanent ; with the quhilk the said bailyeis, counsall, and deykins, being ryplie avysit, after lang ressoning, for ansuer to the said articles, hes thocht expedient statute and ordainet as followis :—First, anent sic persounis as wes maid burgessis. before the decreit arbitrall and vnioun of the merchants and craftsmen, that thai be resauet and admittet gild brether for the awld dewtie of ten pund allanerlie, beand alwayes tryet and fund qualefeit and worthie thairof, and all vtheris having na rycht be thair fatheris, wiffes, or prentessis, to pay the vtter dewtie, quhilk is fourtie pund, for thair gildrie, and

[1] C. R. vol. vii. fol. 167–8.   Extracts C. R. vol. iv. p. 402.
[2] C. R. vol. vii. fol. 170.   Extracts C. R. vol. iv. p. 404.
[3] Register of Burgesses and Guild Brethren.

all vther dewteis awand thairfor. Item, becaus the sone, dochter, or prenteis can be in na better estaitt nor thair fayther or maister wes be thair rycht, thairfore, quhair the maister or fayther wes na burges or gild brother, the said prenteis, the son, or yitt the husband of the dochter, nocht to be resauet burges or gild brother bot for the vtternest dewtie before mentionatt. Item, anent the prenteissis of gild brether and burgessis, first, for thair better tryell and pruif of thair guid conditiouns ; nixt, in respect thai aucht to be far inferiour to thair maisteris bairnis as twicheing thair richt throw thair maister ; and thridlie, to move thame to tak in marriage thair maisters dochteris before any vtheris, quhilk sall be ane greitt comfort and support to friemen, that thairfore na pren-teis be resauet burges be rycht of his prenteisschip, without he haif seruit after the ische of his prenteisschip ane frieman for the space of thrie yeir for meitt and fie, and than to be resauet burges as ane prenteis, and als nocht to be rasauet gild brether be that richt without he haif bene ane burges for fyve yeir, swa to abyde threttein yeir before he be gild brether be rycht of his prenteis-schip ; bot gif he marie his maisters dochter, or the dochter of any freman burges and gild, and beis fund worthie and qualefeit, in that caise to be resauet gild brother at any tyme be rycht of his wyfe. And ordanis the said dene of gild and his counsall and thair successouris to obserue and keip inviolablie this present act and ordinance as ane law in all tyme cumming.'[1]

On 11th May 1586 it was ordained by the council

'that yeirly thair be affixet and sett ane thrid court for creating of burgessis and gild brether after the Trinitie Sonday, to wit, vpoun the Wedinsday nixtt thairafter, that the pairties suittand the sam gif in thair supplicatiouns, and thai sall be callit in and hard, and sic as ar fund worthie, that thai be wairnet to compeir the next counsall day thairafter, to compeir bringand with thame thair dewteis to be payet to the dene of gild and collectouris, and that day to be sworne and resavet.'[2]

On the 8th of June 1586, Grisell Seytoun and William Blair were allowed, at the request of the king, to exercise the privilege of burgess-ship, though they had not been 'made free,' on the following curious condition, viz. :

'ay and quhill thair sall be ane generall taxatioun of the realme and the guid towne taxet, with provisioun that thai obtene the dewteis of thair burges and gildschipis allowet to the towne in the foirend of the townis taxatioun ; and gif thai failyie thairinto, this present tollerance and licence to expyre and be of na effect vnto thame.'[3]

---

[1] C. R. vol. vii. fol. 179.     Extracts C. R. vol. iv. p. 412.
[2] C. R. vol. viii. fol. 12.     Extracts C. R. vol. iv. p. 459.
[3] C. R. vol. viii. fol. 20.     Extracts C. R. vol. iv. p. 462.

On 20th July 1586 the council advised proclamation to be made of the conditions on which they would feu portions of the Common Muir. These conditions were as follow :—

'First, That the said acres sall nocht be sett to any maner of persouns butt to ane burges of the said burgh and his aires quha sall actuallie remayne and dwell in the towne with hous and familie, scatt and lott, and beir all portabill chairges with the inhabitants thairof, with provision to be contenit in the few chairtour that gif the air will nocht be ane burges, remayne in the burgh, scat and lott as said is, he sall be oblist to sell and dispone the said acres be avyse of the towne to any burges that will gif maist thairfore, kepand the conditioun foresaid. Item, the said acres to be tailyeitt to the aires maill, quhilks failyeing to the eldest famele but diuisioun. Item, at the entrie of ilk air the air to pay of entres syluer to the towne for ilk acre in the wester mwre twa merk and in the eister mwre fourty schillings. Item, gif the wedow, coniunct fear, mareis any persoun that is nocht burges and nocht kepand the first conditioun scho to tyne hir coniunct fie or lyfrent. Item, it sall nocht be lesum to the fewares to annalie, wedsett in all or in pairt the said acres, or tak any annuell thairvpoun, without the speciall consent of the provest, bailyeis, counsale and deykins, vpoun payne of tynsall of the few. Item, quhen the said acres sall be sawld fra ane hand to ane vther, with consent foresaid, the new tennent to pay to the towne at his entrie the dowbill of the entres of ane air.'[1]

On 2d August 1586 various parts of the Wester Muir were feued by public roup in terms of the above act, and on the following day proclamation was made that portions of the Easter Muir would be set in feu to burgesses on the following Tuesday.[2] This was accordingly done on 9th August 1586.[3]

The practice of admitting burgesses after the head courts only having been considered unsatisfactory, ' in respect of the multitude that bringis confusion, and thairby may nocht be sufficiently tryet bayth in the qualiteis of thair persouns and rychtis,' the council, on 5th October in the same year, resolved to admit burgesses and guild brethren on each council day.[4]

On 1st February 1586-7 a seal of cause was granted by the provost, bailies, council, and deacons to the cordiners. It narrates

[1] C. R. vol. viii. fol. 28.　Extracts C. R. vol. iv. p. 467.
[2] C. R. vol. viii. fol. 31, 32.　Extracts C. R. vol. iv. p. 469.
[3] C. R. vol. viii. fol. 33.　Extracts C. R. vol. iv. pp. 470, 471.
[4] C. R. vol. viii. fol. 48.　Extracts C. R. vol. iv. p. 473.

that by negligence and oversight the privileges of the craft had not been ' putt to sic executioun as the necessitie thairof requyret, quhairby all things is grown to ane grett abuse,' and the craft ' grittumlie hurt and preiugeit be vnfriemen and be the unsufficiencie of the ledder.'  It then ordained, *inter alia*, as follows :—

' First.  Forswamekill as the prediccssoures of the said provest, baillies, counsall and deykins, of guid memorie, diligentlie considering and vnderstanding vpoun the supplicatioun gevin in to thame be the maisters and hedismen of the said craft for the tyme, thair nichtbouris and conburgessis, that oure Souerane Lords lieges ar grittumelie skaithet and defrawdet be insufficient wark of ignorant persouns, lawborers bayth in blak wark and barket ledder, than daylie bocht and sawld, within this burgh, als weill be fremen as vnfremen and owtland men, on the wolk dayes als weill as on the merket dayes, the fredome and priveleges of burgessis destroyet thairthrow, contrar the commoun weill ; for reformatioun thairof, be thair lettres patent, vnder thair seill of caus, limitt and ordanet certane persouns maisters and owrismen of the said craft, sworne in thair presens, quha suld euery merket day diligentlie serche, visie, and sie all maid wark and barket ledder cumand and presentet in the merket, and if that thai fand sufficient till mark it, and quhair thai fand fals feignyeit wark or barket ledder the sercheris till bring it to proüest and baillies for the tyme, and at the will of thame till escheitt the stufe faltive and the persouns to pvneis as affeires, swa that the Kingis lieges be nocht dissavet, and that na sic stufe be sawld on the merket day quhill the sercheris haif visit the samyn, nor yitt that nane be strikkin vp to sell quhill vij houris at somer and ix houris in wynter before none, vnder the payne of escheitt and pvnesing the persouns as said is ; and that na owtlands folk dwelland without this burgh nor vnfriemen by any rwch hydes nor barket ledder within this toun bot on the merket day allanerly, vnder the payne abonewritten.'

It constituted the deacon and six quarter masters of the craft and their successors to be general searchers for putting the provisions of the seal of cause into execution, with the assistance of their officers, and it provided that the burgesses and freemen of the burgh might sell their ' barket ledder at all tymes, the samyn beand guid and sufficient stufe,' but that no unfreeman should come to the market to buy leather before

' eleven houris past, to the effect that friemen may be first staiket that beiris portabill charges, vnder the payne of wairding of the said vnfriemen and paying of ane vnlaw of xx s. ; '

that no unfreemen

'bring any bwits or schone or vther maid wark to sell within the fredome of this burgh bot on the Monondayes and present the samyn to the merket in tyme and place appoyntet, vnder the payne of escheitt thairof ;'

that no cobler's booth be kept by 'habill young men,' but only by persons upwards of thirty years of age, 'that the friemen may haif thair seruands to serue them.'

'Item, that na frieman of the said craft being burges pak nor peill nor be pairtiner with unfriemen nor mak conventiouns with thame, vnder the payne of ten pund or tynsell of his friedome, and that na friemen and burgessis of the said craft dwell owtwith the fredome of this burgh nor wirk his wark owtwith the fredome vnder the payne foresaid. Item, that na maister ressett ane vthers prenteis or seruand without leif or ane resonabill caus first schawin and tryet, vnder the payne of xx s. Item, at the taking of any prenteis that tryell may be tayne gif the resauer be worthie to tak ane prenteis and to instruct him and gif him meitt and drink sufficiently, to statute that all indentouris be subscryuet be the deykin or his clerk, vtherwayes the prenteis nocht to be bwiket in the townis prenteis buik. Als that na maister of the said craft tak ane vther prenteis quhill thair be thrie year owtrin of his former prenteis, to the effect that the awld prenteis may be habill to teache the secund, for eschewing of vnsufficient work, under the pane of five pund. Item, that nane be maid maister of the said craft except he haif bene ane prenteis for fyve yeir and seruet ane frieman for meitt and fie thre yeiris thairafter, or ellis marie ane burges dochter, vnder the payne of ten pund to be payet be the deykin and quarter maisters that admitts him maister and als meikill be thame that procures in contrair heirof.'[1]

During the year which ended on 24th March 1586–7, thirty-four persons were enrolled as burgesses, eight as guild brethren, and thirteen as burgesses and guild brethren.[2]

Production of the ticket of burgess-ship or guild-brotherhood was the regular evidence of being a burgess or guild brother, but these tickets were occasionally lost; and as the records of admission do not appear to have been kept with scrupulous accuracy about this time, questions were sometimes raised as to whether individuals had been admitted, and as to whether their children

[1] C. R. vol. viii. fol. 70, 71.    Extracts C. R. vol. iv. pp. 480–484.
[2] Register of Burgesses and Guild Brethren.

were entitled to the privileges of the bairns of burgesses or guild
brethren.  On such occasions the council seem to have taken a
liberal view, and when the father had filled positions which pre-
supposed his being a burgess or guild brother, they admitted his
children on payment of the modified dues exigible from the children
of burgesses and guild brethren.  Of this there are illustrations in
the case of the family of James Wood, sometime deacon of the
bakers, on 12th April 1587, and of Robert Forret, sometime bailie
of the burgh, on 12th May 1587.[1]

On 4th July 1587 the convention of burghs in Dundee took
into consideration a complaint by the deacons of crafts of that
burgh in regard to the prejudice sustained by all the burghs by
the resorting and residence of all kinds of craftsmen in the suburbs,
who enjoyed as great privilege as freemen subject to taxations and
all burdens imposed on the burghs.  Thereafter the burgh of Edinburgh was advised to represent the complaint in the approaching
Parliament, and to desire 'remeid' to be provided.[2]

On 28th July 1587 the following addition was ordered by the
town council to be made to the burgess oath:

'Heir I protest before God and your lordschips that I profes and allow
with my hairt the trew relligioun quhilk at this present is publictly preachet
within this realme and authorizitt be the lawes thairof, and sall abyde thairatt
and defend the sam to my lyves end, detesting the Romayne relligioun callit
papistry.'[3]

On 29th July 1587 the Act of Parliament 1587, c. 119, was
passed to encourage Flemish craftsmen to settle in Scotland and
manufacture 'searges, growgrams, fusteanis, bombesies, stemmingis

---

[1] C. R. vol. viii. fols. 82, 83, and 88.  See also the cases of Robert Gal-
braith's widow and children, 27th September 1588 [C. R. vol. viii. fol. 183];
Margaret Aitkenhead, 17th September 1591 [C. R. vol. ix. fol. 104]; the
children of John Arnot and Andrew Symsoun, 22d September 1591 [C. R.
vol. ix. fol. 105]; the widow and children of James Johnston, merchant, 12th
February 1613 [C. R. vol. xii. fol. 112].

[2] Printed Records of Convention, vol. i. p. 238.

[3] C. R. vol. viii. fol. 98.  Extracts C. R. vol. iv. p. 497.

beyis, covertouris of beddis, and vthers.' By this act the settlers
were bound to take no apprentices save Scottish boys and girls, and
before any others the burgess bairns of Edinburgh.  The settlers,
with their servants and apprentices, were relieved from all taxations, subsidies, tributes, impositions, watching, warding, and stenting and all other charges within and without burgh, and the
magistrates of Edinburgh, and other burghs in which the Flemings
settled, were ordained to make them burgesses of their burgh, and
to grant them the liberty thereof during their remaining.[1]

The accounts of the dean of guild for the year to Michaelmas
1587 show that the total dues paid for the admission of burgesses
and guild brethren during the year amounted to £828, 1s. 4d.
Scots, but furnish no details.[2]

On 29th December 1587 the council ratified the act of June
1583 against unfreemen and others.[3]

. The following act affords a curious illustration of the care which
was taken to prevent guild brethren from engaging in work which
was considered derogatory to the guild.  On 5th March 1587–8
Robert Vernour, skinner, having been admitted guild brother,
became bound

'to obserue and keip the lawes and consuetudes of burgh concerning the gild
brether thairof, and to desist and ceis fra all tred and occupatioun in his awin
persoun that is nocht comely and decent for the rank and honesty of ane guild
brother, and that his wyfe and seruandis sall vse and exerce na poynt of commoun cwikry outwith his awin howse, and namely that thai sall nocht sell nor
cary any meitt disches or courses throw the toun to priuatt chalmeris, hostillare
howssis, or ony vther pairt owtwith his awin howse, vnder quhatsumevir cullour or pretense, nor pas to brydellis or banketis within or without this burgh
to vse the occupatioun of commoun cuikry, or yitt be sene in the streitis with
thair aiprounes and seruiets as commoun cuikis and thair seruands vses to
do, and that vnder the payn of tynsall of his liberty and fredome of ane gild
brother without all favour for euir.'[4]

---

[1] A. P. S. vol. iii. p. 507.
[2] Accounts of the Deans of Guild.
[3] C. R. vol. viii. fol. 131.
[4] C. R. vol. viii. fol. 142.   Extracts C. R. vol. iv. pp. 514, 515.

During the year which ended on 24th March 1587–8, sixty-one persons were enrolled as burgesses, eleven as guild brethren, and ten as burgesses and guild brethren.[1]

On 19th June 1588 the provost, bailies, dean of guild, and deacons of the crafts ordained that when any officers or servants of the burgh, who got their burgess-ship as in right of their office, were deprived of office for misbehaviour, they should forfeit their burgess-ship, and they, their wives and children, should not enjoy the benefit and privilege thereof in all time thereafter, unless admitted of new and sworn and received thereto.[2] On 11th October in the same year,[3] and again on 22d October 1589,[4] the act of June 1583 against unfreemen and others was ratified and proclaimed.

The accounts of the dean of guild for the year to Michaelmas 1588 show that the total dues paid for the admission of burgesses and guild brethren during the year amounted to £522, 13s. 4d. Scots, but furnish no details.[5]

On 6th November 1588 the council ordained

'that na burgessis be resauet nor admittet in tyme cuming bot sic as sall compeir the tyme of thair admissioun before the counsall with sufficient airmour, sic as thai will tak thame to for serving of the Kingis grace and the toun, to witt, other with hakbut and furnessing belanging thairto, sic as flaske, pulder and bullet, and ane murrioun, or ellis with jak, knapskall, speir or pik, and mak fayth that the said airmour is thair awin proper geir, and this by and attoure thair sworde; and quhen euir thai sall want the said airmour in tyme convenient, to be poyndet or wardet for ane vnlaw of fyve pund.'[6]

[1] Register of Burgesses and Guild Brethren.      [2] C. R. vol. viii. fol. 158.
[3] C. R. vol. viii. fol. 178.      [4] C. R. vol. ix. fol. 12.
[5] Accounts of the Deans of Guild.
[6] C. R. vol. viii. fol. 186.      Extracts C. R. vol. iv. p. 532.

## CHAPTER III.[1]

On 14th April 1589 the convention of burghs ordained that 'na maner of chepman' or other unfree person, inwith or outwith burghs, should in open market or otherwise sell 'ony maner of staipill gudes in greit or small,' under the penalty of confiscation of the goods[2]; and two years afterwards each burgh was directed to report its diligence in executing the act.[3]

On 17th October, 1589, the town council resolved

'that na maner of personis, men or wemen, huiksteris or topsteris of fysche, butter, eggis, cheise, or vther siclyke stufe, quhilk are not friemen or friemenis wyffes, hald ony maner of bwrdes or craymes to sell siclyke stuf vpoun the hiegait, nor vnder stayres, bot in thair awin howsses, fra this day furth, vnder the payne of xviij s. ; and that nane of the saidis huiksteris or topsteris be sene in the merket amongis byers or sellaris ony tyme of day, vnder the payne of standing in the jogs ane haill day ; and that thai bye na butter or cheise bot on the merket day, and quhen the merket is ceist, vnder the payne of xviij s. ; and siclyke that na vther/ personis, vnfriemen, hald the said stufe in privat howsses to sell, bot that thai bring and present the samyn in oppin merket, and thair to wey and sell the samyn under the payne of escheitt thairof.[4]

By the convention of burghs held at Montrose on 9th June 1591,

'it wes statut and ordanit that all merchandis resortand to France, Flanderis, or any pairt of the Easter seyis, sall at na tyme herefter depairt fra ony

---

[1] The preceding chapters were revised for the press by Sir James Marwick, and the sheets were nearly all printed off many years ago. What follows consists almost entirely of material collected or noted by Sir James for continuation of the work.

[2] Printed Records of Convention, vol. i. p. 304.

[3] *Ibid.*, p. 358.

[4] C. R. vol. ix. fol. 18.

U

burght or sey port of this realme without speciall tikitis, wnder the sub-scriptionis of the denis of gild, quhair thei ar, and quhair nane is, to be subscryuit be the magistratis of the burght or sey portis quhairfra thei pas ; and the saidis tikitis to contene speciall mentioun of thair fredome and actuall residence within frie borrowis or sey portis as said is ; and that ilk merchand present thair saidis tikittis to the conseruitour in Flanderis to be anis sene and buikit in his buikis allanerlie ; and in vther pairtis, sic as France and Easter seyis, to be schawin and producit to the maist discreit merchand beand in the schippis for the tyme, passing to ony of the portis thairof, quha salbe halden to mak report of his diligence to the deine of gild or magistratis of the burght and sey portis quhairfra he passis as said is.[1]

### On 3rd November 1591 the town council

'Vnderstanding that dyveris personis quha ar maid burgess of this burgh takis nane or littill regaird to the keiping of thair aith gevin at thair ressaving, and in speciall of that pairt thairof concerning the bearing of burding in extents with thair nychtbouris, quhilk cummis to pass threw the wanting of the extract and copy of the forme of thair said aith, quhilk gif thay haid or wald raise, it micht serve to call to thair rememberance of thair dewitie, and mak thame inexcusabill in that pairt, and thairfoir it is thocht expedient, statute and ordanit that the forme of thair said aith be at lenth insert or extractit with the act of creatioun of all personis that sal be maid burgessis in tyme cumming, and delyuerit to the pairtie vpoun thair expensis, quhilk sal be ten schillingis, to be payit to the commoun clerk for the extract of the said aith and act of admissioun.'[2]

### On 19th January 1592–3 the town council,

'for dyuers guid causis and consideratiouns moving thame hes thocht ex-pedient, statute and ordanit that nane of the townis almous contributiounis or collectiounis sall be gevin or grantet in tyme coming to ony maner of persounis that hes or sal heirafter exeme thameselffis be any kynd of preve-leges frome beiring of burding with thair nychtbouris in extenting, watche-ing, wairding and siclyke ; and als the saidis prouest, baillies, and counsall be thir presentis ratefeyis and apprevis the actis and statutes maid of before aganis the gevin of burgesschipis or gildries gratis, with this additioun, that quhatsumeuir of the counsall or [others] bering offices for the tyme sall consent to the gevin thairof in tyme cuming, directlie or indirectlie, without the reall payment of the sowmes that aucht to be gevin thairfore, it sall be lesum to thair successouris, prouest, baillies, dene of gild, thesaurer, and

---

[1] Printed Records of Convention, vol. i. pp. 358–9. Subsequent acts to similar effect will be found in the records, as on 5th July 1597 (*Ibid.*, vol. ii. pp. 4, 5), and 1st July 1598 (*Ibid.*, pp. 25, 26).

[2] C. R. vol. ix. fol. 119.

counsall to call thame for the samyn, and caus thame mak payment of thair awin purses of the dewties quhilk suld haif bene payet be the personis admittet be thame without payment as said is.'[1]

On 5th June 1592 parliament ratified previous acts whereby it had been ordained

'that na persoun within this realme suld exercise the traffique of merchandice bot the burgesses of frie burrowis, quhilkis have nocht bene nor yit ar obseruit, be reasone that thair is na penaltie irrogat to the personis contravenaris thereof,'[2]

and therefore it was further enacted

'that whatsoeuir exercisis the said traffique of merchandice nocht being frie burgess thair haill guidis and geir sall becum in escheat, the ane half to our souerane lord, and the vther half to the burgh whais commissioner or collectour sall first apprehend the same.'[3]

It was farther ordained that all manner of persons dwelling in burghs and exercising traffic or merchandise therein, whether admitted free burgesses or not, should bear their part of 'all taxtis, stentis and taxationis, watching and warding, in all dewties and services pertening to our soverane lord, the weill of the realme, and the utilitie of the burgh,' subject to the condition that it should be lawful to the King to exempt 'ane persoun of ilk craft for his hienes particular usé and service'; and it was farther provided that the act should not be prejudicial to the privileges and immunities of the members of the College of Justice.'[4]

On the preamble that the exercise of craftsmen in the suburbs of free burghs was not only hurtful to the lieges, 'for the insufficiencie of the wark,' but also gave occasion to prentices and servants in free burghs undutifully to leave their masters, and that the free craftsmen dwelling in the burgh were injured, seeing they

[1] C. R. vol. ix. fol. 182.
[2] See the Acts 1466, c. 1; 1487, c. 13; *supra*, pp. 44, 51; and 1567, c. 56. A. P. S. vol. iii. p. 41.
[3] 1592, c. 74.  A. P. S. vol. iii. p. 578.
[4] 1592, c. 75.  A. P. S. vol. iii. p. 578.

bore a great part of the charges of the burgh and the advantage
of the work that should relieve them was drawn away to the
suburbs, parliament likewise enacted that

'thair sal be na exercise of craftis in the suburbis adiacent to the saidis burrowis, but that the samyn sall ceis in all tymes heirefter, and that it sal be
lesum to the provost and baillies of the saidis burrowis and thair depuittis
and officiares, to intromett with all the warkis that sal be fund wrocht or in
.wirking, quhether the materiallis thairof appertene to the craftisman him
selff, or to whatsumevir vther persoun, and to escheat the samyn to be
applyit to the commoun warkis of the burgh nixt adiacent to the saidis
suburbis.'[1]

On 13th June 1593 the convention of burghs directed the
several burghs to cause the above act of parliament to be put to
execution and to elect commissioners and collectors to that
effect;[2] and two days later it was ordained

'that na burgh admit or resaue ony person to be thair burges in tyme cuming
that is nocht ane actuall induellar thairof, vnder the pane of ane vnlaw of
ane hundreth poundis to the burrowis; and quhair ony sic persounis ar
alreddy admittit, that thay be callit and causit to cum and remane within
the burgh or els depryvett of thair libertie, vnder the pane foresaid, and ilk
burgh to repoirtt thair diligence heirvpoun in the next general conventioun
of burrowis vnder the pane of twentie poundis.'[3]

The convention likewise at their meeting on 13th June

'thocht expedient, statute and ordanit, and for ane vniformitie to be haid
amang thame selves, vniuersally aggreit that quhensoeuer it sal happin ane
burgess and frieman of ony burgh, be the magistratis and counsall thairof, to
be depryuet *simpliciter* of his libertie and friedom within the samyn, for
vsurpatioun contrair the common weill of thair burgh, breking of his ayth,
or for ony vther just and reasonabll cause quhilk mycht mereit the said pane of
deprivatioun, that than and in that caice na vther burgh in this realme, knawand
of his deprivatioun foresaid, tak vpoun thame to resaue him in thair fellowschip
and admit him thair burges, vnder the pane of ane hundreth poundis to be
payit to the burgh in the quhilk he was depryueit, and quhow sone it sal
happin his deprivatioun to be notifeit vnto thame that salhappin to have

---

[1] 1592, c. 76.   A. P. S. vol. iii. p. 579.
[2] Printed Records of Convention, vol. i. p. 404.
[3] *Ibid.*, pp. 413-4.

resauit him, nocht knawing of the samyn befoir, that they incontinent call him befoir thame and depryue him of his libertie resaueit, vnder the pane abone written, to be payit as said is.' [1]

## On 22nd June 1594 the town council

'being convenit anent the supplicatioun gevin in before thame be Adame Haliburtoune, merchant, beiring that he hes to his lawfull spouse, Katherein Nesbet, dochter lawfull to umquhile Hew Nesbet, merchant, burges and gild brother of this brugh, be quhais richt he is alredy maid burges of this brugh, and haiffing desyret the dene of gild and his counsall to admit him gild brother, be the samyn richt they have refusit him becaus he is nocht responsall presentlie in guides the soume of ane thousand merkis, conforme to the actis of counsall laitlie maid thairanent, albeit it be of weritie that sen he mareit the said Katherein he was of far gritter substance in lands and guidis abone the valour of the said soume, and hes nocht tyne the samyn in his defalt or throw his misbehaiviour bot alanerlie throw schipwrak at Veire, as is notourlie knawin, and the said act can nocht be extendit aganis the rycht quhilk was competent to him lang before the making thairof, althocht that throw seiknes and troublis and throw his absence furthe of the realm he hes nocht socht the samyn quhill now, and thairfoir desiring command to be gevin to the said dene of gild and his counsall to admit him to his lawfull richt of gildrie, as at lenthe is contenit in the said supplicatiouns, the said baillies, counsall, and deykins, understanding the said Adame was anis of habilitie and substance agreing to the calling of ane gildbrother, and tynt nocht the samyn in his defalt, thairfoir and for dyuers vther guid caussis and consideratiouns moueing thame thairfoir, thai ordane the dene of gild and his counsall to admit and resaue him gildbrother of this burgh be rycht forsaid.' [2]

The act of parliament passed in June 1592 'aganes unfrie trafficque and the crafts in suburbs,' was again taken under consideration by the convention of burghs on 29th June 1594, when it was ordained that at next convention each burgh, 'every ane within their awn bounds,' should produce farther diligence in putting the act to execution.[3] At the ensuing meeting on 27th

[1] Printed Records of Convention, vol. i. p. 402. The latter part of this act 'aganis sic as ar admitted burgessis in any burgh and ar nocht actuall indwellare thairof' was ratified by the convention on 3rd July 1594, and each burgh was ordained to put the same to execution and to report their diligence to next convention (*Ibid.*, p. 446). Ratified also on 5th July 1597 (*Ibid.*, vol. ii. p. 4).

[2] C. R. vol. x. fol. 17.　　[3] Printed Records of Convention, vol. i. p. 436.

June 1595 the convention 'findis them selffis to have bene verry slak and negligent' concerning the execution of the act in time past, and gave instructions for more strict observance of its provisions in future.[1] Three days later the subject was again discussed and certain proceedings were resolved upon, a tax on the burgh being imposed to meet expenditure.[2]

On 5th July 1596 the convention of burghs

'vnderstanding that thair is dyuers foirstalleris and regratouris quha resortis to fairis and mercattis of free burrowis, calling thame selffis burgessis and fremen of burrowis, thay nather beand burgessis but plane forstalleris and regratouris, to the grit hurt and preiudice of burrowis, and speciale of the brugh of Aberdein, at the fairis and mercattis of the schirefdome of the samyn; for remeid quhairof it is thocht expedient, statute and ordanit that all merchandis, burgessis of quhatsumevir brugh within this realm, quha cumis to the somer fairis and mercattis of the said brugh and schirefdome of Abirdein, or to ony vther fre fair or mercatt within the libertie of ane frie brugh, that thay bring and produce with them owther thair ticket of bur-geschip, or ellis ane sufficient testimoniall of the deyne of gild of thair brugh testefeing thame to be burgessis actuall induelleries and residentis of that brugh quhair thay are fre; and gif it be ane fremanis seruand that comes to the saidis fairis and mercattis, by and attour the tiket or testemoniall of his maisteris fredome and residence, to bring and produce alsua with him his maisteris attestatioun, beiring that he is his actuall seruand remayneing in hous at bed and buird with him; and quhasoevir dois in the contrair heirof that it salbe lesum to ilk fre brugh to persew, arreist and vse him as ane unfreman, regratour or forstaller.'[3]

On 7th July 1597 the convention ratified an act passed, on 24th April 1595, by commissioners of burghs in the west who had been appointed to treat on affairs for the weal of the burghs, to the effect that all burgesses should be resident in their respective towns and bear their share of the common charges;

'and siclyk the saidis commissioneris hes statute and ordanit that in tyme cuming thair salbe na persoun maid freman and burges in ony of the saidis touns bot sic as ar actuall induelleris, resident within the samyn, and mak securitie for remaning and induelling thairinto and doing of his dewty of the

[1] Printed Records of Convention, vol. i. p. 454.
[2] Ibid., pp. 462–3. See also acts passed on 2nd July 1596 (Ibid., p. 476).
[3] Ibid., pp. 486–7.

samyn, as becumes ane freman ; and incais he makis nocht residence to tyne his fredome *ipso facto*, and to be repute vnfre in all respectis fra thine forth. *Item,* that ewerie ane of thair touns sal be thair commissoneris geve up ane report of the haill nameis of all vnfremen that vsis traffik of fremen within thair boundis to the nixt generall assemble of burrowis that thai may be. persewit be the agent thairfoir.'[1]

On the roll of burgesses for the year 1596 occurs the name of Principal Rollock, who, on 1st October of that year, was admitted a burgess and gild brother of the city, by right of Helen Barroun, his spouse.[2]

On 29th June 1598 parliament ratified an act of the privy council 'anent provisioun of armoure,' dated 26th February preceding, whereby it was directed that the provosts, bailies and council dwelling within every burgh should take order within their respective bounds

'that euerie ane of thair nychtbouris, burgessis, induellaris within thair toun, worth fyve hundreth pundis of frie geir, be furnist with ane compleit licht corslet, ane pik, ane halbert or tua handit suorde or ells ane muscat with forcat, bendrole and heidpece ; and that for euerie licht corslat and pik within thair burgh thair be tua muskattis.'[3]

Keeping in view the rules as to burgesses being resident in the burgh the town council on 26th September 1599

'fyndis be the actis of the burrowes and off this burgh that Johnne Fairlie of Colinestoune, desyrand to be burges and gild of this burgh, aucht nocht to be resauet nor admitted thairto quhill he be first actuall indwellar and resident within this burgh.'[4]

On 30th November 1599 the town council

'for dyuers caussis and consdderationes moveing thame, grantis and gives full licence, power, and libertie to Duncan Dunkiesone, tailyeour, and Helen Broun, his spous, to vse and occupy the libertie and fredome of ane burges of this burgh within all the boundis and jurisdictioun thairof, induring all the dayes of thair lyftymes, inhibiting and dischargeing thair dene of gild and

---

[1] Printed Records of Convention, vol. ii. pp. 11, 12.

[2] C. R. vol. x. fol. 89.

[3] 1598, c. 13 ; A. P. S. iv. pp. 168-9. The act of privy council was again ratified by act of parliament 1600, c. 32 (*Ibid.*, p. 235).

[4] C. R. vol. x. fol. 249.

officeris of all trubling and molesting of thame in the peceabill possessioun thairof induring the said space.'[1]

On 25th January 1600 the town council directed

'David Williamsoun, dene of gild, to caus trye [them] that vses the tred of ane burges and gild, and are nocht admitted frie thairto, and to pvneis thame with all rigour according to the touns acts.'[2]

The following act of council was passed on 15th January 1602:—

'The baillies, counsall and deykins of crafts findis that the meane and small dewteis tayne and payit for making of burgessis and gild brether of this burgh gevis occasioun to sindry persouns of small substance and less industrie to cum and remayne within this burgh, and to seik to be admittet frie within the samyn, quha in schort spaice thereafter falling in pouertie, ar verray chargeabill to the toun be thameselffis, thair wiffis, children, and seruandis, and sic as thai tak in hous with thame, throw sustening and supporting of thame in thair necessiteis with gritter sowmes nor euir thai payet for thair burgesschipis; and als fyndis that the inhabitantis of the suburbs and villages about this burgh takis gritter dewteis nor the toun dois of all sic persounis as thai permitt to vse any occupatioun amangis thame, quhairby the honour, dignitie, and estimatioun of this burgh is vilipendit and disgraceit, being ane frie burgh royall, and thairfore hes thocht expedient, statute and ordanet that na maner of persounis be resauet or admittet burges or gild brother of this burgh in tyme cuming but sic as sall pay and delyuer to the deyne of the samyn for the tyme, in name of the guid toun, the sowme and dewteis following, that is to say, ilk persoun for his burgesschip the soum of ane hundreth markis vsuall money of this realme, by and attoure the comoun and vset dewteis for his vpsett, and to pay for his gildrie the soum of ane hunder pundis money foresaid, and with prouisioun alswa that thai be persouns in substance and conversatioun worthie of the said plaices, and siclyke it is expreslie provydet that thir presentis be na wayes preiudiciall to the richtis and prevelegeis of burges bayrnis, thair sonnes, nor husbands of thair dochteris, nor to the prenteissis of the saidis burgessis and gild brether quha sall pay the awld dewtie vset and wont allanerlie, conform to the decriett arbitrall; and as to sic persounis as ar burgessis of this burgh before the daitt heirof, and as yitt ar nocht gild brether, they to be admittet to the said gildrie, beand fund worthie and qualefeyet for the same, for the sowm of fourty pundis allanerlie, without preiudice of the bayrnes and prenteissis of burgessis and gild brether as said is. And becaus thai fynd that sindrie deykinis of craftis hes in tymes bygane admittet dyuers persounis frie with thair craft before thai wer maid

[1] C. R. vol. x. fol. 258.          [2] C. R. vol. x. fol. 267.

burgessis of this burgh, contrar to thair seill of caus, and to the hurt and preiudice of the toun, thairfore it is fund expedient, statute and ordanet that na deykins of craftis tak vpoun thame in tyme cuming to admitt or resaue any maner of persoun frie to thair craft before he be creattet and admittet burges of this burgh, and schaw and produce before him and his brether his tikket of burgesschip; and gif it sall happin any person to be fund resauet frie with his craft fra this tyme furth that is nocht burges as said is, it is statute and ordanet that he that sall be fund deykin of that craft for the tyme quhen the falt is challenget sall pay to the tounis thesaurer in name of the toun the sowme of twenty pund money vnforgevin.'[1]

On 10th February 1602 the town council

'findis expedient, grantis and ordanis that all sic persones as ar or hes bene auld servandis to ane merchand or craftis man, diligent and faythfull in ther calling and weill reportit of all men, and hable to beir burding in the toun, sall be ressauit and maid burgessis therof for payment of the double of all deuties, . . . with all vther deuties usuallie payit be ane prenteis of their calling quhan he is admittit burgess; and it is fund and declarit that nane sall be reput nor haldin for ane auld servand bot sic as hes servit with ane maister burgess of this burgh, haill and togither be the space of aucht yeris continuallie, and that he was servet vther aucht yeris with that or ane uther maister burgess as said is of his occupation; and the premisses being sufficiently tryit and provin, ordanis the deanes of gild, present and to cum, and his brethren and assessors, to ressaue and admit them burgesses upon the deuteis foirsaides.'[2]

With reference to previous acts, anent the mater of vnfre traffiqueris, saillers without tickettis, regrateris and foirstallers and outlandis burgessis,' the convention of burghs on 5th July 1602,

'forther statutis and ordanis that na brugh tak vpoun thame to grant ony owirsicht, tollerance or dispensatioun to thair outlandis burgessis to dwell or remayne without the burgh, or vse ony tred or traffik, without thai haue thair actuall remaining and residence within the brugh, and that thai ressaue na taxatioun nor guid deid of thair depryweit burgessis, bot that thai caus thair nameis to be delet furth of thair buikis and call in thair burges tickettis, cancell and destroy the samyn, that vther burrowis be nocht abusit be the saidis deprywit burgessis; and the brugh quhais magistratis salbe fund to haue contrauenit this present ordinance at ony tyme heirafter to pay ane vnlaw of ane hundrethe pundis to the burrowis *toties quoties.*'[3]

---

[1] C. R. vol. xi. fol. 74, 75.

[2] C. R. vol. xi. fol. 77, 78.

[3] Printed Records of Convention, vol. ii. p. 128. See also pp. 156, 174, 196.

During the year which ended on 24th March 1605, sixty-one persons were enrolled as burgesses, eight as guild brethren, and twenty-one as burgesses and guild brethren.[1]

On 27th November 1605 the deacon of the wrights was found to have done wrong in admitting a slater to the freedom of his craft before he was made burgess, contrary to the act of 15th January 1602, and he was therefore decerned in an unlaw of £20, which was modified to £12. At the same time the council ratified and approved of the said act in all points, but extended the penalty for contravention to £100 in all time coming.[2]

On 7th July 1606 the convention of burghs at Dundee renewed the act against outland burgesses.[3]

On 11th July 1606 parliament approved and confirmed all the acts of parliament and laws, with all freedoms, privileges, immunities, and liberties granted to burghs royal in all time preceding.[4]

During the year which ended on 24th March 1606, sixty-nine persons were enrolled as burgesses, sixteen as guild brethren, and seventeen as burgesses and guild brethren.[5]

On 2d January 1607 the council prohibited any old servants to be made burgesses under the act of 10th February 1602, until the council were further advised.[6]

On 8th May 1607 the town council ordained proclamation to be made through the burgh, discharging all unfreemen

'to pas thro the burgh and libertie thereof at ony tyme heirafter with ony claith, plaids, or merchandise to sell but on the mercat day and tyme, under payne of confiscatioun of thair guids and punishment of thair persons at the will of the magistrats.'[7]

---

[1] Register of Burgesses and Guild Brethren.
[2] C. R. vol. xi. fol. 189.
[3] Printed Records of Convention, vol. ii. p. 212.
[4] 1606, c. 15.  A. P. S. vol. iv. p. 288.
[5] Register of Burgesses and Guild Brethren.
[6] C. R. vol. xi. fol. 221.
[7] C. R. vol. xi. fol. 228.

The convention of burghs at Dumbarton on 1st July 1607 renewed the act against outland burgesses, and received the reports of several burghs thereanent.[1]  And on 11th August in the same year parliament ratified all previous acts of parliament and laws in favour of free royal burghs.[2]  On the same day an act was passed by which,

'considering the greate hurte and skaith daylie sustenit be the burgessis, inhabitantis of his Majesteis royall burrowes wha vnderlyis and beiris all burdingis imposit vpoun the estaitt of burrowes in all his Majesteis seruices, throw the continuall incresce of vnfrie traffiquerris duelland in diuerse partis of this realme, nocht being burgessis of the saidis royall burrowes, and neuirtheless keip and haldis oppin buthis, buyis and sellis merchandice, and vtherwayis vses the liberties and privileges of frie burgessis as gif they wer burgessis and actuall residentis within the saidis royall burrowes, in manifast defraude of our souerane lordis customes, and to the preudice of the liberteis of the saidis frie royall burrowes ; and thairfoir statutis and ordinis that all vnfrie persones nocht beand actuall burgessis of the saidis frie royall burrowes, wha beiris nocht burding and payes nocht taxt and stent to his Majestie sall desist and ceise fra vsing of ony trade of merchandice, or of the liberteis and privileges foirsaidis of the saidis frie royal burrowes, vnder the panis contenit in the actis of parliament maid anent vnfrie traffiqueris of befoir.'

The same act also authorized letters of horning to be direct upon all acts and decreets of burghs given at their convention, between burgh and burgh and burgesses of free burghs, upon a simple charge of ten days without calling of party.[3]

During the year which ended on 24th March 1607, ninety-nine persons were enrolled as burgesses, nine as guild brethren, and sixteen as burgesses and guild brethren.[4]

On 1st January 1608 the council found Master Robert Stevin, sometime doctor in the High School and burgess of the burgh,

---

[1] Printed Records of Convention, vol. ii. p. 233.
[2] 1607, c. 12.   A. P. S. vol. iv. p. 375.
[3] 1607, c. 13.   A. P. S. vol. iv. p. 375.
[4] Register of Burgesses and Guild Brethren.

'to haif contravenit his ayth of burgesschip in the takyng vp of ane grammer schole in the Kannogaitt, and in drawing the burges bayrnis of this burgh frome thair hie schole to himself, in contrair the liberteis of this burgh and contrer to his ayth of burgesschip, and thairfoir decernis him ane vnlaw of j^c li., and ordanis him to remayne in ward quhill the sam be payet.'[1]

On 5th July 1608 the convention of burghs at Selkirk renewed the act against outland burgesses.[2]

During the year which ended on 24th March 1608, one hundred and ten persons were enrolled as burgesses, nineteen as guild brethren, and fourteen as burgesses and guild brethren.[3]

On 24th June 1609 parliament, on the narrative that the course intended by the king,

'for dischargeing noblemen and gentlemen to be electit provestis and magistraitis of burrowis (whereof nane sould be capable bot burgessis, actual traffikeres, and inhabitantis of the saidis burrowis) hes tane sic effect as is maist necessar for preservatioun of the liberties and good estait of the saidis burrowis, and hindering the dissipatioun of thair common good and perverting of their privileges ; for remeid whereof' [it was ordained]—
'that na man sall in ony tyme cuming be capable of provestrie or magistracie within ony burgh of this realme, nor to be electit to ony of the saidis offices within a burgh bot merchandis and actual traffikeris inhabiting within the saidis burghis alanerlie and na otheris, and that the saidis magistratis of burrowis to be heirafter elected, and thair commissionaris of parliament, shall have and wear at parliamentis, conventionis and other solemne tymes and meetingis, when the dignitie shall require it, sic comelie and decent apparell as his Majestie shall prescryve, conuenient for thair rank and estait, whereby they may be decerned from other commoun burgessis, and be mair reverenced be the people subject to thair charge.'[4]

While the council exacted the prescribed penalties from those who carried on business without being burgesses and freemen, they seem to have sometimes given defaulters indulgence by agreeing to credit them with their penalties exacted in the event of their entering as burgesses within a limited time. Of this there is an illustration in an act dated 25th August 1609, when

[1] C. R. vol. xi. fol. 244.
[2] Printed Records of Convention, vol. ii. p. 250.
[3] Register of Burgesses and Guild Brethren.
[4] 1609, c. 15.   A. P. S. vol. iv. p. 435.

'James Nevein and Alexander Ramsay in Leyth payet euery ane of thame thair vnlaw of twenty li. quhairin thai wer decernit, with provisioun in cais thai mak thameselffis burgessis of this burgh betuix and Michaelmes next that the sam be allowit in thair burges dewty.'[1]

The conventions of burghs at Cupar on 4th July 1609, at Crail on 3rd July 1610, at Stirling on 2d July 1611, and at Arbroath on 7th July 1612, renewed the act against outland burgesses, and received the reports of several burghs as to their diligence in enforcing the act.[2]

On 19th May 1613 the Marquis of Hamilton was made burgess and guild brother.[3]

On 7th July in the same year the convention of burghs at Dunbar received reports from several burghs as to their proceedings against outland burghs and unfree traders, and renewed their instructions.[4]

On 16th July 1613 the Lord President and the Bishops of St. Andrews and Glasgow were made burgesses and guild brethren, and dry confections, wine, and cherries were appointed to be given to them.   On 18th August 1614, John Murray of Lochmaben and other gentlemen of his Majesty's bedchamber were made burgesses and guild brethren.   On 13th August 1616 the Duke of Lennox and the noblemen with him were appointed to be burgesses and guild brethren.[5]

On 6th July 1614 the convention of burghs at Kirkcaldy received reports as to diligence done against several outland burgesses in several burghs.[6]

---

[1] C. R. vol. xii. fol. 10..

[2] Printed Records of Convention, vol. ii. pp. 273, 288, 310, 342.

[3] Register of Burgesses and Guild Brethren.

[4] Printed Records of Convention, vol. ii. pp. 402, 403.

[5] Register of Burgesses and Guild Brethren.

[6] Printed Records of Convention, vol. ii. pp. 446–7.

On 11th February 1620 a committee was ordained to report as
to 'the raising of the burgess-ships, gildships, and the prenteissis
against Wednesday next.'[1]   On 8th March, in the same year, the
council appointed a committee to reason and report 'anent the
hechting' of the burgess-ships and guildships.[2]

On 7th July 1626 the Marquis of Hamilton, the Earl of Cassillis,
and several other gentlemen, were appointed burgesses and guild
brethren.[3]   On 16th November 1627 the council passed the following act :

'The same day, forsameikle as the necessitie of the present effaires and of
the preservatioun of the burgh against forraine or intestein invasioun requyres,
and for the better encouragement of the neighbours of this burgh it is fitt that
thair be ane publict airmorie provydit in some publict hous appointed to that
vse, that the same may be readie quhen occasioun sall present of anie publict
seruice : thairfore statuttis and ordanis that ane voluntar contributioun and
supplie salbe maid through the neighbouris of this burgh, quha will voluntarie
offer the same, of such armour as they sall frielie give, and ordanis the deyne of
gild and his counsall to collect the same and put vp the same in the publick
armororie to be keiped thair to publick vse ; and ordanis theme to call and con-
veyne the neighbouris of this burgh before them and require thair voluntar
contributioun, and to mak inventar of ane buik of such armour as salbe gevin.
And als ordanis that in all tyme cumming ilk man quha is admitted burges of
this burgh ather be his birthricht, mariage, prenteischip or vtherwayes, sall give
to the publict armorie ane sufficient muskett, muskett staff and heidpeice, ane
bandilier.   And if the partie quha is admitted burges hes richt to the gildschip,
that then he present to the publict armorie ane corslett, pick, and heidpeice ;
and if any quha is admittit burges, haiving no richt to the gildschip the tyme of
his admissioun, at anie tyme therefter obtaine himselff maid gildbrother, then
and in that caice he salbe obleist and give to the publict armorie ane corslett,
pick, and heidpeice, by and attour that quhilk he gaive the tyme of his admissioun to be burges.   It is alwayes heirby provydit that, notwithstanding of
quhat salbe givin in to the publick airmorie, ilk burges and gildbrother salbe
bunden and obleist, conforme to his aith, to haue his awin airmour appointit to
him the tyme of his admissioun, and quhilk he presents as his awin, and keip
the samin as his awin to serue the guid toun as he salbe requyrit, conforme to
his aith.   And ordanis the deyne of gild and his successouris to have caire of
the publick airmorie, and to find out ane man to have the oversicht thairof for
preservatioun of the same frome roust and vther inconveniences.'[4]

---

[1] C. R. vol. xiii. fol. 100.          [2] C. R. vol. xiii. fol. 101.
[3] C. R. vol. xiv. fol. 7.          [4] C. R. vol. xiv. fol. 76–7.

On 18th April 1632 the Earl Marischall was made burgess and guild brother, and with him Lord Kilpont and others were allowed to be booked in the guild book.[1]   On 3d July 1632 the commissioners of burghs, at their convention in Montrose, passed the following act:

'There being maney persons of the merchand estate projectors of monopolies which are very prejudiciall to the interest of burrows, therefor it is ordained to be added to the burges oath that no freeman shall project any monopolies, directly or indirectly, prejudiciall to the burgh or burrows, and that none putt to their hands and give declarations in favours of any patent prejudicial to the 'merchand estate without advyce of the council of the burgh whereof he is a member.'[2]

And on 31st July 1633 the town council ordained the dean of guild to make the addition so ordered to their burgess oath which he administers to each burgess at his admission.[3]   At St. Andrews, on 7th July 1633, the convention of burghs passed an act whereby,

'for restraineing of unfree skippers dwelling at unfree ports, it is statute and ordained that in no tyme comeing merchands be partners either in ships or goods with the saids unfree skippers, under the paine of ane hundred pund and deprivation of their liberties.   And the said commissioners ordaines that all such burgesses as are for the present partners with them shall, betwixt and the next generall convention, free themselves of the ships belonging to them, or otherwayes draw them to their own ports, under the said paine.   And ordaines ilk commissioner to intimat the samen to their burghs, and ilk burgh to intimat the samen to their nighbours, and putt the samen to due execution, under the paine of fourty pound, and to report their diligence thereanent to the next general convention.'[4]

---

[1] C. R. vol. xiv. fol. 228.
[2] Printed Records of Convention, vol. iv. p. 531.
[3] C. R. vol. xiv. fol. 271.
[4] Printed Records of Convention, vol. iv. p. 536.   The commissioners who attended the convention at Edinburgh on 28th February 1662, 'considering the great prejudice the royall burrowis of this kingdome susteanes by taking pairtis of schippis or güidis with unfreemen leiving at unfree places within this kingdome, notwithstanding of severall actis of burrowis dischargeing the samyn, wndir the paine of ane hundreth pundis and los of thair freedome, and

In July 1635 the convention of burghs

'ordaines that when any outland person is admitted burges that he shall first make faith solemnly that he is not pursued be any other burgh, or be the agent in generall, for usurping against the libertyes of any other burgh, which declaration being taken and the person found to be pursued in manner forsaid, it shall not be lawfull to any burgh to admitt him before first he satisfie the desire of the said pursuit and become ane actual resident with them and find caution not to remove, under the paine of j^c lib. and deprivation of their liberties.[1]

On 22d April 1640, General Alexander Leslie was admitted burgess and guild brother.[2]   On 1st June 1640 the council passed the following act :

'The same day, forsameikle as the proveist, baillies, and counsall of this burgh, finding that ane gritt pairt of the burgessis and gild brether of this burgh, neglecting both thair aith givin at ther admissioun to the libertie of this burgh and thair bund dewtie in thir tymes of necessitie, quhairin they ar obleist before God for the weill of this burgh, hes to thair disgraice left this guid toun, leving the same exposed to all hasert, and in maner separatt themeselffis frome the rest of thair nichtbouris, in which cariadge if they sall continew they can nott be thocht worthie to bruik anie libertie within this burgh : Thairfore they haue statutt and ordaynitt that all persounes, burgessis and gild brether of this burgh, repair to the same betuixt and the sext of this instant, and mak ther actuall and continuall constant residence therin with the rest of thair nichtbours, that they may be readie at all occasiounes to vndergoe all such labour, haesert, and burdein as they, with the rest of thair nichtbours, sall be commandit, with certificatioun to theme if they sall failzie they sall be depryved of thair libertie of this burgh, and they and thers declaired vncapabell thairof in all tyme heirefter, and ordanis this to be intimat be sound of trumpett at the mercatt croce of this burgh, that none pretend ignorance.'[3]

On 28th January 1642 the following act was passed by the town council :

'The same day, forsameikle as the provest, baillies, and counsell finding that divers of their burgessis hes transported themselffis from hence and hes

---

in particular' the above act of July 1633, ordained that all these acts should be enforced, and directed that partnerships then existing with unfreemen should be terminated at the ensuing Whitsunday (*Ibid.*, vol. iii. p. 552).

[1] Printed Records of Convention, vol. iv. p. 539.

[2] C. R. vol. xv. fol. 129.

[3] C. R. vol. xv.

placed themselffis *animo remanendi* without the countrey, and yet does trade within this countrey, to the no small prejudice of the inhabitants of this brugh, and calling to mynd that the commissioneris of the borrowis hes by divers actis decerned and ordained that all non-residenting burgessis should be halden as unfremen, and finding that some of their burgessis resideing abroad does dayle vse trade in thir places, theirfoir decernis all such to be halden as unfriemen, and fra this tyme ar content that they sall make offer of their goods to the effect they may be sold in ane touns blok.   And if at any tyme heireftir any such sall trade in thir places, decernes their goods to be vsed as the goods of unfremen, and the actes of parliament to be put to executioun agains them.   And ordaines intimatioun and publicatioun heirof to be maid be towk of drum threw this brugh.'[1]

On 17th May 1643 a committee was appointed by the following act to consider as to increasing the fees payable on the entry of burgesses :

'The quhilk day the provest, baillies, dean of gild, counsell, and deakens of craftis being conveynit in counsell : Quhairas it being complenit upoun that the little pryce quhairwith the friedome of this burgh is sett occasiouns many poor people to suit the same, and quhairby the same is contemned be men of qualitie ; and it being universallie regraitted and thoght that the same aught to be highted : Thairfoir the counsell ordaines the provest, Edward Edgar, Robert Fleyming, and the rest of the baillies, deane of gild, old provest, Sir William Gray, John Trotter, Peter Blackburne, Robert Meiklejohne, James Denniestoun, Mitchell Gibsone, Andro Halyburtoun, James Rae, John Maknaght, James Cochrane, George Suittie, Thomas Chairtres, James Rucheid, John Binnie, David Douglas, Thomas Patersone, to meitt and convein and consider the expediencie of the said matter, and to report their advyse to the counsell thairanent ; as also ordaines the saids persones to take to their consideratioun the fewing of the South Loche and conditiouns thairupon.'[2]

On 25th February 1646 the following act was passed :

'The same day, the provest, baillies, and counsell, considering the great prejudice and los the good toun susteins by the multitude of friemen admitted on small or no pryce, ordaines that from hencefurth there be a totall restraint of admitting any burgessis except such as have just right thairto, till a committee of the counsell sall make ane report of quhat pryce they find expedient to be set doun as competent for the freedome and the counsell sall condiscend thairupon, and appoynts the baillies, dean of gild, thesaurer, Sir William Gray, Archibald Tod, Edward Edgar, John Bynnie, Andro Sympsoun,

---

[1] C. R. vol. xv. fol. 220.          [2] C. R. vol. xv. fol. 295.

Robert Achesoun, Robert Mackean, Gilbert Sommervell, Adam Lamb, Robert Meiklejohn, with James Twedie, Patrick Stenhoppis, and William Sklaitter, to meitt, convein, and report to the counsell.' [1]

And on 19th May in the same year the council

'appoyntis for highting the pryce of the gildrie and burgeship of this brugh, James Rucheid, baillie; George Suittie, dean of gild; Sir William Gray, old provest; Archibald Tod, Edward Edgar, John Brynnie, Robert Mackean, Adam Lamb, Gilbert Sommervell, James Twedie, Thomas Patersone, Robert Meiklejohne.'

On 14th August 1646 the council prohibited all burgesses from frequenting unfree places and selling goods there under a penalty.[2] On 27th August 1647 the council passed the following act:

'The same day, forsamekill as the provest, baillies, and counsell finding the great dammage and prejudice the towne suffered be admitting of burgessis and gild bretherne att such low pryces for the saids fredomes as they were of old accustomed to pay, quhairby the said fredome becomes contemptable and the towne overburthened with numbers of poore strangeres, quho bought thair said fredomes for the most pairt for no vther vse but to tape wyne and beir, they, vpone the tuentie-fourt day of Junij j^m vj^c fourtie and six yearis, after rype advyse, did condiscend that the louest pryce for quhilk the fredome of being maid burges could be sold for to a stranger sould be aught scoire poundis, togeather with ten poundis for armes by and attour thair vpsett, and the pryce of being admitted gildbrother to be tua hundreth and fourtie punds and sexten punds for armes, with thair vther ordinar dewes, and accordinglie gave verball ordour to thair deane of gild from thencefurth to admitt of no stranger to be maid burges or gild brother without paying the pryces afoirsaid for thair fredome, and were resolved to have maid ane ample act for that effect, quhilk act was to contein many vther clauses and conditiounes for the right ordouring of the bussiness of the friedome of the brugh, quhilks as yet are not fullie condiscendit on be reassoun of the troubles of the tyme and many vther incident occasiounes quhich have hindered the conclusioneis of the said act; conforme to quhilk verball ordour George Suittie, thane and now present dean of gild, with his counsell, have cairfullie and faithfullie performed thair dewtie in admitting no stranger burges bott vpone the conditiounes afoirsaid, thairfor the provest, baillies, and counsell doe heirby vnanimouslie approve and ratifie the proceidings of the said deane of gild and his counsell, as haveing done acceptable and guid service in all kynd, sicklyk as if the said act of counsell had at that tyme beane concludit and registrat in our buikes of counsell; and because the said act is not as yet

---

[1] C. R. vol. xvi. fol. 74-75.          [2] C. R. vol. xvi. fol. 104.

concludit, and that it is necessar that the said deane of gild and his counsell continue in ressaveing the said last pryce condiscendit on, thairfor, they heirby ordane him and his counsell to admitt of no strangers fra hencefurth to be burgessis or gild brether without paying the afoirsaid pryce of ane hundreth and threscoir of poundis for a burges, and ten pound for thair armes, and tua hundreth and fourtie pound for a gild brother, and sixtene pound for thair armes, by and attour thair vpsettis, ay and quhill the counsell sall discharge the samyne or give a warrand to the contrair; quhairanent thir presents sall be thair warrand.'[1]

On 3d September 1647 the Right Honourable Lieut.-General David Leslie and many other officers of the army were made burgesses and guild brethren.[2]　On 14th June 1650 the council appointed a committee

'to meitt and try quhat actis of burrowis and counsell ar maid for debarring of gratis burgessis, and to report with diligence, that ane act of counsell may be maid to that effect for tyme to come.'

On 4th August 1652 the following act was passed :

'The same day, the provest, baillies, and counsell, taking to thair consideratioun the great hurt and prejudice sustenit from tyme to tyme be thair burgessis and gildbrethren threw the vsurpatioun of unfrie tradders, who tak upoun them to exerce the trade of frieman and not being lyable to the samyn burdens quhairwnto frieman ar, and considering withall how in the tym of thes lait troubles all sort of people have repaired to this burgh for shelter, and have taken upoun them all sort of trading at their pleasour, for the quhich they ar all lyable not onlie to great fynes and paymentis of soums of money for their fault of vsurpatioun of the said priviledge of frieman, bot also ar lyable to be seased upoun in their persons and imprisoned, conforme to the actis of parliament and lawis of this countrey ; yet, nevirtheles, to the intent that nether the gildbrethren nor burgessis may be further wronged in their liberties, nor the stranger have occasioun to complein of hard deilling, bot that it may be manefest how tender the good toun is towards all such quho have suffered in thes lait tymes : Thairfoir, they have thoght fitt at this present to mitigat the pryce of burgeship to all such as sall upon the pryce efter specifiet be admitted thairto betuix and the twentie-nyne of September nextocum ; that is to say, quhairas the pryce of burgeship wes formerlie eight scoir pounds money, and the pryce of the gildship twelff scoir pounds, making together the soume of six hundreth merks money, the saids provest, baillies, and counsell have now for the encouragment and ease

[1] C. R. vol. xvi. fol. 203.　　　[2] C. R. vol. xvi. fol. 205.

forsaid statute and ordained, and be thir presents statutis and ordaines that
all such wnfreemen quho resorted to this toun in the tyme of thes lait troubles
and now ar desyreous to make themselfs friemen sall be admitted be the
dean of gild and his counsell at a third pairt les pryce then formerlie wes in
vse and custome to be payit, viz. the soume of eight scoir merkes ilk burges,
and the soume of twelff scoir merkis ilk gildbrether, extending both to the
soume of four hundreth merks, with the fies and wther small dewes vsit and
wont ; with certificatioun alwayes, that if from hencefurth they sall take
upoun them to sell wyne or aill, or buy or sell any other sort of merchandice,
to the prejudice of the said burgessis and gildbrether, befoir such tyme as
they sall obtein thair libertie as is aforsaid, in that caice the provest, baillies,
counsell, and deakins of (trades) will proceid agains them with all rigor,
conforme to the lawis of the land and statutis of this burgh maid agains
wnfrie tredders and abusers of the favour granted unto them.'[1]

On 8th October 1652 the following act was passed :

'The same day compeird George Suittie, dean of gild, and présented a list
of the burgessis and prenteissis buikit be him in the tyme of the trouble,
desyreing the counsell to ratifie and approve the same, to the effect they may
have thair friedome and libertie as if the court had bein sitting. The
burgessis ar thes : Alexander Coltherd, flesher, buikit upon the twentie ane
of May $j^m$ $vj^c$ fiftie-ane, to be burges be rycht of his prenteiship as prenteis
to Adam Steill, fleshour, burges of the said burgh. Item [etc. etc.]. The
counsell ratifies and approves the buiking of thair names as is abovewritten,
and agries and consents that they be resaved wpon the sight of the buiking of
thair names, as if they had bein resaved after the forme and maner vsit of
before, and will and grant that thir presents be als sufficient to them and
everie ane of them for purcheseing of thair libertie of burgeshipp and
gildshipp and friedome as if they had bein buikit efter the forme and
maner vsit of before, they preiving thair service sufficientlie, as effeirs
according to the ordour.'[2]

On 30th March 1653, Robert Leighton, Principal-elect of the
College, was made burgess and guild brother.[3]   On 7th September
1653 the council appointed a committee to meet anent the
regulating of the prices of making burgesses and guild brethren.[4]

On 10th March 1654 the council adopted the following
resolution :

'Forsamekle as in tymes bygane thair hes bein many burgessis and gild
brether made gratis, upoun requeist and utherwayis, to the prejudice of the

---

[1] C. R. vol. xvii. fol. 335.          [2] C. R. vol. xvii. fol. 348.
[3] C. R. vol. xviii. fol. 11.          [4] C. R. vol. xviii. fol. 48.

fridome of the nighbors and losse of the casualities dew to the gild box, the counsell doe hierby vnanimouslie agrie that no Scottsmen be received burges or gild brother gratis in tyme comeing without payment of the vsuall pryce and dewes, reservand alwayis the provestis priviledge for one, if neid beis.' [1]

On 26th May, 1654, General Monk was made burgess and guild brother.[2] On 8th September 1654· the following act of council was passed :

'Forsameikle as the pryce and rate of the burgeship and gildship hes bein altered from the les to the mair and from the mair to the les, according to the exigencie of the tyme, as appeirs be the acts of counsell of the twentie-seven of August j<sup>m</sup> vj° fourtie-seven, and fourt..of August j<sup>m</sup> vj° fyftie-twa ; and sieing thir tymes hes their awen pressing reasones for diminutioun of thes pryces thairin conteined, as the long-continued troubles of a calamitous tyme, the great indigence and povertie of the people, who ar not able to pay for thair friedome at the lait pryces, the indirect wayis of many who purchase their friedomes gratis upoun requeist of great men, who would be the more unwilling to imploy thair requeists if the pryces wer easie and at the old rate, quhilk hes frustrat the gild box of much money and hinders many to enter : Thairfoir, to the effect the people may have ease for the tyme, and thes indirect wayis and meanes may be prevented and removed, and the gild box somequhat better supplied with money, the counsell hes thoght fitt to reduce the pryce of the burgeship and gildship to the old rate dureing the counsellis pleasure ; that is to say, the pryce of the burgeship to be ane hundreth merkis money and ten pund for armes, and the pryce of the gildship to be ane hundreth pundis money and sexten pundis for armes, they payand the small dewes over and above ; and ordaines the dean of gild and his counsell to admitt and receive burgessis and gild brether at the rates and pryces foirsaid dureing the will and pleasure of the counsell.' [3]

On 24th October 1655 the dean of guild and his council were ordained to administer to burgesses on their admission 'the auld aithis of burgesship, *mutatis mutandis,* conform to the last proclamation . . . and the clerk to extract the same conform.' [4] On 28th November in the same year the bailies were ordained to meet with some of the chief officers in the garrison, and the clerk to expede 'half dussone of burges and guild brether ticketts in commoun form, to be disponed upoun at the discreatioun of the

---

[1] C. R. vol. xviii. fol. 83.          [2] C. R. vol. xviii. fol. 96.
[3] C. R. vol. xviii. fol. 117.          [4] C. R. vol. xviii. fol. 223.

saids officers and themselffis.'[1]   On 14th August 1656, Nicoll
records in his *Diary* that the town of Edinburgh feasted Lord
Broghall, Great President of the Council of Scotland, with the
general of the army of General Monk, as also the whole persons
of the Council of State, and likewise the officers and commanders
of the army, the judges of the land, and their followers.   The feast
was given, he says, with great solemnity in the Parliament House,
richly hung for that end.   The 'hail pryme' men, and such of
their followers as were in respect, were all 'resavit burgessis, and
thair burges tickettis delyverit to thaim.'[2]   On the 3rd of the
following month the council ordered that the burgesses so made
*gratis* should be enrolled;[3] and on the 10th of the same month
the clerk was appointed to bring at the next meeting of the
council a list of such persons as are to be admitted *gratis* burgesses, or should have been admitted that day of the town's feast,
to the effect the same might be considered by the council and
they admitted accordingly.[4]   On 30th December 1657 the
following act of council occurs :

'Report being made be the dean of gild that he and his counsell had called
in all the tailyeouris resideing in the head of the Cannogait, and had compelled the most pairt of them, being able men, to enter themselfis burgesses,
and that the persones aftermentioned, viz. . . . pleads much povertie, yet ar
content to enter burgessis provyding the counsell would dispens with their
arme silver, the counsell agries to dispens thairwith, and gives power to the
dean of gild and his counsell to admitt the foirsaidis persones burgesses
without paying for their arme silver.'[5]

On 9th February 1659 the dean of guild having reported to
the council that several neighbours who were gratis burgesses,
and had the benefit of their freedom *ad vitam*, desired to be
admitted burgesses in the best form, but because of their poverty
were unable to pay the whole dues, and therefore desired to be

---

[1] C. R. vol. xviii. fol. 238.

[2] *Diary of Transactions in Scotland* (Bannatyne Club), p. 183.

[3] C. R. vol. xix. fol. 148.

[4] C. R. vol. xix. fol. 148.        [5] C. R. vol. xix. fol. 266.

free of the armour silver and small dues, the council remitted to
the dean of guild and his council to dispense therein as they
should see cause.    Further, the dean and his council were ordained
to admit and receive—

'David Hastie, weaver, burges in Cannogait, to be burges of this burgh for
payment of the soume of fourtie pund Scotts, and to dispens with his arme
silver and wther dewes vsuall to be payit at the admission of burgesses, and
this wpon ane earnest supplication given in to the counsell be the deaken and
brethren of the weaveris of this burgh for his admissioun, to the effect they
may admitt him frieman of thair trade for his dexteritie and skilfulness of
the trade beyond any others of the calling in dameises and hollands worke
. . . the said David obleidging himselfe to take wp his residence within the
toun, wtherwayis to losse the benefite of his burgeship.'[1]

## On 12th October 1659 the council passed the following act :

'Forsameikle as there hes been several acts of counsell for debarring the
admissioun of nighbouris and countrey men to be burgesses and gildbrether
of this brugh gratis, tending much to the prejudice of those quho have just
right thairto, and bringing in a number of wnfrie people, tradsmen and
wtheris, to tak wp a calling at their owen hand and eatt the meatt out of
friemenis mouths, the counsell ordaines that such nighbouris, strangers, or
wtheris, so admitted gratis, wpon requeist or wtherwayis, have no benefite
of prenteisses, nor their children admitted to hospitallis, or hav any friedome
thairby in no tyme comeing, wnles thay pay the ordinar dewtie for the same,
or hav reall right thairto anothir way ; and that no gratis burges or gildbrother for tyme to come be of any longer continuance then their lyftyme
onlie ; and ordaines the dean of gild and his counsell, and thair successouris,
to observe the same for tyme to come.'[2]

## On the 19th of the same month the council

'appoynts Robert Murray, dean of gild, William Johnstoun, thesaurer,
George Jerdon, and Andrew Burrell, to meitt anent the statuts of the gildrie
for debarring of the admissioun of gratis burgesses so much as may be, and to
report.'[3]

## On 11th November in the same year the following act was passed by the council :

'Forsameikle as there ar sundrie acts of parliament and burrowis made
agains burgesses and gildbrether nonresidents within brugh, who, for eschew-

---

[1] C. R. vol. xx. fol. 18.            [2] C. R. vol. xx. fol. 71.
[3] C. R. vol. xx. fol. 73.

ing of the commoun burdens of the brugh quhairof they ar burgesses, doe
withdraw themselfis and their families thairfra, and take wp their residence
and trade in wnfrie places, to the great prejudice of the brugh to quhom they
belong, and contrair to the saids acts and their oath of burgeship, and seeing
there are sundrie nighbouris of this burgh, burgesses and gildbrether of the
samen, who are wnder the same transgressioun as nonresidents, quhairfoir the
counsell appoynts Robert Murray, dean of gild, to put the saids acts of parliament and burrowis to executioun aganis the saids burgesses and gildbrether of
this brugh non residents, conform to the tennour of the samen in all poynts.'[1]

On 11th January 1660 the dean of guild and his council, with
John Denhame, James Borthuik, and the clerk, were appointed
'to revise the auld acts aganis gratis burgesses for establishing
therof for tyme to tyme, and to report.'[2]

On 16th March 1660 the dean of guild was appointed:[3]

'To try what burgesses keip their residence out of toun, and to advertise
them to reside within brugh betuix and the first of Junij nixt ensueing, with
certificatioun in caice of failzie their burgeship and friedome to be declaired
voyd and null in all tyme thaireftir.'

On 8th May in the same year Charles II. was proclaimed
king in London, and on the 14th of the same month he was
proclaimed at the market cross of Edinburgh.[4]  But on the
9th of the month the town council ordained all burgess and
guild brother tickets to be written out in the King's name, as
formerly, 'befoir the invasioun of the English.'[5]  The following
act of council, dated 25th July in the same year, shows that the
Council exercised supervision over the morals of those who were
allowed to exercise the rights of burgess-ship:

'The baillies, dean of gild, theasaurer, counsell, and deakens of craftis,
being conveined in counsell anent the supplicatioun presented to them be
Issobell Dickiesone, relict of wmquhile James Braidfute, merchand, showing
that quhair it is not vnknowen to the counsell how throw her present fall
she hes foirfaultèd her priviledge and friedome of the relict of a burges and
gildbrother, and seeing it depends whollie wpon the counsell to supplie the

[1] C. R. vol. xx. fol. 82.        [2] C. R. vol. xx. fol. 101.
[3] C. R. vol. xx. fol. 126.        [4] Nicoll's *Diary*, p. 283.
[5] C. R. vol. xx. fol. 141.

same; humblie, thairfoir, desyring that the counsell would graunt her the
libertie of the relict of a burges and gildbrother, as formerlie she had befoir
her fall, for the quhilk she humblie submitts herselfe to the discretioun of the
counsell, as the bill in itselfe at mair lenth beirs : The counsell, taking the
supplicatioun to their consideratioun, do heirby graunt libertie to the said
Issobell Dickiesone to exerce the friedome of the relict of a burges and gildbrother as formerlie befoir her fall for payment of fourtie pund Scotts for
this fault, and ordaines the dean of gild to be chairged thairwith in his
accompts.'[1]

On the 27th of the same month the council appointed a
committee to meet with the dean of guild and his council
'anent the statuts of the gildrie and acts of counsell made aganis
gratis burgesses, and to report.'[2] On the 22d of August in the
same year the following letter from the provost in the castle
was produced to the council:

'Compeired John Denhame, baillie, and produced a letter direct be the
provest from the Castle to the counsell of the dait heirof, quhairof the
tennour followis : Right Honorabill, I hear you ar to put a stop to that
former way of making burgesses, quhich occasioned me to trouble you with
this lyne, that yow, on my desyre, allow the priviledges of this brugh to thir
persones so full as your respects to me will allow yow ; and leist any
conceive a prejudice to the towne, all or any of them, I heartilie agrie that
at any tyme heirefter, if it prove so, I sall be obleidged to pay for them
when they make benefice to the detriment of others. Their names ar
George Dalgleish, a verie honest man, my good fatheris fermer ; the other
one, John Campble, quhom I have forgat at my sister the Lady Allentoun
desyre, now a 12 moneth agoe, a young man dwellis in Cambusnethem ; and
the thrid is the bearer, my servant, John Scott, who hes been with me almost
a prenteistyme. In doeing heirof yow sall more engage your honouris affec-
tionat and humble servand, S. Ja. Stewart, Castle of Edinburgh, 22 August
1660. For the right honorable the Magistratts and Counsell of Edinburgh.'

And the council

'in ordour thairto, graunts the desyre, and ordaines the dean of gild and
his counsell to admitt and receive the saidis George Dalgleish, Johne Campble, and Johne Scott to be burgesses and gildbrether of this brugh for
payment of the ordinar dewtie ; and ordaines the dean of gild to repay the
same, and to dispens with thair arme silver and wther dewes, conforme to
the provest his desyre to the counsell be missive.'[3]

---

[1] C. R. vol. xx. fol. 166.          [2] C. R. vol. xx. fol. 167.
[3] C. R. vol. xx. fol. 175.

Z

On the same day the council ordered an 'act for dischairging the admissioun of burgessis and gildbrether in the best forme gratis in tyme coming, to be drawen be advyce of the dean of gild.'[1]

On 12th September two of the committee appointed on 27th July presented the draft of an act for restraining the admission of gratis burgesses and guild brethren, and other statutes of guildry, which were read 'and marked as presented and read, and no more.'[2]  On 5th October, William, earl of Glencairn, lord chancellor; John, earl of Wigton; James, earl of Tulli-, bardane; William, earl of Dumfries; George, earl of Linlithgow; Kenneth, earl of Seaforth; John, lord Fleming; George, lord Ramsay; Walter, lord Torphichen; James, lord Drummond; and other gentlemen were made burgesses and guild brethren, and invited to dinner.[3]  On 10th October the dean of guild and others were appointed

'to meitt wpon the roll of the noblemens servands quho ar to be admitted burgesses and gild brether, and anent the act drawen for stopping of gratis burgesses and what els may conduce or relate thairto for the future, and to report.'[4]

Two days afterwards, John, earl of Rothes; John, earl of Haddington; James, earl of Callander; James, earl of Galloway; John Bell, provost of Glasgow; and sixty gentlemen were admitted burgesses and guild brethren.[5]  On 7th February 1661 the marquis of Montrose; the earl of Glencairn; David, lord Madertie; William, lord Cochran; and twenty-eight gentlemen were made burgesses and guild brethren.[6]  On 16th February seven gentlemen were made burgesses and guild brethren.[7]  On 1st March 1661 the council passed the following act:

'The counsell, taking to their serious consideratioun that betuixt the yeir 1650 and May 1660 there hes been a great many persones admitted bur-

---

[1] C. R. vol. xx. fol. 175.        [2] C. R. vol. xx. fol. 179.
[3] C. R. vol. xx. fol. 188–190.        [4] C. R. vol. xx. fol. 189.
[5] C. R. vol. xx. fol. 192.        [6] C. R. vol. xx. fol. 227.
[7] C. R. vol. xx. fol. 228.

gesses and gildbrether, both of Scotts and Englishmen, alsweill in the best forme gratis as by right for payment and wtherwayis in maner specifeit in the severall acts of counsell made thairanent, and considering that all such acts wer made and done in the tyme of the vsurpatioun which then ruled, and that now his maiestie and the high court of parliament hes disowned that vsurped authoritie and all acts and deids done dureing the tyme theirof; theirfoir they doe by thir presents ordane all such persones as wer received and admitted burgesses and gildbrether dureing the time of the said vsurpatioun, to compeir befoir the gild counsell betuix and the fyft day of August nixtocome, and to produce befoir them thair burges and gildbrother tickets respective, that the counsell may consider thairof and what is necessarie to be done in reference thairto and to the pretendit oath alledgit given be them at their admissioun, with certificatioun to all such quho sall failyie, and not produce their tickets betuix and the said day, the counsell will declaire their libertie as burgesses and gildbrether void and null, as if any such right had never been granted, and heirby dischairges any of the afoirsaid burgesses or gildbrether to sell or vent aill or wyne or vse any trade quhill they produce their burges and gild tickets to be seen and considered.'[1]

On 22d May 1661, John, earl of Athol; William, lord Drumlanrig; James, earl of Hartfell; John Paterson, provost of Perth, and five others were made burgesses and guild brethren.[2] On 26th June 1661, John Jossie, bailie, and eight others were appointed to consider the roll of the noblemen's servants, burgesses lately admitted, and to report.[3] On 4th October 1661, John Jossie, late bailie, appeared before the council, and produced a paper containing overtures by way of recommendation from the former to the present bailies. Of these, the eighth was in the following terms:

'Seeing, praised be God, we ar delyvered from the yok of bondage wnder the late tyranous vsurpatioun, which laid a kynd of necessitie upon the magistratts and counsell to be somewhat profuselie prodigall in creatting burgesses and conferring gild tickets, some expedient would be thoght wpon be the magistrats and counsell for hedging wp of that priviledge of gildrie, that the vulgar throng may not find so easie accesse, and even these who have right be birth or service according to the true meaning of the sett, efter exact tryell, be not found a persone of competent estate and sufficientlie qualified with congruous endowmentis, that they be not capable of admissioun, for

[1] C. R. vol. xx. fol. 236.            [2] C. R. vol. xx. fol. 260.
[3] C. R. vol. xx. fol. 267.

even efter passing all these previous tryells they of old tymes wer admitted, so highlie did they pryse and of such golden worth did they esteem that soveraigne cittie priviledge the gildship . . . The counsell . . . continues the thrid and eight [overtures] till they be further advysed.'[1]

On 31st January 1662 the dean of guild was appointed to 'give in the form and qualifications of such as are to be admitted guild brethren, to the effect the same may be a rule for after time.'[2]

On 4th April 1662 the council passed the following act:

'Forsameikle as be the decreit arbitrall, 1583, betuix merchandis and craftis, it is expreslie provydit that na maner of persone be sufferit to vse merchandice or occupy the hand warke of ane frie craft within this burgh, or yet to exerce the libertie and priviledge of the said brugh, without he be burges and frieman of the samen, and siklyke, be act of counsell the 15 January 1602, it is statute and ordained that na deakens of craftis admit and receive any maner of persone frie of thair craft befoir he be admitted burges, and produce befoir him and his brethren his ticket of burgeship; and if it sall happen any persone to be received frie with his craft fra that tyme furth that is not burges, it is statute and ordained that he that sall be fund deaken of that craft for the tyme when the fault is challengit sall pay to the thesaurer, in name of the good toun, twentie pund Scotts, as the saidis acts in themselfis at mair lenth beirs; and, seeing it is manefest that the saidis acts have been transgressed and punished, as appeirs be act of counsell of the 27 November 1605, quhairin William Melros, deaken of the wrights, is fund to have done wrong in admitting of . . . , sklaitter, to the friedome of his craft befoir he wes made burges of this brugh, contrair to the said act of counsell of the 15 January 1602, and thairfoir wes decerned in ane wnlaw of twentie pund, and the foirsaid act ratified and approven in all poynts, with this additioun, that the penaltie thairof sall be and extend to the soume of ane hundreth pund in all tyme thairefter; and siklyk, seeing it is notourlie knowen that the deakens of the tailyeouris hes bein wnder that transgressioun these many yeirs, by admitting of tailyeouris to be friemen in the head of the Cannogait upon the touns syde thairof without being admitted burgesses, as if the samen wer a place na wayis belonging to the libertie of the brugh, being without ports, but, as it wer, at their awen disposall, albeit the same be als frie as any pairt at the crosse of Edinburgh, and quhilk is their constant and continuall practise, and quhilk doeth evidentlie appeare be act of counsell the 30 December 1657, quhairin the dean of gild for the tyme made report that he and his counsell had called in all the tailyeouris resideing in the head of the Cannogait wpon the touns syde thairof, and had

---

[1] C. R. vol. xxi. fol. 28.        [2] C. R. vol. xxi. fol. 90.

compelled the most pairt of them that wer able to enter themselfs burgesses, and that wthers, pleading povertie, wer content to enter wpon dispensatioun of their arme silver, quhilk was grantit ; and siklyk, that in the tyme when Michell Gibsone wes deaken, William Ewing, tailyeour, payed four scoir of pundis for his friedome of the craft, not being burges ; and that presentlie in John Smyth, deaken, his tyme . . . being laitlie conveind befoir the gild court to admitt himselfe burges, he did declare that he had payed four scoir of pundis for his libertie to the craft, and had not quhairwpoun to make himselfe burges, and David Grahame the lyk, and many wtheris ; all which they have appropriat to their owen privat vse, contrair to the decreit arbitrall, quhairby the samen is ordained to come in to the common box for a common vse, and quhairby they incurre the tinsell of their friedome and libertie for ever. The provest, baillies, and counsell, taking the premisses to their consideratioun, finds that not onlie the afoirsaid deakens of craftis hes been in the aforesaid transgressioun these many yeirs bygane, but that the said Johne Smyth, present deaken of the tailyeouris, hes continued in the same fault, and is lyable to the paines and wnlawis conteind in the said decreit and statute above written, nevertheles quhairof, the provest, baillies, and counsell doe pas by all former transgressiouns preceiding the dait heirof, and ratifies the afoirsaid acts in the haill heads, articles, and clauses theirof, and ordaines the samen to be put to executioun in all poynts in tyme comeing, and doe heirby prohibite and discharge them in any time comeing to committ the lyk, wnder the paine of . . . in caice of failyie *toties quoties*, and farther censure of their persones at the discretioun of the magistratts but favour.' [1]

On 2nd July in the same year the council

'appoynts the dean of gild to caus wairne all the burgesses residing in Leith to come up to Edinburgh and to reside thairin, wnder the paine of fyve hundreth merkis eache of them, in caice of failyie.' [2]

On 1st July 1663 the council,

'taking to consideratione that in tyme of this sessione of parliament thair will be a necessitie to gratifie thes in publick authoritie, and wthir personis of qualitie, by giving to them a kyndlie welcome to the towne, and be admitting them and sume of thair servants and followeris to the freedome of this burgh ; thairfor the counsall, finding it will be most convenient that the lord proveist sall performe thes thingis in the most decent and frugall way, gives power to his lordship to doe accordinglie, and ordaines the thesaurer to pay the expenses, the deane of gild to admitt such as sall be necessarie for him, and the clerk to wryte out burges and burges and gild brother tickettis for such as his lordship sall give ordour for.' [3]

---

[1] C. R. vol. xxi. fol. 113.          [2] C. R. vol. xxi. fol. 138.
[3] C. R. vol. xxii. fol. 50.

On 11th May 1664, the bailies and council having referred to their act of 12th October 1659,.

'upon the which act, becaus there. hes severall disputs and debeatts been made by persones pretending that the words of payment and. repayment inferrs no lesse than a right als full and compleitt as if they had obteind the samen by prenteiship, mariage, or soumes of money reallie payed ; theirforr the counsell, for obviatting of all such debeatts in tyme comeing, and haveing seriouslie considered the true meaning of the said act, have thoght fitt to explane the same as follows, viz. That the saids words of payment and repay-ment beir them to ane sufficient right for themselfis dureing their lyfetyme, and also for their children eftir them, to be frie burgesses and gild brether ; but that they can never have libertie to take in any prenteissis who may exspect any friedome be their service ; and if they sall mak contract or indentouris with any persones to become their prenteissis wnder expectatioun to be made frie thairby, in that caice to be esteemed as dishonest persones and cheatts, unless they procure from the dean of gild and his counsell a speciall libertie for the same upon payment of such soumes of money as they sall agrie for, and ordaines the dean of gild and his counsell to observe this ordour in all tyme comeing.' [1]

On 13th May 1664 packmen were prohibited from setting up stands until they had entered as burgesses.[2]

At the convention of burghs, on 7th July 1665, the com-missioners,

'taking to their serious consideration the great prejudice their estate sustanes through the admitting of burgessis within their burghis residing in wnfrie places and resorting to publick mercats, therefor they have statut and ordained that all frie burgessis repairing to common mercats within this kingdome shall not onlie bring with them ther burges tickitt but also ane testificat from the dean of gild or magistrats of their saids burghs, testifying them to be frie burgessis and actuall inhabitants within. the samyn, bearing all portable charges with thair neighbours thairin ; and any merchant servant coming to the saids mercat shall have ane testificat from his maister that he is either prentise or fied domestick keeping bed and board in his house and that he is buying the goods for his maisters vse, vtherwayes to be reputed and holden as a forstaler.' [3]

On 14th July 1665 the town council passed an act, in which they resolved to admit all the ministers of the burgh to be

[1] C. R. vol. xxiii. fol. 17.        [2] C. R. vol. xxiii. fol. 18.
[3] Printed Records of Convention, vol. iii. pp. 578-9.

burgesses and guild brethren 'in the best forme, for payment and repayment; with all conveniencie.'[1]  On 31st January 1666 the following regulations were enacted respecting the benefit of burgesses and guild brethren:

'It being moved in the counsell anent the meaning of the act of counsell concerning burgesses and gild brether, of the date the 12th day of October 1659 yeirs, it is resolved by the counsell that such persones as have been made burgesses and gild brether before the making of the said act sall enjoy the privileges conforme to the nature of their tickets; but that such who have been made burgesses and gild brether since the date of the said act, or shall be heerefter admitted, though their tickets be of the most ample forme, sall have their friedome discend to their children, bot that they ar absolutelie to be secludit from the benefite of taking prenteissis.'[2]

On 11th April 1666 all burgesses and guild brethren were ordained to pay army silver:

'Forsameikle as there ar many burgesses and gild brether made gratis upon requeist, in the best forme, to the prejudice of the nighbouris who payis and serves for their fredome, the counsell agries that their be no burges or gild brother made gratis upon requeists without giving in of armes or payment of arme silver theirfoir; and ordaines that the wholl arme silver of burgesses and gildbrether be imployed be the dean of gilds for the tyme in buying of armes for the touns magasen in tyme comeing.'[3]

On 18th December 1668 the following act was passed for regulating the clerk's dues of the tickets to burgesses and guild brethren:

'The counsell, consideddering severall compleants given in be the militia burgessis that are stented, a pairt quhairof may pay their stent, and vtheris are wnabell to pay, doe thairfor declare that such of the said militia that ar stented within thrie pund sall be exeimd from payment of stent in tyme cuming.'[4]

In 1669 persons were made burgesses to allow them to enter the militia;[5] and on 16th June of that year certain militia burgesses were exempted from paying stent.[6]  On 16th February 1670 liberty was granted to Christian Bruce to keep a shop as

[1] C. R. vol. xxiii. fol. 91.          [2] C. R. vol. xxiv. fol. 11.
[3] C. R. vol. xxiv. fol. 26.          [4] C. R. vol. xxvi. fol. 36.
[5] C. R. vol. xxvi. fol. 71.          [6] C. R. vol. xxvi. fol. 71.

a burgess.[1] On 23rd February 1670 the council passed an act to admit such officers of the militia regiment as had right to be burgesses and guild brethren in right of their wives or as apprentices, and to dispense with their dues.[2] On 10th June 1670 the council granted liberty to Margaret Lindsay to keep a shop.[3] On 10th August 1670 they granted similar liberty to Helen Bruce.[4] On 12th October 1670 the following act was passed in favour of freemen burgesses:

'The councill, considdering the great prejudice the nighbours that ar freemen burgesses of this city susteans by the daylie commerce and trade that wnfree persons vses by selling waire in great in their chambers, and pairtly by retailing and otherways; and als considdering that their are many persons that keeps chops, taverns, and vses the employment within this city that is only propper to burgesses to exerce, doe, for remeed thereof, appoynt the dean of gild and his councill to meett and conveen befor them all such persones that trades by selling or retailing merchand waire within the city, keeps chops, or vses any other imployment or trading that is propper to burgesses or gildbrether to exerce, and to caus them to admitt themselfs burgesses; and to grant to such of them as hes not present money for payment of their dewes, and to that effect to give their bonds for payment thereof at such dayes as they think most convenient, and for that effect to meett daylie, or ilk other day, as they sall find occasion.'[5]

On the 21st of the same month the dean of guild was empowered to admit a burgess and guild brother yearly.[6] On 4th November 1670 the council approved of the course adopted by the council of the guild on 12th October anent admitting infirm burgesses and taking of their bonds.[7] On 27th December 1671 the council granted liberty to Christian Crew to keep a shop.[8] On 28th March 1673 proclamation was made anent non-resident burgesses in the following terms:

'Forsamikle as the provost, ballyes, and councell, considdering that by severall ackis of the generall conventione of burrowes and statutis of this burgh, it hes bein enacted and ordained that no burges that does not actually

---

[1] C. R. vol. xxvi. fol. 114.        [2] C. R. vol. xxvi. fol. 115.
[3] C. R. vol. xxvi. fol. 135.        [4] C. R. vol. xxvi. fol. 143.
[5] C. R. vol. xxvi.                  [6] Ibid.
[7] Ibid.                            [8] C. R. vol. xxvii.

resede within brugh should enjoye the priveledge of the respective brughs quhairof they are burgessis, and considdering that the saids actis ar maid for the preservatione of the privelege of burrowes, and for their further incres and flourishing conditione, and for keeping good order in the merchand estaite of this kingdome, wherby non wer to be reckoned amongest the number bot those that actually reseed within the royall burrowes, and that non should have the benefeit of ane burges bot those that bear portabill charges within brugh, and which actis being of singulare advantage in this burgh in particular, the counsell resolves to revive and to caus the samyne to be putt to executione with all speed and severity in tyme coming. Therfor thes ar to mak publicatione and intimatione to all thes burgesses, whether at present they dwell in the villadge of Leithe or ellis wher, and actually traffiques in the city of Edinburgh, that they mak their residence and duelling within the samyne within fourty dayes after the publicatione heirof, certifieing all these persones that comes not and reseeds here within the said space, that they sall not enjoy the benefeit nor priveledge of trade and traffique as ane burges during the tyme of ther non-residence as said is.'[1]

On 25th June 1673 liberty was granted to the relict of Andrew Kinnear, minister at Calder, to trade as a burgess during her lifetime.[2] On 20th May 1674 the following act was passed in regard to gratis burgesses:

'The councill, takeing to their consideratione that quhair, be ane act of the convention of burrows, it is statut and ordained that no gratis burgessis nor gild brether be given nor granttit to any persoun or persones within anie of the royall borrows of this kingdome, under certificatione that the consenters theirto shall pay the pryces themselves; as lykwayes by ane act of the councill of this burgh it is ordained that the consenters to the grantting of burges ticketts gratis shall be persewed for the sowmes payable theirfor after they ar out of their offices; and lykewayes taking to their consideratione that the grantting of gratis burgessis and gild brether ticketts is contrair to the primitive and originall priviledges and liberties, which are only competent to burgesses and gildbrether who are made upon onerous caussis, wheirby the samyne are not only made contemptible, but somtymes prostrated and lavished away upon obscure and unworthie persones, to the dishonour of the citie and greatt diminishing of the common good, and that pairtlie through the corruptione of the givers, and pairtlie by the importunitie of great persones, who would not crave such favours iff they were persuaded befoir hand that it wer not in the power of the councill to grant them such concessions as that gratis burgesses and gildbrether can have the priviledges and liberteis of those persones who have the foresaid right upon onerous

---

[1] C. R. vol. xxvii.                    [2] *Ibid.*

accounts, such as those who are burges and gildbrother by right of thair father, or by right of thair wyfe, or by right of thair prentesschip, or having bought the same with thair money, all which ways of obtaining burges and gildbrother are the only caussis of constituting burgesses and gildbrether upon onerous accounts, and by vertew whereof the saidis priviledges descend to their children and qualifies them for receiving of prenteises, and makes them competent be gratis burgesses and gildbrether, thair rights importing originally and naturally no mor nor a reasonable privilege during life ; and also considering that the rates and pryces of burges and gild-brother are verie low and inconsiderable, the pryce of the gildship being diminished from twelve scoir pounds to ane hundred pounds, and the burge-ship from eight scoir merks to ane hundred merks, sua that the said pryces are most moderat and sober, wheirby personnes may be invited to buy their burgeship and gildship, and those persones who are not of mind to buy the same at such low raitts may justlie be reputed unworthie of such priviledges : Thairfor, and to the effect that ane clear distinctione and difference may be made betwixt gratis burgessis and gildbrether and those who are burgessis and gildbrether upon the forsaids onerous caussis, the councill be thir presents statuts, ordaines, and declairs that all persones who lies been, is, or that heirafter shall happen to be, gratis burgessis and gildbrether of this burgh, shall only enjoy the saids priviledges dureing their lyftymes, exclud-ing them heirby in all tyme comeing from the benefite of takeing prenteissis, and their children from the benefeitt of being burgesses and gildbrether. And furder declaires that no gratis burgessis nor gildbrether, nor their children, shall have the benefeitt of the hospitalls of this burgh, nor shall they be capable to be electit to anie office or imployment within the samyne in no tyme comeing ; and wheras their hes bein severall formes of gratis burgessis and gildbrether ticketts made use of by payment and repayment, and by insertting the oath at lenth of ane gild brother and burges in the bodie of the saids ticketts, which seims to import the saids ticketts to be con-ceaved in the best forme, wheras their wes no reall payment of money made, but only in the act of admissioun mentione is made of ane act of councill, which yitt after inspectione appears to have bein given gratis ; thairfor the councill declaires that all such burgessis and gildbrether ticketts that hes bein or heirafter shall happen to be made, though in the best forme, are and shall be halden and repute in all tyme comeing gratis burgessis and gildbrether ticketts, and are only to continwe dureing the lyftyme of the receavers, and that the persones in whose favours they are conceaved are heirby debarred and excluded in all tyme comeing from takeing prenteissis, and from being elected to anie office or imployment within this burgh, or to have the benefeitt of the hospitalls theirof, or that their children shall be capable of the priviledges of · burgessis and gildbrether, heirby declairing all practiqs or acts of councill in contrair heirof to be of no force nor effect, as being against the true meanirg and designe of the ancient statuts and priviledges of this burgh ; and in respect, by old custome and consuetude, the magistrats of

this burgh dureing ilk year of thair offices hes bein in use to make a few
burgesses and gildbrether, which wes almost all the honourarie that they had
for their great paines and fatig in serveing the Good Toun the year of their
office, viz. the present Lord Provost tua burgesses and gildbrother, ilk ane of
the baillies ane burges and gildbrother, and the dean of gild and thesaurer
each of them ane burges and gildbrother : Thairfoir, and in regaird the
makeing of these burgesses and gildbrether are upon als waghtie considera-
tiones and onerous caussis as if the sowmes of money dew theirfor were
actuallie payed in doun told and numerat money, the councill declaires that
all such persones who hes or heirafter shall be made burgesses and gildbrether att the desyre of the saids magistrats, not exceeding the forsaid
number, are and shalbe halden and repute burgesses and gildbrether in the
samyne way and maner as if they had bought the samyne with their money,
and that notwithstanding of anything to the contrair contained in this
present act ; and lastlie, in respect the councill hes determined by thir
presents how farr ane gratis burges and gildbrother tickett does operat, viz.
that it imports and caries no more than a personall priviledge dureing lyfe,
with the exceptiones abovewritten, thairfoir the councill dispensses with all
former acts of councill which aniewayes may irrogat anie fynes or penalties
against those who hes consentted to the grantting of gratis burgesses and
gildbrether ticketts, and that in all tym coming.'[1]

On 4th December 1674, James Young, farmer at Braid, was
made burgess for allowing water-pipes to be laid through his
ground.[2] On 5th May 1675 several militiamen were made
burgesses and guild brethren.[3] On 11th November 1675, Bailie
Hay received for a burgess and guild brother ticket £100, which
the council disposed of to indigent persons. On 18th May 1681
the council agreed to admit 'such fleshers as frequent the Land
Mercat' to be burgesses, for payment of a hundred merks each,
with the poor's-box money.[4] On 8th February 1682 such stablers
as wished to be admitted as burgesses were ordained to be admitted for payment of a hundred merks each.[5] On 1st November
1682 the following act of council was passed :

'Considering that the incorporatione of the taylyeouris and cordiners of
Edinburgh does grant libertie and warrand to severall persons of ther airts

---

[1] C. R. vol. xxvii. fol. 214.        [2] C. R. vol. xxviii. p. 31.
[3] C. R. vol. xxviii. p. 63.          [4] C. R. vol. xxx. p. 31.
                    [5] C. R. vol. xxx. p. 104.

that are not fremen of ther incorporation nor burgesses of this cittie to sett
vp and exerce ther calling vpon the south syd of the head of the Cannogat
outwith the Netherbow, and takes vpsets from them, which tends greatly to
the prejudice of the good toune, doe therfor discharge all such taylyors and
cordiners, and all other tradsmen that exerces ther imployment vpon the said
south syd of the head of the Cannogat, which is within the priviledge of the
good toun, to exerce ther imployment till such tymes as they admit themselves burgesses of this burgh, and discharges all tradsmen to exerce their
trads within the forsaids bounds in tyme coming, till such tyme as they be
admitted burgesses of this city, vnder the penalty of fourtie pounds Scots,
by and attour the.payment of ther dewes as a burgess, and incaice any of
the incorporation shall suffer any of ther airts to exerce their employment
in the bounds forsaid befor they be admitted burgesses, the deacon and boxmaster shall pay ane hundred merkis Scotis.' [1]

On 23rd September 1687 the following act was passed .in
regard to the magistrates' burgesses :

'The lord provost, baillies, and councill, considering that by act of
councill the magistrats have had the freedome of admission of burgesses and
gildbrethren these many years bygane during the years of their offices,
viz. the lord provest the admission of two during each year of his office, and
each baillie, each dean of gild, and each thesaurer the admission of one
burges and gildbrother during the years of their offices yearly, and that
heretofore they have made composition with the respective burgesses that
were admitted, by vertue of the said act of councell, as to their freedome of
admission of burgesses during the years of their respective offices, and that
farr below the ordinary dewes in use to be payed by any persone that has
no rycht as to their freedome, even litle above the dewes that has been
payed by apprentices who served for their freedome during the tyme of
their apprenticeship, and that some others of the magistrats has comple-
mented their friends with that freedome during the time of their saids
respective offices, quhich has tended greatly to the prejudice of the merchants
of this cittie, who were in use to get great prentice fies with their apprentices,
the councell, for remeid thereof, discharges the magistrats to make ane
composition for their burgesses and gildbrether during the years of their
respective offices, and in lieu of their composition appoints the dean of gild
and his successors in office to give them for each burges gild brother two
hundereth and sixtie merkis.' [2]

On 30th November in the same year the council,

'considering that the magistrates has been at extraordinary pains and
trouble since the ordinary tyme of the election of the magistrates, doe

---

[1] C. R. vol. xxx. p. 153.          [2] C. R. vol. xxxii. fol. 152.

therefor appoint the town thesaurer to pay to them in lieu of their burgess and gild brothership two hundereth and threescore merks Scotis money, and the like soume to such of the magistrats as has not disposed upon their burgess and gild brother tickets the former year of their office, whereanent thir presents shall be a warrand.' [1]

On 17th February 1688 the council passed the following act :

'Anent the petition given in be Mr. Robert Blaickwood, the present Master to the Merchant Company of Edinburgh, for himself and in name of the rest of the members of that societie, mentioning that, whereas many good acts, formerly made upon prudent and weightie considerations by the magistrates of this cittie, for encouragement of the freemen burgesses of the land mercat, tradeing with inlandish comodities, all which being now gone into desuetude, and many abuses being comitted, to the great prejudise of the neighbors, by unfree persons, who vend their goods all the dayes of the week in this cittie, both in publick and privat, without having any regard to the mercat day, the mercat time or place, and therefor craveand the saidis lord provost, baillies, and counsell to cause revive and renew ane former act, made the 17th October 1656 (which was therwith delivered to be read), as also to appoint intimation to be made by tuck of drum thorow this cittie upon ane or more of the next mercat dayes, as the counsell should think most expedient, that none might pretend ignorance, as the petition bears : Which being considered be the councell, together with the act of councell dated the 17th of October 1656 years produced therewith, they doe revive the same in the whole heads and articles therin specified, and appoints the same to be put to dew execution in all poynts, which act bears : forsameikle as the provost, baillies, and councell of this burgh, be their several acts of counsell and statutes of the samen made in favours of the freemen burgesses against unfreemen retaillers and others, . . . who, contrare to all law, good order, and policie observed in all well-governed commonwealths, did dayly and hourly vend and sell sundrie sorts of merchandise, such as webs of linen and woollen cloath, plaids, and sicklyke, quhilk ought to be sold be the freemen burgesses only ; and sicklyke they, their wives, bairnes, and servants, going up and down all the streets and vennells of this burgh to privat houses, selling webs and plaids and sicklyke merchandize, to the great hurt and damnage of the freemen burgesses of this burgh, for remeid whereof several proclamations were then emitted and passed be tuck of drum thorow this burgh, pear and shore of Leith, dischargeang all unfree persones whatsomever to go up and doun the streets and vennells selling privatly, or to keep any mercat, in great or small, except upon the mercat day only, in mercat place and mercat time, betwixt nyne houres in the morning and ane afternoon, under the pain of confiscation of the goods and punishment of

---

[1] C. R vol. xxxii. fol. 173.

their persones at the will of the magistratts : Nevertheles of the which acts, orders, and proclamations emitted as said is, all manner of persons, retaillers in and about Edinburgh, and others coming from all the corners of the countrie, frequents the comon mercat of this burgh in a disorderly way, some of them sitting doun upon stones and stools befor the stands upon the high street, which should be patent and open for passage; others, who are comon re-tailers, should put out stands in the mercat place, not keeping stands, but going up and doun be themselves and their servants throw the haill town, where they may best vent and sell their goods without any respect to mercat day, mercat time, or mercat place, whilk tyme is only proper betwixt nyne hours in the morning and ane o'clock in the afternoon, and the place betwixt the weigh house and lucken booths on both sides of the street; and many of them keeping a privat way of selling all the dayes of the week, some of them both buying and selling again in one and the same mercat day, and others buying in one mercat day, laying up that waire privatly in town till the next mercat day, and selling it over againe, and so keeping a constant course of trade in buying and selling from ane mercat day to another as if they were freemen merchants of this burgh ; and sicklyke many of the saidis retaillers keeping daily mercat in Leith, abuseng the freedome and liberties of this burgh, and all of them eating the meat out of the mouths of the freemen merchants of this burgh, who are lyable to all portable burden wherewith they have been overcharged in tymes past, and rendering them altogether uncapable to bear further burden in tyme coming.  Which ordors by the forsaid act were appointed to be intimate yearly by tuck of drum, that none might pretend ignorance, as at length is contained in the said act.  And the councell farder hereby allows libertie to all freemen burgesses to buy any whole webs upon any day of the week, and also libertie to unfree persons to sell whole webs to freemen burgesses of this citie, and ordains this present act to be published throw this cittie by tuck of drum yearly, that none pretend ignorance.'[1]

## On 5th April 1689 the Estates of Scotland,

'takeing to their consideration the great invasiones that have been made of late yeares upon the priviledges of the royall burrowes, particularly these of Edinburgh, in the election of their magistrats by recommendationes and nominationes, made by the late King in ane arbitrary and despotick way, contrair to the lawes and liberties of the kingdome, so that the present magis-trats and councill of the said burgh are not their true magistrats and councill by them freely elected, but plainly such as have bein (at least by progress) imposed by the foresaid court methods and practises, and the meeting of the Estates considering that the constitutiones, liberties, and priviledges of the said burgh being so far violat and perverted, the only naturall and just way to restore

---

[1] C. R. vol. xxxii. fol. 192.

the same is to allow and authorise the incorporation itselfe and wholl members thereof, to whom the aforesaid liberties and priviledges were originally granted, to make a new choice and election of magistrats and ordinary councill.'

Therefore they authorized the Town Clerks of Edinburgh

'to convein the whole burgesses who hes born and does beare burgadge dewtie and ar lyable to watching and warding within the city (secluding from this number all honorary burgesses, with the toune servants, pensioners, beedmen, and the like) to meet upon Wednesday next, the tenth instant, at eight a clock in the morneing in St. Giles church, with continuatione of dayes, to the effect that the saids burgesses and each of them may give in thair subscrivit lists of tuenty-four persones to be the magistrats and ordinary councill of the said burgh, according as the plurality of votes shall determine.'

The magistrates and council so chosen were to continue till the first Tuesday after the ensuing Michaelmas, when a new election was to proceed in all points, conform to the sett and decreet arbitral pronounced by King James VI.[1]

On the 25th of October the council revived the act of council of 1674,

'declaring that no gratis burgesses shall have libertie to book prentices, or have any priviledge to get their children into the hospital, with this adition, that the councell hereby declares that none of these gratis burgesses alreadie admitted, or that hereafter shall be admitted, shall have noe place of the good town, or have any quarterly pensions in time coming.'[2]

On 12th February 1690 the council rescinded and annulled the act of 30th November 1687, and revived in favour of the magistrates then being, and their successors in office, the act of 1674,

'appoyinting the lord provost to have admission of two burgesses and gild brether each year of his office, and each of the baillies, dean of gild, and the thesaurer, to have ane burges and gild brother; and declayres, if they compliment ther freinds with the said fredome, or what agreements they shall make with the person or persons they give the said fredome, shall be alse sufficient as if they had payed the whole dewes to the dean of gild.'[3]

[1] 1689, c. 22.  Acts of the Parliaments of Scotland, vol. ix. p. 34.
[2] C. R. vol. xxxiii. fol. 46.
[3] C. R. vol. xxxiii. fol. 90.

On 6th March 1691 the council having

'considered the dean of gilds report anent dean of gild Nicolsones accompt the last half year of his office, representing that the auditors of his accompt refuses to allou the said dean of gild Nicolson ane article in his accompt for the soume of threttine hundred and eighty-six pounds threttine shillings and four pennies, and that for the burges and gild brother tickets that was dew to the magistrates their half year, viz. two hundred and sixty merks for each burgess and gild ticket, conforme to ane act of counsell of the date the [30 November 1687], which being considdered be the councill, they approve of the auditor's report in refusing these articles, and they rescind the said act of councill, declaring the same void and null in all time coming. But the councill allowes the provost and magistrats for the said half years service to have the nominatione of their burges and gild brotheris tickets to be disposed off at their pleasure, conforme to custome.'[1]

On 19th August 1691 the following act was passed:

'The councell, taking to their consideration the great abuse that has of a long tyme crept into this city, and still continues, by burgesses and gild brethern obtaining the freedome thereof, and yet makes not their actuall dwelling and residence therein, and, notwithstanding, pretends during the tyme of their non-residence that they ought to enjoy the benefite of the freedome of this burgh ; which practise does destroy, frustrate, and defeat the chief ends and designes of being burgesses and gild brethern, which is, that they, being admitted thereby members of the society and incorporation of the burgh, ought to reside therein, unless absent upon the accompt of their trade, and to bear scott and lott and their pairt in all publict burdens and taxations with the rest of their neighbours, and that the charges of keeping their houses and families ought to be spent within the same. And lykewise, considdering that their are many acts of the royall burrowes of our predecessors, that burgesses and gild brethern non-residenters should lose the public benefite of their freedome during their non-residence, therfor the councill, in pursuance of all acts of conventions of burrowes relative hereto, appoints the samen to be put in full force and execution, and revives all former acts of their own counsell of this brugh against not-residenting burgesses and gild brether, and lykewise enacts and ordaines in all time coming that no burgess or gild brother of this brugh shall enjoy and possess the benefite of the freedome theirof, unless he and family resides eight months in the year within the same, but shall be holden and lookt upon during the tyme of his or families non-residence as ane unfreeman in all caises. Declaring, nevertheless, that whensoever he shall happen thereafter to come and reside within this city, that then his rycht of burgesship or gild

---

[1] C. R. vol. xxxiii. fol. 226.

brother shall revive, and become effectual and beneficial to him in all caises, notwithstanding of his former non-residence. And appoints publication hereof to be made upon Wednesday next by tuck of drum, that none may pretend ignorance hereof.'[1]

On 4th November 1691 the council appointed a committee to consider the draft of an act

'excluding gratis burgesses from having any benefit by their burges tickets, except their burgesships during their lifetime.'[2]

On 8th March 1693 the council appointed another committee, to consider

'how arms may be provyded for the good touns use out of the armes money payed into the dean of gild by the burgesses at their entry, and report.'[3]

On the 28th of April in the same year another committee was appointed, to consider

'how the armes money payed into the dean of gild be burgesses at their entry may be applied for buying of armes for the toune magazine.'[4]

On 19th July 1695 the council ordained, that thereafter all gratis burgesses should take the burgess oath in presence of the dean of guild and his court.[5]  On 3d January 1696 the following act was passed:

'The lord provost, baillies, councill, and deacones of craftes being conveaned in councill, pursuant to general acts of councill made in favoures of the freemen burgesses of this burgh against unfreemen retailers, particularly the acts dated 8th May 1607, 16th July 1647, 17th October 1656, and 17th February 1688, which acts are appointed to be yearlie intimate by tuck of drum throu this cittie and town of Leith, doe, in pursuance thereof, and for the better regulating of the abuses and disorders committed by unfree persones in the land mercat and other places of this cittie and suburbs, statute and ordaine that noe unfree persones goe up and down the streets and vennels of this cittie, or suburbs thereof, or to private houses privately, to sell or keep any mercate, great or small, except in the mercat day, mercat tyme, and mercat place, which is on the Wednesday, betwixt nyne a clock in

[1] C. R. vol. xxxiii. fol. 277.     [2] C. R. vol. xxxiii. fol. 305.
[3] C. R. vol. xxxiv. fol. 153.     [4] C. R. vol. xxxiv. fol. 171.
[5] C. R. vol. xxxv. fol. 177.

2 B

the morning and one a clock in the afternoon, betwixt the Weigh-house and
the west end of the Luckenbooths ; and to the end that the mercat may be
regular, and the High Street left free and patent to his Majestie's leidges,
that non presume to sitt doun upon the High Street before the stands upon
stones or stools, but that all hucksters and others who buy cloath to sell it
again shall be obligded to take stands, and that it shall not be leisome to
them, by themselves or their servants, to goe up and doun the mercat with
their cloath in their armes, but that they shall remaine therewith at their
said stands, (excepting always those who are the makers thereof themselves).
As also that noe unfree persone buy and sell on one and the same mercate
day, nor keep any part of their ware that is unsold in house or sellers within
the good toun or suburbs thereof, but that, after the mercat is over, they
shall remove the same without the liberties of this burgh until the next
mercat day ; with certification to all and every one that shall contraveen any
part of the premisses, their said ware shall not only be confiscat, but their
persons punished at the will of the magistrates, in terror of others to commit
the lyke in tyme coming. And the councill appoints the baillies of the
butter mercat to see the forsaid act put to due execution, with assistance of
one or more of the neighbours, as they shall be from time to time authorized
for that effect ; and ordaines thir presents to be published throw this cittie
and toun of Leith by tuke of drum upon the first Wednesday of July, yearly,
or oftner as neid requires, that none pretend ignorance.'[1]

On 27th March 1700 the dean of guild having reported that in
the accounts of incidents in the treasurer's disbursements considerable sums were entered as paid to the clerks for burgesses and
guild tickets given by the council gratis, which expense might be
saved to the town and paid by the parties,

'the councill appointed that in all tyme coming the pairties who receive
the freedome of burgeses and gild brethern from the councill gratis, should
pay the clerks dues as others doe pay, excepting allwayes such noblemen and
gentilmen as the councill shall think fitt to complement with the freedome of
this city.'[2]

On 11th April 1701 the council,

'taking to their serious consideration the great prejudice the old burgesses
and their children, and these that have served their prenticeships or have
bought their freedome in this cittie, doe daylie sustaine by gratis burgesses,
who oft times doe make moyen with one or other of the councill to get a gratis
burges ticket, upon designe either to get a place or to get their children put

---

[1] C. R. vol. xxxv. fol. 228.        [2] C. R. vol. xxxvi. fol. 502.

in Heriotts Hospitall, or themselves into the Trinity Hospitall, or both, which does much prejudge these who has true right, either by their birth, mariage, service, or money ; therefore it is statute and inacted that heirafter noe gratis burges, either already made or that shall be made hereafter, shall by any gratis burges ticket be capable to get any beneficiall place what-somever belonging to the good toun, or themselfes or their children in any hospitall theirto belonging, but shall be keeped for old burgesses and their children, or such as has served as prentice, or married a burges daughter, or bought their freedome with their money ; declaring always that any persone that has right be their parents, wife or service, or otherwayes, to whom the councill gives their dues gratis, are not hereby understood to be gratis burgesses.' [1]

On 18th March 1702 the council prohibited the incorporation of tailors and other incorporations of the city from communicating the freedom of the trade, in all time coming, to any in the head of the Canongate, or any other place within the burgh, except to such as were burgesses.    And the several incorporations were ordered to cause the act to be recorded in their respective books, and to return an extract of the same to the council.[2]    On 16th July 1703

' the councill, considering that there are severall persons who exercise trade and merchandizeing within the good toune of Edinburgh and suburbs thereof, and doe pretend to have honorary or gratis tickets from the councill of the burgh for warranding their trade and merchandizeing, therfore, to the effect it may be knowen what persons have right to trade and merchandize be virtue of the said honorary and gratis burges tickets, and for the better security of trade within the city and suburbs, the councill have appointed the said persons to produce their saids tickets to the dean of gild and his court once this month of July, with certificatione, if they failzie soe to doe, they shall lose the benefite of their said tickets.' [3]

On 24th September 1703 the following act was passed :

' The counsell, taking to ther serious considderation the great prejudice which the freemen, burgess, and gild brethern of the cittie sustaines by the many gratuitous burgesses that are admitted, who bruke and injoy the same libertie of trade during ther lifetyme with the freemen, for remead wherof in time coming it is statute and enacted that heirafter all such gratuitous

---

[1] C. R. vol. xxxvi. fol. 782.          [2] C. R. vol. xxxvii. fol. 98.
[3] C. R. vol. xxxvii. fol. 533.

burgess as shall be admitted shall only have freedome and libertie to trade
for the space of five years after ther admission, or att least to commence after
ther beginning to trade and exerce ther said libertie, and that after the said
five years is elapsed that they shall be holden as unfreemen ; and that the
dean of gild and his counsell, and ther successors in office, are hereby
appoynted to treat them as such in all tyme coming.  And sicklyke it is
furder enacted that the clerke shall keep a seperat register, wherin all such
gratuitous burgesses shall be recorded.' [1]

On 12th April 1704 the council authorized £165, 14s. Scots to
be paid to Gilbert Kirktoune for 'wrytting and gilding burges
tickets, and furnishing gold, wax, and parchment,' conform to an
account extending from November 1702 to 15th September 1703.[2]
And on the same day the council, considering the great expense to
which the town was put annually for writing gratis and honorary
burgess tickets, regulated the clerk's charges therefor as follows:

'For all burges and gild brother ticketts, wher the persones names and
designations are gilded in capitall letters, ther shall be payd the soume of
three pound ten shilling for wrytting and gilding therof.  As also, for all
other burges and gild brother tickets not gilded, the soume of fourtie shilling
for wrytting therof ; and for single burges ticketts, the priviledge wherof
continues but for fyve years, the soume of twentie-nyne shilling Scotts.'

The following entries illustrate the practice of giving right to
females who were not burgesses to exercise limited rights of
trading in the burgh.   On 8th September 1708 the council
'granted licence to Elizabeth Skeen, daughter to the deceast
Mr. Thomas Skeen, advocat, to trade in this city, liberties and
priviledges thereof, and that during all the days of her life, she
being unmarried.' [3]   On 10th September 1708 the council granted
'licence to the persons afternamed to trade within this city, and
priviledges therof, for the space of seven years, gratis, viz. Anna
Semple, relict of Mr. John Semple, chamberlain to my Lord
Primrose ; Mary M'Callum ; Jean Murray ; Anna Burnet ; and
Mr. Richard Cameron and Margaret Mowbray, daughter to the

---

[1] C. R. vol. xxxvii. p. 642.        [2] C. R. vol. xxxvii. p. 778.
[3] C. R. vol. xxxix. p. 194.

deceast Mr. Patrick Mowbray, late clerk to the chyrurgeons, for all the days of her life, she being unmarried.'[1] On 10th August 1709 they granted 'licence to Sarah Dalrymple, daughter to Charles Dalrymple of Waterside, to use her trade of japaning as a burges of this city all the days of her lifetime, and her continuing unmarried, providing always she employ the freemen of this city for the timber work.'[2] On 31st August 1709 they granted 'licence to Margaret Kennoway, relict of John Stirling, chirurgeon, to trade within this city, liberties and priviledges therof, during her widowity.'[3]

On 31st August 1715 the council,

'considering how prejudiciall it is to the interests of the good toun the selling of burges tickets be the magistrats to fleshers, and particularly that the customs of the House of Muir and sheepflocks is thereby much impaired : Therefore, to prevent the lyke abuse in tyme coming, do heirby prohibit and discharge the magistrats, or others haveing right, in tyme coming to sell or dispose of any burges ticket to fleshers. And siclyke discharges the dean of gild and his councel in all tyme coming to receave or book any such burgesses, in case the magistrats, or others having right, should happen to sell the said burges tickets to fleshers. And to the effect this act may be the better observed, appoints the same to be booked in the dean of gild court books, and to be read yearly in the said courts the first court day after the election.'[4]

On 7th September 1716 the following act was passed :

'The council, with the extraordinar deacons, upon report of Robert Craig, dean of gild, and considering that the eight tickets given to the magistrats yearly being derogative to the credit of the good toun, and prejudiciall to the dean of gild and his court ; for preventing whereof it is statut and ordained, that from and after Mertimas next the dean of gild for the tyme being pay to the lord provost two hundered pund yearly, and to each of the other magistrats one hundered punds Scots yearly, in lew of their tickets. And siclyke statut and ordained, that from and after the said terme the council dispose of burges and gild brother tickets at the rate following, viz., each burges and gild brother ticket not under two hundered merks, and each singall burges ticket not under one hundered merks, Scots money.'[5]

---

[1] C. R. vol. xxxix. p. 206.  [2] C. R. vol. xxxix. p. 409.
[3] C. R. vol. xxxix. p. 421.  [4] C. R. vol. xlii. p. 150.
[5] C. R. vol. xliii. p. 184.

On 22nd March 1717 the council passed the following act:

'The councel, with the extraordinar deacons, considering that hitherto there is no space of tyme determined betwixt and which persons having right to enter burges or burges and gild brother should be oblidged to enter themselves in the dean of gilds books, or otherways loose their priviledge, whereby severall persons take occaission to carry on a private trade without entering, by which they reap the benefit of burgesses but bear no part of the publict taxes, to the great prejudice of the neighbourhood, and soe severall persons, by their delaying to enter, are prevented by death, to the great prejudice of their widows and children; for preventing whereof it is hereby statute and enacted that in all tyme coming every person having right to enter burges or burges and gild brother, either by their faither, or their wife, or as prentice, shall enter themselves in the gild books within the spaice of three years after their majority, or marriage, or the tyme of the expyreing of their indenturs; declairing heirby, that in caise they doe not enter within the spaice foirsaid, they shall amitt and lose their right and priviledge of entering in case it can be made appear that ever they had any trade in the place; att least, that before they be admitted to enter, they shall be obleidged to pay twenty punds Scots for each year they shall soe trade before their entry; and this but prejudice to the former laws made against unfree traders. And the councel, furder considering that by the sett and constitution of this citie, traidsmen as well as merchants are declaired capable of being gild brother, but rarely admitt themselves untill they be chosen to some office that absolutely requirs their being gild brothers; for preventing whereof it is statut and enacted and declaired that all traidsmen who are not gild brethern are and shall be incapable of being elected or chosen to bear any office in this citie that must be born by gild brethern only; lykeas the councel, understanding that of late many women strangers who had no title to the freedome of this city did, for payment of a little money, procure licences to trade from year to year, which gave occaission to many servants to give over their service and keep shops, and trading therein, whereby the neighbourhood not only wanted servants, but many honest indigent relicts and children of burgesses, who had their subsistance for themselves and familys by such trade and shop-keeping, and did bear a share of the burdens of this city, have their livelyhood taken from them, and thereby become a burden to the good toun; for preventing whereof in tyme coming it is statute and ordained that, from and after the term of Whitsunday next, no women whatsomever shall be allowed to keep any shop or merchandize and trade within this city, except the widows, daughters of burgesses and burgesses and gild brethern, upon the said daughters payeing and consyning in the hands of the dean of gild for the tyme being the half of their dues usually payable at the entrie of the children of burgesses. Which payments are to be recorded in the gild court books, and charged upon the dean of gild, and allowed to their husbands at their entrys, in case of their marriage ; certifying the transgressors heirin that they shall have their shops clossed up, and be fyned in ane hundered pounds Scots money.'[1]

On 29th March 1717 the following act was passed :

'Anent an representation given in be the incorporation of the freemen fleshers of Edinburgh, shewing that the fleshers, as being one of the incorporations of the burgh of Edinburgh authorized by the sett of the good toun, have had many usefull and necessary priviledges given and secured to them, both by the acts of the toun council and by acts of the privie council, and also of the parliament itself, and particularly by an act the 27th day of March 1573 years,[2] ratifieing severall other acts made in favours of the said incorporation, all persons whatsoever, sellers of flesh in the toun mercat, are discharged to slay their nolt, sheep, or bestiall within the freedoms of the toun, but to bring the same to the mercat dead and slain, under the penalties mentioned in that act, which is afterwards ratified by the parliament in the year 1693, together with the other acts in favours of the fleshers. This regulation is not only usefull and necessary for the good and policy of the burgh, to prevent driving numbers of cattle through the toun, and many other inconveniences, but is plainly ane undoubted consequence of the freedom competent to the fleshers as an incorporation ; for if this priviledge be encroached upon, it is obvious the freemen fleshers have no right or priviledge in the exercise of their traide above what unfreemen have. It may likewayes be observed, that although the parliament of Scotland thought fitt to retrench the priviledges of the freemen fleshers in some particulars, yet this stands untouched, and indeed could not be altered without disolving the incorporation. It is also notourly knowen that severall inconveniancys are laid upon the countrey, and necessarly follow upon unfreemen being allowed to traide as freemen fleshers. It proves ane incouradgment to servants to desert ther maisters before they be competently skilled in their employment, and gives those runaways ane opportunity to cheat and impose upon the country, by buying bargins of catle under the name and character of fleshers freemen in Edinburgh, while they have no stock whereupon to traide, or wherewith to pay, which hath been too well avouched by too many complaints made to the magistrats against severall of those unfreemen. The incorporation of the fleshers doe therefore humbly expect that the magistrats and councel of the good toun will take such effectuall methods for suppressing abusses of that kind as will preserve the undoubted priviledges of the freemen fleshers, and maintain the good order and policy of the burgh in the manner that hath been thought necessary, and was therefore appointed to be observed by the severall acts above mentioned, as the petition bears. Which being read, the

[1] C. R. vol. xliv. p. 70.
[2] The council record is wanting at this time.

councel remitted the consideration thereof to the magistrats and deacon conveener, and to report their oppinion theranent. Accordingly, Baillie George Haliburton, in absence of Baillie James Cleilland, reported that, they haveing considered the petition, they were of oppinion that all unfreemen, though burgesses, ought to be discharged to slay any nolt, sheep, or other bestiall within this citie for sale in the mercat, under the penalty of confiscation, and such other punishments as the magistrats shall think fitt, as the said report under the hands of the Committee bears. Which being considered be the councel, they, with the extraordinar deacons, approved of the said report, and have discharged, and heirby discharges, any unfreemen fleshers, tho' burgesses, to slay any bestiall whatsomever within this citie for seall in the mercat, under the penalty of confiscation, and such other punishments as the magistrats shall think fitt ; and recomended to Baillie M'Aulay to cause intimate thir presents to the said unfree fleshers in the mercat, that non may pretend ignorance.' [1]

On 9th July 1725 the council appointed a committee

'to bring in the draught of ane act for preventing their making burgess who are not able to bear the caracter, and soon after come to be burdens on the town, and report the same to the councell with all conveniency.' [2]

On 1st September 1725 the following act was passed:

'The councell, with the extraordinar deacons, considering that there are great many arrears arising from the dean of gilds accompts, which is occassioned by the dean of gilds taking bills and other securities for the dues of burges and gildbrother tickets, and that the persons receivers of the said tickets and their children do thereby enjoy the benefite and priviledge of the citie, albeit the dues be not payed for the same ; for preventing of which, the councell, with extraordinary deacons, statute and ordains that whosoever shall purchase a burges ticket, or burges and gildbrother ticket, by bill or other security for the dues thereof, shall not receive their tickets untill first the dean of gild for the time being be satisfyed and payed the dues for the same, and strictly prohibit and discharge the clerks to extend or give out any such ticket without the dean of gilds warrand first had and obtained for that effect ; and appointed thir presents to be recorded in the dean of gild books.' [3]

On 9th April 1729

'the councill appointed a committee to prepare an act empowering the dean of gild and his court to grant licences to those who had a small trade, and were not able to enter burgesses.' [4]

---

[1] C. R. vol. xliv. p. 77.        [2] C. R. vol. l. p. 579.
[3] C. R. vol. l. p. 620.        [4] C. R. vol. lii. p. 250.

On 23rd April 1729 the following act was passed:

'The councill, haveing taken into their consideration that by the laws of the land, and by the rights and infeftments granted in favours of this city, it is unlawful to or for any person to use, exercise, or occupy any branch of trade or craft within this city or libertys, except such as are burgesses and freemen thereof allenarly, and that notwithstanding there are severall unfree persons of both sexes do presume to use, exercise, and occupy severall branches of trade within this city and liberties, which is injurious to the freemen thereof, who have paid for their freedom, and on whom the publick taxes are imposed, and whereby also that branch of the revenue ariseing to the town from the upsets and entries of burgesses is greatly diminished; and likewise considering that severall persons offending as aforesaid would cheerfully purchase their freedom had they ability to do it, and that their poverty only hinders them from acquiring their freedom, and that the executing against them the laws made against unfree traders would not only be a hardship upon them, but also would be hurtfull to the community, by disabling numbers of the inhabitants from holding house, and thereby making them objects of the town's charity: Further, considering that by the antient laws and laudable practice of the royal burrows, such of their inhabitants as were unable to purchase their freedom, and who only occupyed some low and inconsiderable branches of trade, such as the retail of ale, beer, milk, horsehyring, cowfeeding, and the like, were admitted stallangers, whereby they were allowed to carry on their small trade on payment annually of such rates as were imposed on them, in proportion to their trade and ability, and that in the present case it is expedient to take tryall of such a remedy for a term of five years from and after Whitsunday next, in manner hereinafter mentioned, and that the laws made against unfree traders should be put to punctuall execution against every person who is unfree, and who shall not be admitted as stallangers in manner hereinafter specified: Therefore the councill do hereby empower and authorize the dean of gild and his councill, and their successors in office, from and after the term of Whitsunday next, dureing the aforesaid term of five years, to receive and admitt every inhabitant of both sexes as stallangers who shall appear to them to be unable to purchase their freedom, and thereby to give them liberty to deall and trade in retail of ale, beer, fish, milk, herbs, roots, fruit, cowfeeding, horsehyring, poultry, and suchlike small trade, to be setled and specified in their respective act of toleration, and renewed annually, upon payment of such a sum as shall be settled by the said dean of gild and councill, to be accounted for by the said dean of gild for the use of the town, which admissions shall be renewed annually, otherwise to become void and null; and the sums to be severally paid for the said admissions not to exceed ten pound, nor to be under three pound, and that the receipts of the said sums may be regularly brought as a charge upon the dean of gild and his forsaids for the benefite of the town; that all such admissions shall be duly recorded

2 c

in a book to be made and keept for that purpose, bearing the aforesaid
such receipt; and the dean of gild and his councill, and their forsaids, are
hereby ordained, from and after the said term of Whitsunday next, to cause execute the laws made against unfree traders against every person of both sexes
residing within this city, or within any of its liberties, who are unfree, and
who shall not purchase their liberty of being tolerate stallangers as aforesaid.' [1]

The following form of receipt and licence was on 9th July in
the same year approved of, and authorized to be granted to such
persons as fell within the class referred to in the preceding act of
council:

'*Edinburgh*,          *day of*                    *years*.—In consideration that
B has payed to A, dean of guild, for the use of this city, the sum of          ,
          is heirby permitted by the said dean of guild and his councel to exercise
traide within this city and its libertys, by          , allenerly, for a
term of one year from          to          , exclusive, without any
furder right or priviledge to the said          .' [2]

On 22nd October 1729 the following act was passed:

'The council, takeing into their serious consideration that it is highly
necessary for the toun to manage their revenue in the most frugal way, so
that it may answer the true ends and purposes to which the toun is indis-
pensibly bound; amongst other things, it has been observed that considerable
sums annually has been expended upon entertainments, at the making
noblemen, gentilmen, and others burgesses, which by no means the toun was
able to bear without retrenching the more necessary and prestable demands
upon the revenue; And further, taking into consideration the act of
parliament, Georgii primi, anno nono, whereby the persons and estates of
such of the said magistrats and council who shall be accessory to the
increasing the said city's capital debt to any greater sum then what is therby
allowed dureing the said spaice of thirty-eight years from and after the said
first day of July 1723, are subject and lyable to the said city in releif of such
sums as shall be borrowed by them more then what is thereby provided
and allowed; from all which it is most certain the toun will inevitably
involve themselves in dificulties and inconveniences too obvious to be here
expressed: Therefore the council statutes and ordaines that in no time
thereafter any entertainment shall be given at the touns charge on the
account of makeing noblemen, gentilmen, or other burgesses, as aforesaid; and
that all burges tickets which the toun council shall agree that those proposed
have just merit to, and are deserving of, shall be put into the hands of the
member of the council that makes the motion, in order to be delivered to

---

[1] C. R. vol. lii. p. 263.          [2] C. R. vol. lii. p. 327.

them in name of the council, excepting always and from this present act are excepted allenerly all such as are his Majestie's ministers of state and his Majestie's judges of the court of session and exchequer, the commander-in-cheef of his Majesties forces in North Brittain for the time, in which event the toun council shall not only authorize the freedome of the burgh to be given to the persons above excepted, but shall order and authorize the entertainment on that occassion ; and therefore rescinds and anulls all acts of council or practises to the contrary, and enjoins the inviolable observation hereof in all time comeing.' [1]

On 2nd June 1731 the council took into consideration the act of council, dated 24th September 1703, by which the endurance of gratis burgess tickets was limited to five years, and passed an act in the following terms :

'Considering that there is no distinction made in the tenor of gratis tickets that are given to such as are servants to his Majestie's commissioners to the general assembly, and to such like, from the honourary tickets that are given to noblemen and gentlemen in compliment, they ordain that for hereafter, in all gratis tickets which are not given as complements to noblemen and gentlemen, that there shall be ane explicit reference to the forsaid act of council limiting the terme for which the freedom is thereby intended.' [2]

On 30th June 1731 the council took into consideration the acts of council made touching the admission of gratis burgesses, particularly the acts dated the 24th September 1703 and 2nd June then current, and passed the following act :

'Considering that it is necessary to distinguish such gratis tickets as are given to servants of commissioners to the general assemblys and such like from honourary tickets that are given in complement to noblemen and gentlemen, and that the effect of all gratis tickets and terme of their endurance may be plainly settled and determined, doe enact and ordain that all honourary tickets that shall be given in complement to noblemen and gentlemen shall be according to the formula thereof now practised, and that all gratis tickets which shall be given to the said commissioners' servants and such like shall be according to the formula therof hereto annexed ; and that no gratis tickets shall qualifie any person to bear any office within burgh, or shall any person be capable to enter into the right thereof, nor shall be deemed any tittle to the benifite of any of the town's hospitalls, and that the endurance of gratis tickets to the said commissioners' servants and such like shall be, and it is hereby limited to the terme of five years after the date of the same, but

---

[1] C. R. vol. lii. p. 402.        [2] C. R. vol. liii. p. 369.

honorary tickets that shall be given in compliment to noblemen and gentlemen shall endure during their lives only.'

The following is the form of burgess ticket referred to :

'*Edinburgh, the        day of*                    .—The which day, in
presence of the right honourable Patrick Lindesay, Esq., lord provost of this
city ;  Thomas Dick, Alexander Wilson, Robert Blackwood, and James Seton,
baillies ;  John Osburn, dean of gild, and gild council compearing, A. B. is
made burges of this burgh, in termes of and conform to ane act of the town
council dated the thirty day of June 1731.' [1]

On 18th July 1733 the council, on consideration of a complaint
that several persons, unfree of the town, from Musselburgh and
neighbouring places, hawked about and sold earthenware at all
times though neither market day nor market time, recommended
the dean of gild and his council

'to restrain all unfree persons from selling any earthenware except on
mercat day and mercat time, conforme to the laws in that behalf made.' [2]

The authority granted by the council to persons not burgesses
or guild brethren to have an annual licence seems to have been
complained of by the merchants, and their petition was referred to
a committee of the council, who, on 13th February 1736, reported
that they had reasoned upon the several points of the petition and
memorial, and were of opinion that

'at this time it is not proper to make any alteration on the entry money of
burgesses and gild brothers, whither of strangers or apprentices ; but as to
these women who have served apprentiships or are now carying on trade,
tho' not burgeses' children, were of opinion that the dean of gild and his
court should permit them to trade for payment of £6 sterling, which sum is
to be sunk, and not to be allowed at their mariages, they also paying publick
burdens in proportion to their trade ; that the widows and daughters of burgesses and burges and gild brether be admitted to trade without paying any
entry money, untill they are married ; that there being several persons who
have taken up the trade of ale selling, stabling, and albeit they have no title,
which is an incroachment on the burges-rights while they continue that trade
and pay no yearly consideration for it : Therefor, and in regard these
persons are unable to purchase their freedoms, the committee were of opinion
that such persons should be licentiat to deal in the retaill of ale, beer, fish,

---

[1] C. R. vol. liii. p. 412.          [2] C. R. vol. liv. p. 418.

milk, herbs, roots, fruits, cowfeeding, horsehyring, poultry, eggs, and salt flesh, for one year after Whitsunday next, they paying to the dean of gild for their said licence a sum not exceeding £10 and not under £3 Scots yearly, as the same shall be taxed by the dean of gild and his council ; and that the said stallangers be discharged from selling any other goods then those above mentioned, under pain of confiscation of the saids goods, and of being otherwise prosecute as the law directs ; and the committee, considering that there are a great many women servants and others who, turning wearie of their services, have, out of a principle of avarice and habit of laziness, taken up little shops, albeit they have no title to the priviledge of trade in this city, which is evidently hurtfull to the tradeing burgesses, who bear the publick burdens of the place, and·is attended with many other bad consequences, therefore they were of opinion that all persons who possess little shops, who are not the widows or daughters of burgesses, should be strictly prohibited and discharged from keeping any shop or trade within this city after Whitsunday next, under pain of confiscation of their goods, and of being otherwise punished as the laws against unfree traders directs ; and that the council's act hereanent should be published thro' the city by tuke of drum, and the act printed and affixed on all the publick places of the city, that none may pretend ignorance. And that all hawkers of both sexes who go about privately or publickly selling goods should be also prohibited to trade in time comeing, under the penalty above mentioned. As the report signed by the dean of gild bears ; which haveing been considered by the council, they, with the extraordinary deacons, approved thereof, and ordered that a draught of an act of council be extended thereon.'[1]

At the following meeting of council, held on 18th February 1736, the draft of the recent proclamation was submitted.[2] On 28th April 1736 the council passed the following act :

'The lord provost, magistrats, and council, with the deacons of crafts, ordinary and extraordinary, in council assembled, considering that, by the rights and infeftments granted to this city from the crown, and ratifications thereof in parliament, the right to admit freemen, both burgesses and gildbrethren, is vested in the magistrats, council, and deacons of crafts ; and that, by the laws of the land, and constitution of this and other royal burrows, it's unlawfull to or for any person to use, exercise, or occupy any branch of trade or craft within this city or libertys, except such as are burgesses and gildbrethren, or otherwise made free thereof, and that, notwithstanding, upon due enquiry had concerning the same by a committee of council who were thereto appointed, it does appear there are several women, other then daughters to burgesses and gild brethren, and other then those who have served apprentiships with freemen, who are now carying on trade and who are

---

[1] C. R. vol. lvi. p. 256.      [2] C. R. vol. lvi. p. 263.

not capable to be made free, many whereof, from a principle of laziness and avarice, have withdrawen themselves from service, which is the station of life in which they could be most usefull to themselves and to the community, and have creept into little shops, whereby the rights and priviledges belonging to freemen, their widows, their daughters, and apprentices, are vilely incroached on, and is also attended with other consequences, extremely hurtfull to the community, which have been sett furth by a petition from a great body of freemen : Likewise, considering that by an act of council made the 22nd of March 1717, it is, among other things, enacted that the widows of burgesses and gildbretheren dureing their widowity should hold and enjoy a right to trade, and that the daughters of burgesses and gildbretheren, while they are unmarried, should hold and enjoy the same, upon paying to the said dean of gild one-half of the dues in use to be paid at the entry of burgesses and gild-bretheren, and which payments, in case of their marriages, were to be allowed to their husbands in part of their own entry money, if they should think fitt to enter : Furder, considering that by another act of council, dated 23rd April 1729, in respect there were several who were disabled and disqualified by poverty to acquire their freedome, that were, according to the ancient laws and laudable practise of the royal burrows, to be indulged to trade as stal-langers in low and inconsiderable branches, such as the retaill of ale, beer, milk, herbs, roots, fruits, horsehyring, cowfeeding, poultry, and the lyke, upon payment to the dean of gild for the use of this city of an annual rate or duty, not exceeding £10 and not under £3 Scots, as should be settled by the dean of gild and his council annually, and to be specified in an act or order to be granted in that behalf by the dean of gild to every stallanger yearly, which was to endure only for a certain terme of five years that is now expired : Furder, considering from experience it is shewen that the forsaid payment to the dean of gild by daughters of burgesses and gildbretheren of one-half of the dues in use to be paid by burgesses and gildbretheren at their entry and admission is a burden too heavy to be born by the said daughters, also that to exclude women who have or may serve apprentiships with freemen from all manner of trade would be injurious to the freemen, and that women, even by such service, are not capable to be made free, otherwise than by a tollerance to trade, upon paying for it a valuable consideration to this city, yet that a grant of such a tollerance is an equitable and rational deed, and very consistant with the constitutions and laws of the burrows and usefull to the community. Moreover, that even a denyal of such a tollerance to gentle-women while unmarried, haveing pretty good stocks, and haveing been deallers for several years past in the milanary way, or in some such merchan-dise different from that which has been usually caryed on in the little shops complained on, and who shall be willing to pay to this city a valuable con-sideration for it, as hereinafter mentioned, would be an unjustifiable hardship done to them, and would be hurtfull to the community : Likewise, that the indulgeing the poorer sort of householders to trade as stallangers in the particulars hereinbefore and after mentioned, and no other, under the rules

and regulations hereinafter specified, is not injurious to the community, but
a real benifite to it, by putting maney inhabitants in a way to earn their
bread, and thereby prevent their becomeing burdensome to the community,
therefore the said lord provost, magistrats, and council, with the saids deacons
of crafts, did, and hereby do, unanimously enact and ordain, that from and
after the 15th day of May next no woman whatever, other than widows or
daughters or apprentices of burgesses or gildbretheren, or those to be tollerated as hereinafter enacted, shall exercise or occupy any branch of merchandise or traffic by retaill or otherwise within this city or any of its libertys, on
any pretence whatever; otherwise that they shall be prosecuted and punished
as unfree traders, conforme to law.   Further, the said lord provost, magistrats,
and council, with the said deacons of crafts, did, and hereby do, unanimously
ratifie, approve, and confirme the aforesaid in part recited act of council,
bearing date 22nd March 1717, with this variation only, that while the
daughters of burgesses and gildbretheren remain unmarried, they shall not
be lyable to pay to the dean of gild any part of entry money that is due and
payable by freemen burgesses or gildbretheren at their admission.   Also, it
is hereby enacted and ordained that it shall and may be lawfull to and for
such women who have or shall serve apprentiships to any freeman of this
city, and to such gentlewomen who have for some years past been deallers in
the milanary way, or in some such merchandise different from that which
has been usually caryed on in the little shops complained on, to cary on
their trade while they shall be unmarried, and that within this city, or any
of its libertys, upon payment to the dean of gild, for the use of this city, of
the sum of £6 sterling by every one of them, and upon their obtaining from
the dean of gild an act or order for tollerating them in that behalf, which is
hereby directed to be given and to be duely entered in the gild books.
Likewise, the dean of gild and his council, and their successors in office, from
and after the date hereof, dureing the full terme of five years next hereafter,
are hereby authorized and impowered to receive and admitt such householders
to be stallangers as by reason of poverty are not able and qualified to acquire
the freedome of this city, whereby liberty shall be given to them as stallangers to deale and trade in retaile of ale, beer, fish, milk, herbs, roots,
fruits, cowfeeding, horsehyring, poultry, eggs, salt fish, and salt flesh, and in
nothing else, and which are to be particularly settled and specified in their
respective acts of tolleration, which are to be renued annually, else to be of
no force, upon payment to this city of such a rate or sum annually as shall be
raited and settled by the dean of gild and his council, the sum to be severally
paid for every act of tolleration not exceeding £10 Scots nor to be under £3
Scots money; and that the receipts of such sums may be regularly brought
as a charge on the dean of gild and his successors, all such acts of tolleration
shall be duly entered in a book to be made and keept for that purpose, bearing the forsaid receipts.   Further, all and every one who shall be tollerated
as stallangers in manner hereinbefore specified are strictly prohibited and
discharged from dealling or tradeing in any trade or goods other than those

which are to be particularly specified in their several acts of tolleration, otherwise that they shall be prosecuted and punished as unfree traders; and the
dean of gild and his council, and their forsaids, are hereby required and
ordained to cause execute the laws made against unfree traders against every
person of both sexes residing within this city, or within any of its libertys,
who are unfree, or who shall not purchase their liberty, or be tollerated in
manner hereinbefore specified. Further, the dean of gild and his council,
and their forsaids, are hereby required and ordained to put in execution
the act of council, dated the 26th of February 1729, against hawkers and
petty pedlars. And that none may pretend ignorance hereof, it is hereby
ordered that thir presents be proclaimed by tuck of drum threw this city
and its libertys, and that printed copies hereof be affixed on all the publick
places as usual.'[1]

On 13th October 1736 a committee was appointed to consider
the act of council of 28th April, with the objections to the same
given in by several burgesses.[2] On 9th February 1737 the council
passed an act, in which, after narrating the preamble to their act
of 28th April 1736, and reciting the said act, they ratified and
approved of the same, except the clause by which licences were
authorized to be granted to women who have or should serve
apprenticeships to freemen, or to women dealing in the millinery
way, or in some such merchandise different from that usually
carried on in little shops.[3] On 9th March 1737 the following act
was passed:

'Considering that by a clause in the late act of council, dated the 28th
April 1736, for granting of licences, several persons, under collour of being
deallers in the millinary way, or in sume such merchandise different from
that which has been usually carryed on in little shops, has consigned the
sum of £6 sterling in the hands of the dean of gild in order to obtain such
licence to trade, in several ways · highly prejudicial to the right of free
burgesses: Also considering that the said act of council is now rescinded by
another act, dated 9th February last, therefore did authorise and appoint the
dean of gild and his council to enquire narrowly if any of those persons who
have consigned £6 for the use above mentioned are millenars or deallers in
the millenary way, and to give out licence to none but' those, excepting them
who are comprehended in the act last mentioned, and to return the money
of those persons who shall not be found to be millinars as aforesaid.'[4]

---

[1] C. R. vol. lvi. p. 315.          [2] C. R. vol. lvii. p. 87.
[3] C. R. vol. lvii. p. 203.          [4] C. R. vol. lvii. p. 217.

On 19th July 1738 a committee was appointed to revise and examine the rates of upsets and entries of burgesses and guild brethren, and to report how much the same ought to be increased.[1] On 14th February 1739 the price of entering gratis burgess was ordered to be confined to the rate set down in the council's act of 12th April 1704.[2] On 28th April 1742 the following act was passed in regard to the admission of burgesses and guild brethren :—

'In consequence of a late application from the Merchant Company of this city, setting furth the loss and inconveniences that might arise to them by persons getting false and improper designations when they are admitted burgesses and gildbretheren, on purpose to intitle them to priviledges which of right doe allenarly belong to the said Merchant Company, for preventing whereof the magistrates and council did and hereby do enact, statute, and ordain, that in all time comeing the dean of gild and his council shall admit no person burges or gildbrother of this city till a petition by such person be read openly in the gild court, desireing to be admitted burges or burges and gildbrother, and mentioning the title on which he claims the business to which he has served an apprenticeship, and the business he is at the present time in the exercise of, and the truth of all these allegations to be certified by at least two burgesses of character resideing in the place. Further, that the dean of gild and his council, the next dyet of court after the said petition is presented, shall pronounce an interlocutor on the said petition, either granting or refuseing the desire thereof, as they shall think proper; and if the petitioner be to be admitted burges or gildbrother, or both, the interlocutor shall direct what designation shall be in the ticket. And in like manner, that the dean of gild and his council, in their interlocutor, shall order every person to be designed in his ticket from the particular business he is at the time in exercise of, whither merchant or member of any of the incorporations, vintner, stabler, ale seller, etc.; and in case of his not having actually begun business, then he shall be designed son or apprentice to such a person, or simply indweller. As also, that the clerks keep the said petitions, certificats, and interlocutors on record, as a warrand to them for giving extracts of burges tickets; and if any clerk shall give an extract of a burges or a gildbrother ticket before such interlocutor be signed, or not agreeable to the interlocutor, he shall be lyable in a penalty of £10 sterling. And sicklike, that no fees be taken by the clerks, or any other officers of court, for the said petitions, certificats, and interlocutors, further than the dues at present in use to be paid by every burges or gildbrother at his entry. And lastly, that

[1] C. R. vol. lix. p. 150.    [2] C. R. vol. lx. p. 35.

this act be read at least twice a year publickly in the dean of gild court, viz., at their first meeting after the election of magistrates for the city, and at their first meeting in Aprile; and that the minuts of these dyets of court bear the reading of this act, under the penalty of twenty shillings sterling, to be paid by the clerks each time they omit to read and insert the same.'[1]

On 8th February 1744 the council ordained

'that in time comeing, such as shall neglect to enter in right of their wives during their lifetimes, shall not, upon their offering to enter afterwards, be entitled to any abatement of the ordinary dues in use to be payed by unfreemen.'[2]

By the Act 24 George II. c. 31 (1750–1), being an act for further regulating and encouraging the linen and hempen manufactures of Scotland, it was by sect. 3 provided

'that every maker of heckles, spinning-wheels, reels, weaving-looms and weaving-reeds, and also every weaver or manufacturer of linen, flaxen, or hempen cloth, or heckler or dresser of flax or hemp, shall and may and is hereby authorized to exercise the said respective trades, within any city, town, corporation, burgh, or place in Scotland, without any lett or hindrance from any person or persons whatsoever, and without being chargeable or charged with payment of any entry-money or other duty whatsoever, for or in respect of their following such trade or business.'

On 5th September 1759 the following act was passed:

' The dean of gild represented to the council that there were two persons applying to the dean of gild court to be admitted burgesses in right of their wives; that by an act of the town council, of date 19th July 1583,[3] it is enacted that daughters of burgesses shall lose their freedom if they are not reputed virgins; that this act had been so applied that the daughter of a burges could not communicate the freedom of the city to her second husband, although the first had not taken the benefite of entering burges in right of his wife, which was the case of the two persons now applying to the dean of gild court, and moved the council would explain the above act, in order to remove any difficulty arising therefrom in time coming; which being considered by the magistrates and council, they, with the extraordinary deacons, did and hereby do find and declare that the daughter of a burgess has right to communicate the freedom of the city to her second husband, in the event of her first husband's not entering burgess in her right.'[4]

---

[1] C. R. vol. lxiii. p. 31, 32, 33.        [2] C. R. vol. lxiv. p. 194.
[3] *Antea*, pp. 134–5.        [4] C. R. vol. lxxv. p. 379.

On 11th August 1762 the council admitted the five masters
of the High School to be burgesses and gild brethren, dispensing
with the dues, for good services done by them; but it was resolved,

'that for the future, none of the masters of the High School shall be admitted burgesses untill after they are five years in office.'[1]

On 13th May 1767 the council, while admitting Dr. Alexander
Carlisle, minister of the gospel at Inveresk, his Majesty's almoner,
to be burgess and guild brother, enacted as follows :

'Considering that a practice has for some time prevailed of giving the
freedom of the city to many persons indiscriminatly, which has been attended
with great inconvenience, the council do therefore enact and declare that no
burges ticket shall be granted in time comeing to any person whomever but
such as are invested with public character, or shall have signalized himself in
the service of his country or this city.'[2]

On 6th June 1770 Adam Smith, LL.D., was made burgess and
guild brother.[3]    On 17th July 1782 the following representation
was made by the dean of guild :—

'Dean of guild Cleghorn represented that, after entering upon his office,
he was at pains to enquire into the number of burgesses, and of persons
carrying on trade within the city not burgesses; that he discovered a considerable number who for many years had been altogether overlook't, and
others who had traded upon a licence in a line of business which did not
entitle them to that indulgence; that instead of ordering prosecutions, as
has been sometimes practised, he caused an advertisement to be published in
all the newspapers, and afterwards ordered circular letters to be sent to every
person trading who had not been admitted burges. In consequence of this,
one hundred and thirty-two persons had been admitted burgesses, and
seventy-six burges and guild brother, since Michaelmas 1781 ; that the sum
thus raised amounts to £972 sterling, and the roll of persons allowed to trade
by licence has not been diminished, and for the current year will yield about
£60 sterling, in all £1032 sterling; that the medium of this revenue for ten
years preceding Michaelmas 1780, including the licence money, is £262, 8s. 6d.
sterling annually, so that it has increased already £770 sterling.  The dean
of guild hoped it would not appear any presumption to propose that the
money thus raised this year over and above the ordinary income shall be

---

[1] C. R. vol. lxxvii. p. 293.        [2] C. R. vol. lxxxiii. p. 43.
[3] C. R. vol. lxxxvii. p. 26.

applied for the benefite and ornament of the city in some public work, and
what in his own judgment he would preferr, is the building a steeple for St.
Andrew's Church in George Street.'[1]

The council remitted the representation to the lord provost's
committee for report, and the lord provost, at the unanimous desire
of the council, thanked the dean for his attention to the city's
interest in the matter. On 30th August 1786 the following
representation by the old dean of guild was submitted to the
council, and ordered to lie on the table :

'Mr. M'Dowall, old dean of guild, represented that the dues payable
by burgesses and gildbretheren at their admission was established more than
a century ago, and as the money arising therefrom is applicable to such
public works as fall more immediately under the direction of the dean of
guild, the expence of which has been quadrupled since that establishment,
there must consequently be a very great deficiency in the fund for carrying
on these public works. Many of the corporations within the city, sensible
of the difference of the expence of all kind of works since the times that their
entrie moneys were fixed, have raised the same ; and the town of Aberdeen,
upon the same account, has augmented the dues payable by burgesses and
gildbretheren at their admission. He therefore submitted it to the council
if it would not be proper to take this matter into consideration, and to raise
the dues for admission of burgesses and gildbretheren in such manner as
shall appear equitable.'[2]

On 1st November 1786, and again on 13th June 1787, the
representation was remitted to a committee, but nothing seems to
have been done upon it. Several years afterwards, however, the
city chamberlain seems to have made a representation to the
council on the subject, and the same having been remitted to a
committee, they, on 25th January 1797, made a report, the substance of which, with the action that followed upon it, is embodied
in the following act :[3]

'The council, having heard read a report from the magistrates, old
magistrates, and convener, of the 24th instant, upon a motion by the
chamberlain for raising the entry money payable by persons when admitted

[1] C. R. vol. cii. p. 311.        [2] C. R. vol. cviii. p. 185.
[3] C. R. vol. cix. p. 342.

burgesses, stating " that the money t present payable was less than it was two centuries ago, and that, considering the difference in the value of money, and the many additional advantages since that period, the money at present payable was no ways adequate to the benefit derived from being a burges ; " and having taken the same under consideration, they unanimously approved of the said report, and in the terms thereof appointed and ordained, that from and after the 15th day of May next the following sums of money shall be paid to the community by persons to be admitted freemen, to wit—by a stranger when admitted a burgess, £12, 10s. : and when admitted a burgess and guildbrother, £25 ; and by all and every other person, either in right of a father, of a wife, or of a master, when admitted burgess, £6, 5s., and when admitted burgess and guildbrother, £12, 10s., all sterling money ; and authorized the dean of guild to grant licences to persons not able to pay their entry money, and to women, for such annual sum as he and his council may think adequate, according to the circumstances of the case of each individual ; and that a list of the persons so to be licensed, with the money annexed payable by them, shall yearly be made up and delivered to the town council at their first meeting in September next, and in every subsequent year ; and directed and required the dean of guild for the time being to order prosecutions according to law against all and every person and persons concerned who shall not either enter a freeman or obtain a license in manner before mentioned ; and appointed an extract of this minute to be made out, and delivered to the dean of guild without abiding a reading in council.' [1]

## On 5th April 1797 the following act was passed :

'Read memorial for Mr. Francis Braidwood, convener of the Incorporated Trades of Edinburgh, for himself, and in behalf of the whole incorporations of said city, and which memorial is of the following tenor :—" That in consequence of a resolution in council passed on the 25th of January last, the entry money payable by persons when admitted burgesses and guildbrethren is to be raised from and after the 15th day of May next, to a sum very considerable above the present. This determination of the council, though manifestly for the benefit of the comunity, and to the conviction of the memorialist and his brethren of the conveenery, yet has produced a good deal of agitation, and created a considerable degree of alarm, amongst the freemen and relatives of the masters of the different incorporations, many of whom have been induced, from motives of interest as well as conveniency, to bind their children or grandchildren to the same profession with themselves, and calculating, no doubt, upon the present reduced state of admission fees as one of the advantages attending it, and to which, by the sett of the city, they could with confidence claim. The memorialist, with a view to allay this alarm, and to obtain the sentiments of his brethren collectively, called a

---

[1] C. R. vol. cxxvi. p. 440.

meeting of the conveenery on the 31st day of March last, and they authorized
the memorialist to state the case of those relations of the freemen burgesses
of the different incorporations already mentioned, in a short but respectful
memorial to your lordship and the honourable council, and to request that
an abatement of the admission money for burgesses and guildbrethren, so far
as respects them, might be granted by an act of council passed to that effect.
The memorialist herewith produces the minute of the conveenery, and without urging argument or plea of favour further than what must naturally
occur to your lordship and every member of council, that the sons and sons-
in-law of freemen, burgesses, and tradesmen of Edinburgh are surely and
have a just title to be admitted burgesses and guildbrethren of this city in
virtue of the priviledge they derive from their father and wife to any
indifferent person.  The memorialist will not presume to say what this
abatement ought to be, but leaves the same solely to the discretion of the
council, and it is certain that, by their passing an act agreeable to the wishes
of the convenery, it will manifestly tend to the harmony and relief of the
whole trades of Edinburgh.  Signed by appointment of the convenery."
    'All which having been considered by the magistrates and council, they
agreed to reduce the fees payable to the city by sons and sons-in-law of
tradesmen, as well as merchants, to the sum of £9 on their entering burgesses
and guildbretheren, and to the half of that sum on their entering burgesses
only.'[1]

On 21st May 1800 a remit was made to a committee to consider
a motion to have the act of council raising the entry money of
burgesses rescinded, so far as it affected the members of the fourteen incorporations.  On 12th August the committee reported
against any alteration of the act, and their report was approved of
by the council on the following day. [2]

So matters appear to have remained until 15th October 1817,
when the following act was passed:

    The Lord Provost felt it to be his duty to represent to the council, that,
considering the benefits resulting to the individuals entering burges and
guild brother of this city, by the diminished rate of charge made on goods
imported by them into Leith, by the great and solid advantage which they
derive in case of adversity by the admission of their children into George
Heriot's, George Watson's, the Merchant Maiden, and other hospitals, in all
of which they are reared and educated in such a way as would reflect credit
upon their own parents in their best days of prosperity, and considering that

---

[1] C. R. vol. cxxvii. p. 181.          [2] C. R. vol. cxxxiii. p. 271.

no alteration has taken place upon the rate of fees. of admission for either burges or guild brother for a period of twenty years, during which the value of money has materially depreciated : The Lord Provost therefore moved that a committee be appointed to enquire into the present rate of fees of admission for burges and guild brother, and how far it may appear to be expedient and proper to encrease the same, and more particularly the fees paid by aliens or persons not having a claim to be entered guild brothers in right of consanguinity or relationship or of servitude, and whether these should not be materially encreased, so as more effectually to meet the intention of the pious founders of the before-named humane institutions, whose sole object must have been that of affording relief to the children of decayed citizens, and who were *bona fide* such.'

The magistrates and council having considered the foregoing representation, approved of the same, and remitted it to a select committee.[1]

In the year 1819 the Convention of Royal Burghs resolved that it was unnecessary and inexpedient, in the present state of society, to impose any oath upon entrant burgesses, and gave directions to the magistrates of all royal burghs to forbear in future to exact any oath; recommending that in lieu thereof a clause should be inserted in the tickets of admission, declaring that by the acceptance of his privileges the entrant becomes solemnly bound to discharge every civil duty incumbent by law on a true and faithful burgess. This resolution was reported to the council on 4th August 1819, and although it was stated that the burgess oath had gone into complete desuetude in Edinburgh, yet it was agreed immediately to adopt the same, trusting that the other burghs, on receiving the official notice of the act of convention, would be induced immediately to follow the example of Edinburgh.[2]

In 1818 a long standing dispute between the members of the guildry and the town council assumed the form of legal proceedings, and on 20th May the council remitted to the city's agent a summons which had been served upon them at the instance of

---

[1] C. R. vol. clxxv. p. 123.          [2] C. R. vol. clxxviii. p. 421.

certain persons styling themselves 'members of the Incorporation of Guildry.' This summons contended

'That it ought and should be found and declared that the guildry of Edinburgh is an existing body corporate, with all the rights and priviledges annexed to a body corporate by the laws of the kingdom, and the complainers, and the whole remanent members thereof, entitled in particular to exercise and enjoy the whole privileges and immunities conferred upon them by being entered therewith, according as the same have been enjoyed heretofore, or as they may establish their right thereto to the satisfaction of our said Lords : And the said lord provost, magistrates, and council of the city of Edinburgh ought and should be decerned and ordained, by decree foresaid, to admit and receive the said incorporation and its members into a full and free participation of all the rights and privileges which as a corporation, or individual members thereof, they are entitled to exercise and enjoy in common with the other societies and corporations of the said burgh, and also to communicate and preserve to them the whole of the exclusive rights and privileges to which as members of the guildry they are or shall be found entitled to lay claim : And it ought and should be also found and declared, by authority aforesaid, that the members of the said corporation, or any ten of them in number, having an undoubted right to call upon the dean by requisition to convene them, and if he shall refuse to comply with the terms of such requisition, that the members shall then be entitled to assemble, after advertisement or otherwise, as may be consistent with law ; that the various meetings above referred to, called after requisitions to the dean of guild, have been regularly and legally summoned, the proceedings thereat valid and effectual : And the said whole defenders ought and should be also decerned and ordained to cease and desist from interfering with the affairs of the company, in any manner of way, in all time hereafter ; and also to make payment to the complainers of the sum of £100 sterling, or such other sum as our said Lords shall modify as the expences of the process to follow hereon, over and above·the expences of extracting the decree to be pronounced therein, conform to the rights and privileges of the said corporation, and in its members and laws, and daily practice of Scotland, used and observed in the like cases, in all points, as is alleged.'[1]

Pending this action, a select committee of the House of Commons was appointed in 1819 to examine the matter set forth in the several petitions presented to the House from the Royal Burghs of Scotland during that and the two previous sessions of Parliament, and to report their observations and opinion thereon

---

[1] C. R. vol. clxxvi. p. 202.

to the House. The committee thus appointed appear to have investigated the claims of the guildry of Edinburgh, and their report, which was ordered to be printed on 12th July 1819, contains the following passage on the subject:—

'Your committee are of opinion that there is abundant evidence of the original existence of the guildry of Edinburgh as a corporation ; that persons admitted guild-brethren in terms of the sett of the burgh still possess certain privileges ; and that the power exists of continuing the body, by means of the admission of members to participate in these privileges in perpetual succession, by the dean of guild and his council, members of the body—a power which it does not appear to your committee can be supposed to exist in any but a corporation. Whether they have lost the right of administering their funds, or of assembling for the regulation of their affairs, is a question which your committee does not think it necessary to decide. That the funds originally destined to the support of their decayed members, among others, have been long diverted from that purpose ; and that rights and privileges they once possessed have been allowed to fall so much into disuse as now to be questioned in a court of law, your committee consider to be just subject of complaint, and to have arisen from the cause to which the petitioners ascribe it, namely, to the want of any vote or voice in the council.'[1]

On 11th January 1820, however, the Lord Ordinary (Cringletie) decided that the pursuers had failed to make out their case. The following is a copy of his note and interlocutor, which were reported to the council on 12th January 1820 :[2]—

'The Lord Ordinary has attentively considered this case, and thus communicates to the parties what has occurred to him.

'Originally the word "gild" seems to have applied to a society of merchants only—see Statutes of the Gild in 1283—and by the Statutes of William cap. 35, the whole merchants of the realm *are declared to enjoy and possess their merchant gild*, with liberty to buy and sell in all places within the *bounds of the liberties of the burghs* ; so that, according to this, if the guildry were an incorporation, it comprehends all the merchants of Scotland, all of whom were equally free to buy and sell within the city of Edinburgh as those individuals who lived in the city.

'Nothing, therefore, can be derived from the mere name of *gild* to show that the merchants of Edinburgh in particular ever were an incorporation. They were part of a guildry belonging to all Scotland. As, however,

---

[1] Report from the Select Committee (1819), pp. 14, 15
[2] C. R. vol. clxxix. p. 403.

merchants were a more respectable class of the community than tradesmen, it is easy to suppose that the government of burghs would in early times have been committed to their exclusive management, who, again, would naturally secure to themselves certain privileges ; and it seems equally clear that this created dissensions and dissatisfaction in the city of Edinburgh— as much as the privileges of the senators did in ancient Rome—and made way for the admission of the trades to participate in the government and privileges of the city ; but the government of the town having been committed to the guildry or merchants, and their having obtained privileges, by no means prove that they were an incorporation, the more particularly—1*st*, As the right to buy and sell was granted to them by statute, and *was not exclusive in Edinburgh to them alone*, the same right being competent to the whole merchants of the realm ; and 2*d*, That out of this same guildry arose all the different corporations of craftsmen. If the Lord Ordinary mistake not, the craftsmen of Edinburgh are many of them brethren of the guild ; at least if they be not, certain it is that by the decreet arbitral of King James the Sixth in 1583 they all may be so, as is there ordered :—" Item, toward the long controversies for the guildry, it is finally with common consent appointit, agreeit, and concludit, that *as weill* craftsmen as merchants shall be receivit and admittit gild brether, and the ane not to be refusit nor secludit therefra mair nor the other, they being burgesses of the burgh alsmeit qualified therefor, and that gild brether to have liberty to use merchandise ; " and by the same decree it is ordered that no person shall act *as a merchant* or as a craftsman unless he be a burgess and freeman of the burgh. This decree was ratified in Parliament, and therefore after this period the general right of the original guildry or society of merchants of the realm was abridged so far that they could not trade in Edinburgh unless they were admitted as burgesses ; but, on the other hand, there was no incorporation of the merchants and craftsmen of Edinburgh into one corporation. In short, it appears to the Lord Ordinary that originally the term " gildry " applied to a description of persons, viz. merchants, as much as the terms clergy, navy, or army characterize particular descriptions of subjects, having each particular privileges, but by no means can entitle these or either of them to be considered incorporations in the proper legal sense of that word.

Accordingly the guildry of Edinburgh never chose their own dean, neither did they chuse his council nor any of the officers of his court. 2*dly*, They do not even admit members, who by said decreet arbitral are admitted by the provost, magistrates, and council, dean of guild and his council. 3*dly*, They have no funds peculiar to themselves, all fees arising from their own admission, or on account of their apprentices, being at the disposal of the magistrates and council. Of course they have no boxmaster, all of which are decided evidence of their not being an Incorporation.

In these answers it is said that since 1487 downwards there is no evidence of the guild brethren having ever held courts or meetings for the purpose of transacting business of any kind, and opposite to this passage on the margin of the page are written with pencil these words—"Disproved by the recently discovered entries in the Guildry Records, *circa* 1500." For sake of argument, the Lord Ordinary will admit this note to be correct. But what follows? Just this, that after the crafts were to be admitted as well as the merchants into the guildry, such meetings were considered to be highly exceptional, as leading to turbulence, since by the said decree all meetings were prohibited, and since that date it is not even alleged that there have been meetings of the guildry till those giving rise to the present action ; and indeed there could not properly be meetings of the guildry, since that word, instead of applying as originally to merchants only, now comprehends not only them but all craftsmen of Edinburgh, and as all of these are incorporated into separate corporations, having their separate officers, there cannot exist any common interest in the guildry (*i.e.* the whole) other than what is common to all the inhabitants of the city, who may as well claim to be a corporation as the collective body of merchants and tradesmen.

'Accordingly, the very purpose for which some of the members of the guildry lately called on the dean of guild to assemble the whole, was avowedly one in which every inhabitant of the city was as much interested as the guildry. It was one which, prior to 1583, disturbed the tranquillity of the city, and of course was chiefly in the view of the King and arbiters when they prohibited all conventions.

'The Lord Ordinary is therefore of opinion that the term "guildry" applied originally to the merchants of the whole kingdom, and that those of Edinburgh never were embodied into a corporation. Consequently that they are not now a "corporation," and in a particular manner that they have no right to call on the dean of guild to call meetings of the guildry, or failing of his doing so, for any number of the members of it to call meetings.

'As to the title to pursue, the Lord Ordinary of course thinks that as a body the guildry has none, and particularly without concurrence of the dean and his council, who have disclaimed the action ; but he thinks it was competent for individuals to pursue for the purpose of having it found that they are members of an incorporation, as much as they can sue for any privilege, honour or emolument.

### INTERLOCUTOR.

'11*th January* 1820.—The Lord Ordinary having advised the summons, defences, the condescendence for the pursuers, their answers, productions for both parties, and the whole process, for the reasons explained in the foregoing note, sustains the title of the pursuers as individuals to carry on this action, but assoilzies the defenders therefrom, and decerns ; finds the pursuers liable for expences, to be taxed by the auditor of court, to whom remits the account when the same shall be given in.          (Signed)        J. Wolfe Murray.'

Eventually, the whole of the legal proceedings between the guildry and the council were abandoned, and subsequently the

Burgh Reform Act, 3 and 4 William IV. cap. 76, passed on 28th
August 1833, declared that from and after the passing of the act,
every guildry should be entitled to the free election, in such form
as should be regulated by them, of the dean of guild, or director,
or other lawful officers for the management of their affairs without
any interference or control whatsoever on the part of the town
council or any member thereof. It also declared, that from and
after the time when it came into operation, the person elected
dean of guild by the guild brethren in Edinburgh should be a
constituent member of the town council of the city, and should
enjoy all the powers and perform all the functions then enjoyed or
performed by such office-bearer in the city. The passing of this
act gave a new impulse to the questions at issue between the
guildry and the council. The former contended that the legislature had recognised not only their right to elect the dean, but
their character and privileges as an incorporation. The latter, on
the other hand, insisted that the provisions referred to were not
intended to confer on the members of the guildry any rights which
did not previously exist, but that on the contrary such rights are
reserved, and that the important questions in dispute were still left
upon the footing of the ancient law and practice.[1] In November
1833, accordingly, when a meeting of the members of the guildry
was called by circular and advertisement in the newspapers, to elect
'the dean of guild court, including the clerk and officer, a
treasurer, a clerk or secretary to the guildry, and twelve assistants,' the lord provost called the attention of the council to the
subject, and observed that—

'Heretofore there was no incorporation of guildry in this city; that by the
Burgh Reform Act a power was for the first time given to the guild brethren
of Edinburgh to elect their dean of guild, who is *ex officio* to have a seat in
council; and that for time immemorial the election of the members of the dean
of guild court, of the clerk of court, and of the officer of court had belonged

---

[1] Special Report on Edinburgh by the Commission on Municipal Corporations in Scotland, 1835, p. 319.

to the magistrates and council. Not content, however,' he added, 'with the boon conferred on them of electing their own dean, or an officer, a clerk or treasurer, or as many assistants as they might think proper, this new incorporation had thought fit unequivocally to declare its intention of encroaching on the patronage of the magistrates and council, in such a way as to render it incumbent on them to defend their right, so as to hand down the same unimpaired to their successors. The lord provost therefore moved the council that instruction be given to the agents to present a bill of suspension and interdict to stop the meditated election by the guildry of the members of the dean of guild court, the clerk of court, and officer, and the motion was agreed to and the agent instructed accordingly.'[1]

A few days afterwards, a committee was appointed to confer with a committee of the guildry in regard to the appointment of certain officers,[2] and on 20th November 1833 the dean of guild submitted to the council the names of the persons whom he wished to form his court, declaring that he proposed their names to the Council without in any way compromising the rights of the Guildry if they should be found entitled to elect the dean of guild court. The magistrates and council therefore elected the persons so proposed to be old dean of guild and guild councillors, and remitted to the dean to qualify them in the usual manner.[3] On this being done, the council withdrew the interdict which had been obtained. At a subsequent meeting of council, a deputation from the guildry presented a memorial, in which they craved the council to

'relinquish, now and in all time coming, any interference with the admission of members of the guildry, and make restitution to the treasurer of the incorporation of whatever sums had been received on this account since the passing of the Burgh Reform Act.'

The memorial was remitted to the lord provost's committee, but no concession has been made to the guildry. The council still claim, in point of law and usage, the exclusive right of admitting burgesses and guild brethren, which they have enjoyed since the year 1573; having exercised it by the dean of guild, not as the

---

[1] C. R. vol. ccxiv. p. 374.          [2] C. R. vol. ccxiv. p. 397.
[3] C. R. vol. ccxiv. p. 413.

representative of the guildry, but as one of their own body, whose duty it has been to admit such members without any interposition whatever on the part of the guild brethren. In practice, the town-clerk signs the tickets of admission, receives the fees, and pays them over to the city chamberlain. The magistrates and council thus claim, and have in practice received, the whole of the entry-money.

Since the passing of the Burgh Reform Act, the dean of guild has been elected by the guildry annually; and the certificate of election has borne that the election was made by the 'Incorporation of the Guildry.' The assumption of this title has, however, been invariably met on the part of the council by the declaration 'that there is no Incorporation of Guildry or Guild brethren in this city.' [1]

On 10th March 1835 a remit was made, on the motion of Bailie M'Laren, to the treasurer's committee, with the dean of guild, to consider and report

'whether a reduction might not be made on the entry-money payable by the burgesses, which, by encreasing the number of entrants, would have the effect of encreasing the revenues of the city.' [2]

Under this remit the following report was adopted by the committee :—

'*Edinburgh, 3d October* 1837.—The Treasurer's Committee, to whom was remitted on the 10th March 1835 " to consider and report whether a reduction might not be made on the entry-money payable by burgesses, which, by encreasing the number of entrants, would have the effect of encreasing the revenues of the city," have hitherto delayed reporting, in the expectation that the roll of the Parliamentary constituency for the election of councillors would ere now have been declared by act of parliament to be the burges roll of the burgh, as has been done in regard to the burghs of England. As this expectation has not been realized, the committee have taken the subject into

---

[1] The above paragraph was written in 1873, since which time the practice has changed. The declaration referred to was discontinued subsequent to the year 1886.

[2] C. R. vol. ccxviii. p. 380.

consideration, and beg leave to report as follows, beginning with a tabular view of the number of burgesses entered annually from 1825 to the present time:—

| Years. | | | Number of Burgesses. | | | Additional number entered as Councillors. |
|---|---|---|---|---|---|---|
| 1825 | . | . | 133 | . | . | ... |
| 1826 | . | . | 71 | . | . | ... |
| 1827 | . | . | 83 | . | . | ... |
| 1828 | . | . | 53 | . | . | ... |
| 1829 | . | . | 52 | . | . | ... |
| 1830 | . | . | 64 | . | . | ... |
| 1831 | . | . | 46 | . | . | ... |
| 1832 | . | . | 28 | . | . | ... |
| 1833 | . | . | 20 | . | . | 14 |
| 1834 | . | . | 11 | . | . | 2 |
| 1835 | . | . | 13 | . | . | 6 |
| 1836 | . | . | 21 | . | . | 2 |
| 1837 | . | . | 17 | . | . | ... |
| | | | 612 | | | 24 |

'It will be observed from the above statement, that the yearly average number admitted during the last four years (excluding those who entered as councillors) was 15½, while during the first four years the average number admitted was 85, the decrease being nearly in the proportion of from six to one. This fact shows that unless some very great change shall be made regarding their admission, the term "burgess," in place of being nearly synonymous with "householder," as it was in ancient times, will be applicable only to a very small fraction of the householders of the burgh.

'The committee are of opinion that to the comparatively high rate of the entry-money must be ascribed the small number of entrants, when it is considered that for this entry-money the burgesses now enjoy no exclusive privileges whatever from the public; for the committee do not regard the fact of their children being eligible for admission into George Heriot's Hospital as an exception to the rule, that institution being supported solely from the funds invested for that purpose by the munificence of a private individual. With this conviction, the committee are unanimously and decidedly of opinion that the entry-money ought immediately to be greatly reduced.

'Of the 636 burgesses admitted during the last thirteen years, 229 were what is technically called "strangers"—that is, persons who had no claim under any act of council to be admitted at less than the maximum rate of £16, 9s., which includes £3, 1s. 4d. for stamp-duty and engraving of the burgess ticket.

'The remaining number of 407 were all privileged persons. Of these, there were 121 apprentices of burgesses, who were admitted at the modified rate of £8 each, including £1, 1s. 4d. for stamp and engraving of ticket ; and 286 sons or sons-in-law of burgesses, who were admitted at the modified rate of £6, 5s. 6d. each, including £1, 1s. 4d. for stamp and ticket. The average rate payable by each of the total number admitted was £10, 5s. 4d., including £1, 15s. 9d. for stamp and engraving of ticket, or, after deducting this sum, the average rate was £8, 9s. 7d., which was paid partly to the city, and partly to the city clerks, dean of guild clerk, and dean of guild officer. For a stranger, the sum was divided as follows :—To the city, £12, 10s. ; for stamp and ticket, £3, 1s. 4d. ; city clerks, 4s. 10d. ; dean of gild clerk, 10s. 5d. ; dean of gild officer, 2s. 5d. It is unnecessary to particularize the items of the payments by the other classes. Taking the average of the whole number of burgesses admitted during the period embraced in the statement, the sum received by the corporation from each, after deduction of all the claims referred to, was £7, 14s. 3d.

'The committee are of opinion that the future entry-money payable by all burgesses, without exception, should be equal to one-fourth of the maximum rates presently chargeable to strangers on account of the city, the city clerks, dean of guild clerk, and dean of guild officer, according to the following scale :

| | | | | |
|---|---|---|---|---|
| The city . | . | . | . | £3 2 6 |
| City clerks. | . | . | . | 0 1 3 |
| Dean of guild clerk | . | . | . | 0 2 10 |
| Dean of guild officer | . | . | . | 0 0 7 |
| Stamp and ticket . | . | . | . | 3 1 4 |
| | | | | £6 8 6 |

'The Stamp duty for the sons, sons-in-law, and apprentices of burgesses being £1, 1s. 4d., the total charge to all these classes will be farther reduced to £4, 8s. 6d.

'The average sum formerly payable to the city for each entry, after deduction of all expenses, being £7, 14s. 3d., and the sum proposed to be charged by the city in future being £3, 2s. 6d., it follows that if the number of entries on an average of the next four years shall increase from the present rate of 15½ annually to 38, the revenue derived by the city from the entry of burgesses will be the same as it has been during the last four years. If the number of entries shall encrease to the average rate of the first four years of the period referred to, namely to 85, the revenue will be encreased threefold. That the number of entries will encrease to the extent of 85 per annum, your committee do not expect, but they entertain no doubt that they will encrease to such an extent as to render the revenue under the proposed arrangement greater than under the present system. The establishment of the schools of George Heriot's Hospital, to which the children of burgesses, by the act of Parliament under which they are erected, enjoy a preferable right, will be an additional inducement for the humbler classes of citizens to become burgesses when the entry-money shall be reduced to a sum within their reach, as it will be by the proposed alterations.

'In this way these classes of the inhabitants will be greatly benefited, by having their children educated at little or no expense, while their anxiety to obtain this advantage will effectually prevent any decrease in the revenues of the city.

'If these recommendations shall be agreed to, the committee are of opinion that all persons admitted as simple burgesses should really be citizens of Edinburgh in the proper sense of the term, *bona fide* residents as house-holders, or carrying on business as masters, in some part of the ancient or extended royalty of the city, and consequently bearing some share of the city burdens, or, as it is technically called, "paying scot and lot." There can be no doubt whatever that no other classes are, or ever have been, properly entitled to become burgesses of the city, and that it was for such only that George Heriot's Hospital and other hospitals wer eestablished. Indeed, it is apparent from the records of the town council, that at the time George Heriot's Hospital was founded, so strictly was this rule enforced, that when any burgess went to reside beyond the limits of the royalty, he ceased to be a burgess of Edinburgh, and was incapable of enjoying any of the privileges of a burgess.

'For a number of years great laxity has been observed in the admission of burgesses—parties having frequently been admitted solely with a view to get their children into George Heriot's Hospital, who never resided within the city, and who never bore any part of the city burden ; and in some recent instances parties have even been admitted who, at the period of their admission, and for many years before, had resided in distant parts of the kingdom. It is perfectly evident that in every case in which the children of such persons are admitted into the hospital, the children of *bona fide* citizen-burgesses are inevitably excluded, the number who can be received being necessarily limited. Hence, by the indiscriminate admission of burgesses who have no connection with or interest in the ancient or extended royalty of the city, the children of the citizen-burgesses are deprived of a positive right, which was intended exclusively for their benefit by the munificent founder of that institution.

'The committee are of opinion that the very least residence which can be required within the royalty of the city, either by carrying on business as masters, or by the occupation of dwelling-houses as proprietors or tenants, should be—for masters, uninterrupted occupancy for one year, and for house-holders, uninterrupted occupancy for three years at the date of admission ; with the exception of the apprentices of burgesses serving for the freedom of the city, within the royalty, from whom such residence should not be required, and that proper evidence of occupancy, such as the production of tax receipts, or other evidence to the satisfaction of the dean of guild clerk, should be required in all other cases.

'The committee intend these regulations regarding residence to apply only to those who enter as simple burgesses, and not to those who enter as burgesses and guild brethren, and who derive any advantage in return for the payment made to the city, by a modified rate of shore-dues on goods imported by them into the harbour of Leith.'

The report was submitted to the council on 3d October 1837, and was ordered to be printed and circulated, with a view to its being considered at the following meeting.[1]  The report was accordingly considered on 10th October 1837, with the following addition to it:[2]—

'Since the foregoing report was laid before the council, it has been represented to the committee, that to enforce residence within the royalty, in the case of surgeons wishing to enter as burgesses with the sole view of being admitted Fellows of the Royal College of Surgeons, would be productive of great hardship to individuals, because all applicants for admission must produce a burgess ticket, and cases may occur in which it is of great importance that persons should be admitted who are not qualified in respect either of residence or apprenticeship.  It has been suggested by members of the Royal College, that from the scientific character of that body, and the fact that its fellows enter without any view to the admission of their children into the hospitals, the council should permit all applicants who have neither resided within the royalty nor served as apprentices for the freedom of the city, to be admitted burgesses at the present maximum rate of £16, 9s.  The committee are of opinion that this representation is well founded, and that for the reasons stated an exception should be made in favour of all applicants for admission as Fellows of the Royal College of Surgeons, to the extent of allowing those who are not qualified in respect either of residence or apprenticeship, to enter as burgesses on their paying the present maximum rate of £16, 9s.

'The committee recommend that this minute should be extracted and communicated to the dean of guild clerk, without abiding a reading, in order that the new regulation may come into immediate operation.

(Signed)          D. M'LAREN, Treasurer.'

In consequence of a protest by the clerk to the Trustees of the City Creditors against the proposed reduction of entry-money, it was resolved on 18th October 1837 to delay acting upon the resolution come to by the council.[3]  Afterwards, on 24th October

<hr>

[1] C. R. vol. ccxxv. p. 75.          [2] C. R. vol. ccxxv. p. 108.
[3] C. R. vol. ccxxv. p. 139.

1837, a remit was made to the lord provost's committee, to request a conference with the Trustees of the City Creditors on the subject.[1] A conference accordingly took place between them on 30th October 1837, but the Trustees declined to agree to the proposed reduction, and the declinature was reported to the Council on the following day.[2] At the same meeting an interdict against the proposed reduction of dues was served on the council, and ordered to be answered.

On 11th September 1838 the council adopted a motion made by Treasurer M'Laren, and resolved that the act of 10th October 1837 regarding the reduction of the burgess dues (the operation of which was suspended at the instance of the Trustees for the Creditors) should be immediately carried into effect.[3] And on 2d October 1838 they further resolved, on the motion of Treasurer M'Laren,

'that the dues payable on the admission of guild brethren be reduced to the same rates and subject to the same conditions as the dues payable by burgesses, as contained in the report sanctioned by the town council on the 11th September last.'[4]

On 27th August 1839 the council adopted a motion by Councillor M'Laren, and remitted to the treasurer's committee to consider what dues should in future be charged on the admission of burgesses and guild brethren.[5] Under this remit, the committee on 10th September submitted the following report, which was approved of by the council:—

'*Edinburgh*, 3d *September* 1839.—The treasurer's committee, in terms of the remit to them to consider what amount of dues should be charged in future on the admission of burgesses and guild brethren, beg leave to report that the existing regulations enacted on 10th October 1837, and 11th September and 2d October 1838, should be altered in the following respects :—

'I. That the dues to be charged on the admission as a burgess of a person being the son, son-in-law, or apprentice of a burgess should be—

---

[1] C. R. vol. ccxxv. p. 204.     [2] C. R. vol. ccxxv. p. 234.
[3] C. R. vol. ccxxvii. p. 473.     [4] C. R. vol. ccxxviii. p. 101.
[5] C. R. vol. ccxxxi. p. 65.

| | | | | | |
|---|---|---|---|---|---|
| For the city | . | . | . | . | £3 14 0 |
| The city clerks | . | . | . | . | 0 1 3 |
| The dean of guild clerk | . | . | . | . | 0 2 10 |
| The dean of guild officer | . | . | . | | 0 0 7 |
| For vellum and engraving ticket | | . | . | | 0 1 4 |

In all . . . £4 0 0

'II. That the dues to be charged on the admission as a burgess of a person in the character of a stranger should be—

| | | | | | |
|---|---|---|---|---|---|
| For the city | . | . | . | . | £4 14 0 |
| The city clerks | . | . | . | . | 0 1 3 |
| The dean of guild clerk | . | . | . | . | 0 2 10 |
| The dean of guild officer | . | . | . | | 0 0 7 |
| For vellum and engraving ticket | | . | . | | 0 1 4 |

In all . . . £5 0 0

'III. That the same amount of dues respectively should be charged on the admission of persons as guild brethren of the city.

'IV. That in cases where persons enter both as burgesses and guild brethren at one and the same time, and where, therefore, only one ticket is necessary, the dean of guild clerk should be authorized nevertheless to charge the expence of the vellum and engraving of the ticket, as if the parties had entered burgesses at one time and guild brethren at another.'[1]

On the motion of Convener Maclagan, it was remitted to the treasurer's committee, on 3d January 1843, to consider the following motion :

'That any person, upon satisfying the dean of guild clerk that he is a member of any of the fourteen incorporated trades, and carrying on business within the city, shall have a right to a burgess ticket upon payment of the usual fees ; and the regulation regarding apprentices shall be effective only regarding indentures entered into after this date.'[2]

And on 31st January 1843 the following report by the committee was submitted to the council :—.

'The committee had before them the motion of Convener Maclagan, which was remitted to this committee on the 3d inst. ; and it having been explained by Convener Maclagan that the object he had in view was to obviate the difficulty thrown in the way of entrants with the incorporations of the city obtaining their burgess tickets under the regulations adopted by the council in

---

[1] C. R. vol. ccxxxi. p. 65.          [2] C. R. vol. ccxxxviii. p. 232.

1837, inasmuch as the party applying for a burgess ticket is required to produce evidence of his having occupied premises and carried on business for one year, while by the laws of the incorporations no person can open shop or commence any business affecting their privileges until he shall have become a member of incorporation, but which he cannot be without producing his burgess ticket.

'The committee having considered the matter, are of opinion that this anomaly may be obviated by making the following regulations in regard to the granting of burgess tickets to applicants for admission into any of the incorporations, viz. that as soon as an essay shall have been appointed to any applicant for admission into any of the incorporated trades, or an order made for taking him upon trials towards his admission, the dean of guild clerk shall issue a burgess ticket to such person on production of a certificate from the clerk of the incorporation that his essay had been appointed, or an order made for taking him upon trials.'

The report was approved of by the council, with this further condition, that the entry-money of the applicant, or the first moiety thereof, if payable by moieties, shall also be certified to have been paid.[1]

On 7th February 1843 the council, on the motion of Councillor Murray, remitted to the treasurer's committee to consider and report on the regulations for the admission of burgesses and guild brethren.[2] And on the 14th of the same month the following motion was remitted to the same committee for consideration:

'That the privilege granted to the sons of members of the incorporated trades, and what are called free apprentices, of obtaining burgess tickets upon other terms than are applicable to other members of the community, be rescinded;'

along with a petition on the same subject by sundry burgesses.[3] On 12th November 1844 the dean of guild clerk was directed, on the motion of Councillor Johnston, to prepare a return of the gross number of burgess tickets issued annually during the last five years, distinguishing the number of persons who have in addition become guild brethren during the same period.[4] And on

[1] C. R. vol. ccxxxviii. p. 289.　　[2] C. R. vol. ccxxxviii. p. 330.
[3] C. R. vol. ccxxxviii. p. 356.　　[4] C. R. vol. ccxlii. p. 463.

19th November 1844 this return was printed and laid on the table of the council.[1]

On 24th December 1844, the council, on the motion of Treasurer Thomson, adopted the following resolution :

'That it be remitted to the treasurer's committee to consider and report whether an increase might not be made on the entry-money payable by burgesses and guild brethren, and some arrangements made for more effectually securing the rights of the children of *bona fide* burgesses, whose parents had paid scot and lot.'[2]

And on 7th January 1845 the following report, dated January, was submitted to the council, and ordered to be printed :[3]

'The treasurer's committee have repeatedly and deliberately considered the remit made to them, to report whether an increase might not be made on the entry-money payable by burgesses and guild brethren, and some arrangements made for the more effectually securing the rights of the children of *bona fide* burgesses, whose parents had paid scot and lot.

'The committee have had before them the successive regulations on this subject enacted by the magistrates and council from 10th October 1837 downwards, and they have inquired into the different attempts which of late years have been made to alter or amend those regulations, and the causes of the failure of those attempts.

'On a careful review of the whole subject, the committee are unanimously of opinion :—

'1. That the expectation entertained in the act of council 10th October 1837, that the revenue, under the arrangements then proposed, would be greater than under the former system, has not been realized.

'2. That a large proportion of the persons who have entered burgesses of late years did not belong to the class of merchants, tradesmen, and shop-keepers, from which chiefly the burgesses used to be drawn ; and did so enter chiefly from the hope of benefiting by the admission of their sons into George Heriot's Hospital, thus injuring the rights of *bona fide* burgesses, who have paid the local taxes, and done good service to the city.

'3. That this is an evil which is growing, and that the only remedy for it is to fall back on the rates of admission charged previously to the act of council 10th October 1837, which appears to have been devised with a due regard to the rights and circumstances of all parties.

'The treasurer's committee therefore unanimously recommend :—

'1. That the act of council 10th October 1837, and all other acts of council

---

[1] C. R. vol. ccxliii. p. 8.　　　　[2] C. R. vol. ccxliii. p. 93.
[3] C. R. vol. ccxliii. p. 132.

subsequent thereto regulating the admission of burgesses and guild brethren, should be repealed.

'2. That the rates of admission payable anterior to the said act should be enacted of new : of these a table is subjoined.

'3. That with the exceptions after mentioned, it shall be a necessary qualification to admission that the person applying *bona fide* resides or carries on business within the parliamentary boundary of the burgh.

'4. That, in terms of the Burgh Reform Act, this qualification shall not be enforced in the case of entrants who have been elected councillors of the burgh.

'5. Neither should this qualification be required of apprentices who have regularly served for the freedom of the city.

'6. Nor of persons residing or carrying on business beyond the parliamentary boundary, and not apprentices, who are applying for admission into the Merchant Company, or into any of the trades incorporations ; provided always that in these cases a certificate shall be produced from the treasurer or clerk of the company or incorporation, bearing that the entry-money of the applicant, or the first moiety thereof if payable by moieties, has been paid.

## 'TABLE OF RATES OF ADMISSION.

### BY PURCHASE.

'1. Burgess and guild brother :—

| | | | | | | | |
|---|---|---|---|---|---|---|---|
| To the city | . | . | . | . | £25 | 0 | 0 |
| City clerks | . | . | . | . | 0 | 9 | 8 |
| Dean of guild clerk | . | . | . | . | 0 | 16 | 8 |
| Dean of guild officer | . | . | . | . | 0 | 4 | 10 |
| Stamp duty, vellum, and engraving | . | . | | | 3 | 1 | 4 |
| | | | | | £29 | 12 | 6 |

'2. Burgess or guild brother :—

| | | | | | | | |
|---|---|---|---|---|---|---|---|
| To the city | . | . | . | . | £12 | 10 | 0 |
| City clerks | . | . | . | . | 0 | 4 | 10 |
| Dean of guild clerk | . | . | . | . | 0 | 10 | 5 |
| Dean of guild officer | . | . | . | . | 0 | 2 | 5 |
| Stamp duty, vellum, and engraving | . | . | | | 3 | 1 | 4 |
| | | | | | £16 | 9 | 0 |

### IN RIGHT OF MASTER, UPON A REGISTERED INDENTURE.

'1. Burgess and guild brother :—

| | | | | | | | |
|---|---|---|---|---|---|---|---|
| To the city | . | . | . | . | £12 | 12 | 0 |
| City clerks | . | . | . | . | 0 | 9 | 8 |
| Dean of guild clerk | . | . | . | . | 0 | 10 | 8 |
| Dean of guild officer | . | . | . | . | 0 | 4 | 10 |
| Stamp duty, vellum, and engraving | . | . | | | 1 | 1 | 4 |
| | | | | | £14 | 18 | 6 |

'2. Burgess or guild brother :—

| | | | | | | | |
|---|---|---|---|---|---|---|---|
| To the city | . | . | . | . | £6 | 5 | 0 |
| City clerks | . | . | . | . | 0 | 4 | 10 |
| Dean of guild clerk | . | . | . | . | 0 | 6 | 5 |
| Dean of guild officer | . | . | . | . | 0 | 2 | 5 |
| Stamp duty, vellum, and engraving | | . | . | 1 | 1 | 4 |
| | | | | | £8 | 0 | 0 |

IN RIGHT OF FATHER OR WIFE.

'1. Burgess and guild brother :—

| | | | | | | | |
|---|---|---|---|---|---|---|---|
| To the city | . | . | . | . | £9 | 0 | 0 |
| City clerks | . | . | . | . | 0 | 9 | 8 |
| Dean of guild clerk | . | . | . | . | 0 | 10 | 2 |
| Dean of guild officer | . | . | . | . | 0 | 4 | 10 |
| Stamp duty, vellum, and engraving | | . | . | 1 | 1 | 4 |
| | | | | | £11 | 6 | 0 |

'2. Burgess or guild brother :—

| | | | | | | | |
|---|---|---|---|---|---|---|---|
| To the city | . | . | . | . | £4 | 10 | 0 |
| City clerks | . | . | . | . | 0 | 4 | 10 |
| Dean of guild clerk | . | . | . | . | 0 | 6 | 11 |
| Dean of guild officer | . | . | . | . | 0 | 2 | 5 |
| Stamp duty, vellum, and engraving | | . | . | 1 | 1 | 4 |
| | | | | | £6 | 5 | 6 |

The report was considered on 21st January, when, after discussing the whole matter, it was recommitted to the treasurer's committee for further consideration.[1] Nothing appears, however, to have followed on this remit.

By the act 9 and 10 Vict. c. 17 (14th May 1846) the exclusive privileges of carrying on or dealing in merchandize, and of carrying on or exercising trades or handicrafts in burghs was abolished, and it was declared that

'it shall be lawful for any person to carry on or deal in merchandize, and to carry on or exercise any trade or handicraft in any burgh and elsewhere in Scotland, without being a burgess of such burgh, or a guild brother, or a member of any guild, craft or incorporation.'

A memorial by the Merchant Company, complaining of the operation of the rules with regard to the admission of burgesses

[1] C. R. vol. ccxliii. p. 155.

and guild brethren enacted in 1837 and 1838, and requesting the
magistrates and council to take these acts under their consideration,
and to modify the same, to the effect of allowing all parties resident
in Leith and the suburbs of Edinburgh, otherwise qualified, to
become burgesses and guild brethren, the purpose of such parties
being, by that means, to become also members of the Merchant
Company, was remitted to the Lord Provost's committee, by whom,
on 4th August 1847, the following report was prepared, and
approved of by the council on 10th August:

'The Lord Provost's committee having considered this memorial, and
referred to the act of council 31st January 1843 in favour of the trades
incorporations, without admitting the correctness of all the statements made
and arguments used by the Merchant Company in support of the memorial,
are of opinion that, following out the precedent established by that act, the
magistrates and council should agree to admit as burgesses and guild brethren
all persons not admissible by the present regulations who may apply to be
admitted as members of the Merchant Company, and who shall produce a
certificate from the treasurer of the Company of their having so applied.'

On 3d June 1849 a sub-committee of the treasurer's committee,
while reporting upon the establishment of a superannuation fund
for the officials of the city, recommended—

'That all the officials of the city, both present and future, and including
those not appointed directly by the council, and also those not paid directly
from the city's revenues, should enter themselves as burgesses of the city, and
so make some provision against a time of adversity, both for themselves and
for their children. The present rules as to the admission of burgesses throw
difficulties in the way, inasmuch as these require, as a preliminary qualification, that all entrants shall have carried on business on their own account
within the royalty for twelve months, or have been householders, also within
the royalty, for three years. These restrictions the sub-committee recommend should be entirely done away in the case of the persons referred to;
and if this shall be agreed to, they would humbly suggest that a similar
privilege should be held out to the teachers and others in the service of
George Heriot's Hospital.'[1]

This report was approved of by the treasurer's committee, and considered by the council in part on 5th June, when it was approved

[1] C. R. vol. cclii. p. 72.

of.[1] This resolution also includes the above recommendation in regard to burgesses, and which recommendation forms part of a report by the treasurer's committee on 'the proposed super-annuation fund,' dated 22d February 1849. Subsequently, on 9th October 1849, the council, on the recommendation of the treasurer's committee, instructed the dean of guild clerk to give effect to so much of the council's resolutions of 5th June last as relates to the admission of the officials of the city and of George Heriot's Hospital as burgesses of the city; and also agreed to request the treasurer of Heriot's Hospital to communicate to the teachers and others in the service of the hospital the resolution as to admitting them burgesses.

On 17th October 1854 the council, on the recommendation of the Lord Provost's committee, resolved that the entry-money on the admission of burgesses and guild brethren should be paid directly to the chamberlain in each case, by means of pay-slips to be prepared and printed for the purpose.[2] On the same day the council, on the motion of Councillor Sibbald, remitted to the Lord Provost's committee,

'to consider the mode of admitting parties as burgesses and guild brethren, and whether any new regulations should be made as to the persons to be admitted and the fees payable on admission, and to report.'[3]

On 9th September 1856 the council remitted to the Lord Provost's committee, for consideration and report, (1) the following motion by Councillor Ritchie:

'That the burgesses of the Canongate shall be enrolled as burgesses of the city, and that their names be added to the roll of the city burgesses without farther payment;'

and (2), letter from the clerk of Canongate, transmitting statement by the Canongate deputations in regard to the Municipal Bill on the subject of Councillor Ritchie's motion.[4] On 30th September

[1] C. R. vol. cclii. p. 377.          [2] C. R. vol. cclxiii. p. 372.
[3] C. R. vol. cclxiii. p. 384.          [4] C. R. vol. cclxix. p. 77.

1856 the council considered the following report of the Lord Provost's committee on the subject :

'*Edinburgh*, 24 *September* 1856.—In terms of the remit to them of 9th instant, the Lord Provost's committee have considered the motion of Councillor Ritchie, "That the burgesses of the Canongate shall be enrolled as burgesses of the city, and that their names be added to the roll of the city burgesses, without farther payment." The committee have also considered the statement of the Canongate deputations in regard to the Municipal Bill, transmitted by the clerk of Canongate, and which was remitted to the committee of the above date, and heard a statement of the deputation who had charge of the Bill on behalf of the magistrates and council, who do not admit the accuracy of the allegations contained in the statement first before mentioned, and beg to report that as the present burgesses of Canongate have already paid for being entered as such, it is reasonable that they should be admitted as burgesses of the city at a reduced rate, and therefore recommend that the magistrates and council should agree to admit as burgesses of the city such persons, being otherwise qualified, as had been duly admitted burgesses of Canongate on or before 31st December 1855, being the date when the petition for leave to bring in the Municipal Bill was deposited in the private bill office of the House of Commons, and that on payment of the reduced entry money of £2, 4s. or of £3, 4s., according as the parties are or are not the sons, sons-in-law, or apprentices of burgesses of the city ; being an abatement of £1, 10s. in each case respectively. These reduced entry-moneys are of course exclusive of the stamp duty and fees.'

(Signed)     JOHN MELVILLE, *Lord Provost*.[1]

The report was approved of by the council, Councillor Ritchie dissenting, and on 14th October, he tabled reasons of dissent against the resolution.[2]

In 1859 some communications passed between the council and the governors of George Heriot's Hospital, in regard to the claims of James Richmond, pianoforte maker, Westminster, who was stated to be a descendant of George Heriot, to be admitted a burgess under the act of council dated 15th April 1719. The result of their communication is embodied in the following report of the Lord Provost's committee, dated 19th October 1859, which was approved of by the council on 25th October 1859, and a copy was ordered to be transmitted to the governors :[3]

[1] C. R. vol. cclxix. p. 107.          [2] C. R. vol. cclxix. p. 159.
[3] C. R. vol. cclxxix. p. 90.

'The Lord Provost's committee, in terms of the remit to them of the 4th instant, having considered the report by the law committee of George Heriot's Hospital on the application by James Richmond for the admission of his son to the hospital, and deliverance by the Governors thereon; and having also considered the act of council therein referred to, of date 15th April 1719, "statuting and enacting that all the relations of George Heriot, proving their propinquity of blood, are thereby made and declared virtually burgesses and freemen of the good town, so as to entitle their children to the benefit of being chosen and admitted into the said hospital," are of opinion and report that that act of council should be rescinded, and that when any person claiming relationship to George Heriot shall apply to be admitted a burgess on that ground, his case should be favourably considered, but, at the same time, should be disposed of on its own merits.'

On 3d September 1861 the council remitted the following motion by Bailie Johnstone to the Lord Provost's committee for consideration and report:

'That unless on special motions for admission of honorary burgesses, no person shall in future be admitted a burgess of the city who shall not produce satisfactory evidence that he has carried on business as a master within the city for at least three years, or that he has resided at least six years within the city, and occupied, as owner or as tenant, a private dwelling-house assessed at not less than £15 sterling annual rent for at least three of these years: Remit to the Lord Provost's committee to consider and report to the first meeting of council in October next; and in the meantime delay consideration of applications for admission as ordinary burgesses until the report of the committee shall be taken under consideration.'

At the same time it was resolved that the disposal of applications for admission as ordinary burgesses should be delayed until the report of the committee was received.[1]

On 7th October the committee adopted the following report on Bailie Johnstone's motion:

'The committee having fully considered the above motion, which was adopted by the council and remitted on 3d ultimo, beg to recommend, that unless a special motion for admission of honorary burgesses, and in the case of persons elected members of council, no person should in future be admitted a burgess of the city who shall not produce satisfactory evidence that he has carried on business as a master within the city for at least three years immediately preceding the date of application, or that he has resided at least six

---

[1] C. R. vol. cclxxxiii. p. 36.

years within the city immediately preceding the date of application, and occupied, as owner or as tenant, a private dwelling-house assessed at not less than £15 sterling of annual rent for at least three of these years.

'The committee have to remark, that while there was a division of opinion among members of committee as to the rental qualification above expressed, the committee were otherwise unanimous as to the foregoing recommendation.'

The report was considered by the council on the following day, when Councillor M'Laren moved as an amendment to the motion for the approval of the report: 'That so much of the report as fixes a rental of £15 be not approved of.'

The council, however, by a majority of nineteen to sixteen, approved of the report,[1] and this resolution was confirmed, at the following meeting of council on 22d October, by a majority of twenty-one to seventeen.[2]

At a subsequent stage of the proceedings of the same meeting, Councillor M'Laren gave in the following protest against the approval of the minutes:

'Councillor M'Laren protested for himself and all who may adhere to him—

'1. Against the decision of the council come to this day approving of the second reading of the minutes of the last meeting of council, in so far as the council have therein fixed a rental of £15, below which all householders are hereafter to be excluded from the right to enter as burgesses of the city, although willing to pay the dues of entry, such exclusion being, in the opinion of the protestors, beyond the power of the council, and therefore illegal and of no force or effect in law, no such rule or any other rental rule having ever existed in the history of the burgh.

'2. He likewise protests in particular against the approval of the minute fixing the £15 rental, because of the hardship which it would entail on many respectable classes of inhabitant-householders, very few of whom could hope to be admitted under the regulation admitting traders carrying on business as masters for three years within the city.

'3. That it appears from a return prepared by the assessor under the Lands Valuation Act, to an order of the House of Commons in May 1860, that there were then occupying houses under £15 of yearly rent, amongst others, the following number and classes of persons, all of whom will be excluded, viz. :—

---

[1] C. R. vol. cclxxxiii. p. 86.          [2] C. R. vol. cclxxxiii. p. 113.

| | | | | |
|---|---|---|---|---|
| Accountants | . . | 6 | Brought forward . | 578 |
| Architects | . . | 9 | Missionaries . . | 32 |
| Artists | . . | 15 | Naval and military | |
| Cattle salesmen | . | 5 | officers . . | 3 |
| Church officers | . | 15 | Overseers and managers | 4 |
| Clerks (of these, above | | | Reporters . . | 2 |
| £10, 124) . | . | 291 | Shopmen and ware- | |
| Commercial travellers | 83 | | housemen . . | 133 |
| Government officials | 120 | | Students . . . | 3 |
| Inspectors | . . | 25 | Surveyors . . | 7 |
| Surgeons and medical | | | Teachers . . . | 41 |
| doctors . | . . | 7 | Writers . . . | 20 |
| Ministers . | . . | 2 | | |
| | | 578 | | 823 |

The following members adhered to the protest :—The Dean of Guild, Convener Cox, and fourteen councillors.

On 4th February 1862 a letter from Mr. William Fraser, jun., clerk to the convenery of the incorporated trades, representing that the alterations in the qualification for the admission of burgesses will injuriously affect the interests of the incorporated trades, was remitted to the Lord Provost's committee,[1] but no action was taken upon it.

On 19th May 1868 a representation by the town clerk of the following tenor was submitted to the council:

' *Edinburgh*, 14*th May* 1868.—The city clerk begs to refer the magistrates and council to the act of council, dated 8th October 1861, relative to the admission of burgesses.

' By a previous act of council, dated 5th June 1849, all officials of the city, present and future, and other persons therein enumerated, were authorized to be admitted without reference to other qualifications.

' An application has been made by one of the officials of the city to be admitted a burgess. The applicant does not possess any of the qualifications specified in the act of council of 8th October 1861 ; and the city clerk suggests that the magistrates and council should formally renew the act of 5th June 1849.;

The clerk was authorized to admit the applicant on payment of the usual fees, and *quoad ultra* the subject of the representation was remitted to the Lord Provost's committee,[2] who, on 7th July

[1] C. R. vol. cclxxxiii. p. 383.            [2] C. R. vol. ccxcix. p. 467.

1868, recommended that the act of council of 5th June 1849, providing that all officials of the city, present and future, and the teachers and others in the service of George Heriot's Hospital, should be admitted burgesses on payment of the usual fees, without other than such official qualification, should be renewed. Their report was approved of by the council on 7th July 1868.[1]

In May 1869 an application was made by a married woman, to allow her to purchase a burgess ticket in name of her husband, from whom she lived apart. The woman occupied a shop in her own name, and supported her family by her own earnings, and her avowed object in making the application was to secure for her children the benefits which might accrue from their father being a burgess. The application was remitted to the Lord Provost's committee, who, on 12th May, submitted the following report:

'The Lord Provost's committtee beg to report that, having carefully considered this petition, they are not prepared to allow the petitioner "to purchase a burgess ticket in the name of her husband," from whom she lives apart, and who appears to have no claim or qualification whatever. Having regard, however, to the fact that the essential condition of burgess-ship in this city, at the earliest times, has been, as it is expressed in the old records, that they should "hald stob and staik therein, and walk, ward, pay extentis and skattis within the burgh, conforme to thair substance," and that there is sufficient precedent for doing so, the committee are of opinion that the woman herself should be admitted a burgess. She fulfils all the conditions above mentioned, and there appears no good ground in reason or equity why she should be excluded from any benefit attaching to the fulfilment of these conditions.          (Signed)          'W. CHAMBERS, L. P.'

The council, on 18th May, approved of the general principle laid down in the report, and re-committed the special application to the committee, with powers,[2] and the woman was admitted a burgess in her own name.

On 10th July 1871 the following motion by Bailie Lewis was remitted to the Lord Provost's committee for consideration:

'That the conditions of entry as burgesses of the city be restored to what they were previous to 1860.'[3]

---

[1] C. R. vol. ccxcviii. p. 132.     [2] C. R. vol. ccc. p. 23.     [3] C. R. vol. ccciv. p. 419.

And on 20th September the committee adopted the following report:

'Previous to the passing of the act of council 8th October 1861, it was a sufficient qualification for admission as burgess of the city that the applicant had carried on business on his own account for one year, or been a householder for three years of uninterrupted occupancy within the ancient or extended royalty, at the time of admission. And these conditions were subject to exceptions in favour (1) of persons entering in right of their masters; (2) of persons entering any of the city trades incorporations; (3) of persons entering the Merchant Company; (4) of the officials of the city and Heriot's Hospital.

'By the act of council of 8th October 1861, above referred to, it was declared that, unless on special motion for admission of honorary burgesses, and in the case of persons elected members of council, no person shall in future be admitted a burgess of the city who shall not produce satisfactory evidence that he has carried on businsss as a master within the city for at least three years immediately preceding the date of the application, or that he has resided at least six years within the city immediately preceding the date of application, and occupied, as owner or as tenant, a private dwelling-house assessed at not less than £15 sterling of annual rent for at least three of these years.

'By act of council of 4th February 1862, the exception in favour of persons entering the Merchant Company was revived, and by another act, of date 7th July 1868, the exception in favour of the officials of the city and Heriot's Hospital was renewed. The difference between the existing conditions and those in force prior to October 1861 consists, therefore, in the exclusion (1) of persons entering in right of the masters in the incorporated trades to whom they have served regular apprenticeships; (2) of persons desirous of becoming members of such incorporations, burgess-ship being a condition of entry; and (3) the condition of six years' residence instead of three, or carrying on business for three years instead of for one year.

'The committee unanimously recommend that the exception in favour of apprentices and proposed members of the trades incorporations be revived, and that the former condition shall qualify citizens for admission, viz. that the party shall have carried on business on his own account for one year, or been a householder for three years of uninterrupted occupancy at the time of admission within the city, with this qualification, that the claimant shall instruct payment by him of the police and poor rates chargeable against him during such periods.'

On 28th September the council approved of the report, and resolved as therein recommended.[1]

[1] C. R. vol. cccv. p. 150.

On 24th September 1872 the council remitted the following motion by Councillor Cranston to the treasurer's committee for consideration :

'Considering that it is the duty of the town council to foster provident habits in all classes of the community ; that the working classes would be specially benefited by participating in the privileges and advantages derivable from the education and training of Heriot's Hospital and schools, and that these privileges can only be obtained through possession of burgess rights ; it be remitted to the treasurer's committee to instruct the city chamberlain to receive partial payments, in instalments of not less than two shillings, towards the purchase of burgess tickets, the tickets to be delivered when the chamberlain is in receipt of the full fees.'[1]

---

[1] C. R. vol. cccviii. p. 41.   With this motion,·which did not result in any new resolution of the town council, the information collected by Sir James Marwick, as noted on p. 153, is brought to a close.

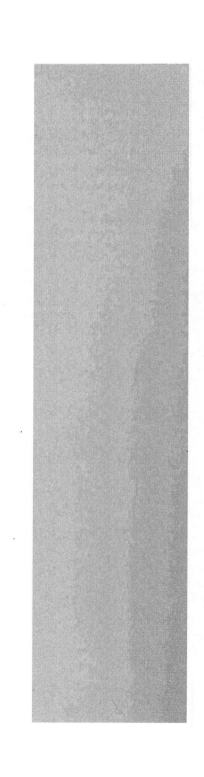

# INDEX.

*Printed by* MORRISON & GIBB LIMITED, *Edinburgh.*

Lightning Source UK Ltd.
Milton Keynes UK
UKHW022111080223
416681UK00011B/2676